Show Me a Story!

Show Me a Story!

Why Picture Books Matter

Conversations with 21 of the World's Most Celebrated Illustrators

COMPILED AND EDITED BY

LEONARD S. MARCUS

WITH A FOREWORD BY DAVID WIESNER

CANDLEWICK PRESS

First Candlewick paperback edition 2013
Originally published as *Ways of Telling* by Penguin Young Readers Group

The Library of Congress has cataloged the hardcover edition as follows:

Show me a story! : why picture books matter :
conversations with 21 of the world's most celebrated illustrators /
compiled and edited by Leonard S. Marcus. — 1st Candlewick ed.
p.   cm.
ISBN 978-0-7636-3506-0 (hardcover)
1. Illustrated children's books. 2. Illustrators — Interviews.
I. Marcus, Leonard S., date.
NC965.S56 2012
741.6'420922 — dc23   2011045897

ISBN 978-0-7636-6464-0 (paperback)

13 14 15 16 17 18 SCP 10 9 8 7 6 5 4 3 2

Printed in Humen, Dongguan, China

This book was typeset in Minion.

Candlewick Press
99 Dover Street
Somerville, Massachusetts 02144

visit us at www.candlewick.com

For my sister, Maris J. M. Kramer —
who taught me to play "Twenty Questions" —
with love

Why do picture books matter? Of course part of the reason is because they're books, but the heart of the matter is right there in the name; it's the pictures. Before they read words, children are reading pictures. In picture books, the illustrations work in concert with the text in a way that is unique among art forms.

Picture books tell stories in a visual language that is rich and multi-leveled, sophisticated in its workings despite its often deceptively simple appearance. It is through the book's images that a child first understands the world of the story—where it is set, when it takes place, whether it's familiar or new. They read the characters' emotions and interactions in facial expressions and body language. They may notice secondary pic-torial storylines happening alongside the main action, like a secret for them to follow. And nowhere is visual humor explored more fully than in the picture book. Possibly only Charlie Chaplin or Buster Keaton could equally run the gamut from gentle kidding to sophisticated wit to pie-in-the-face slapstick to anarchic postmodernism.

Such visual reading is as important to a child's development as read-ing written language is. Take away the pictures and you deprive kids of a wealth of understanding—not to mention a lot of fun.

The first art that most children see is in picture books. That's a big responsibility for the illustrator. Leonard Marcus showcases a group of artists who recognize that responsibility and respond with work that challenges and inspires kids' burgeoning visual literacy. In twenty-one captivating and intimate interviews, *Show Me A Story!* offers an in-depth look at the passion and vision that these amazing artists bring to their work. No two are alike, except in their remarkable levels of creativity. Their books leave kids amazed and moved. They leave their imagina-tions energized. And quite often, they leave the kids giggling maniacally on the floor.

That is why picture books matter.

David Wiesner

CONTENTS

INTRODUCTION

T he picture book came of age in the United States during the 1930s as the nation was recovering from the Great Depression. Americans, until then, had looked primarily to Europe for culture and to England in particular for the finest examples of illustrated books for the young. Picture books by British artists Randolph Caldecott, Kate Greenaway, Walter Crane, Beatrix Potter, and L. Leslie Brooke filled library shelves alongside those created by a small but growing number of American illustrators, including E. Boyd Smith, C. B. Falls, Wanda Gág, and Robert Lawson. As America's industrial might grew, so did the conviction that the time had come for American illustrators to rise to the challenge of matching, or even surpassing, the high standard set by artists from across the Atlantic. It was with this ambitious goal in mind that in 1937 the American

Library Association established a prize for illustration and named it the Randolph Caldecott Medal after the greatest of England's picture-book masters.

In 1942, Robert McCloskey became only the fifth illustrator to be honored with a Caldecott Medal. It is amusing to learn that when McCloskey's editor, May Massee of Viking Press, telephoned him with the good news, the creator of *Make Way for Ducklings* had to ask her to explain just what it was that he should be so happy about. He had not yet heard of the medal. The episode suggests the degree to which the American children's-book world of the 1930s and '40s remained a young and insular cottage industry. Few of the major illustrators of McCloskey's generation started out with dreams of making their names as juvenile artists. Most wandered into the field by chance. McCloskey, for instance, had wanted a career as a muralist and painter. But he needed to make a living, and because his best friend happened to be May Massee's nephew, he had shown his portfolio to her. The editor, who immediately recognized his promise, gave him encouragement and a thoughtful critique. Then, sealing his loyalty to her for life, she took the young artist out to dinner.

By the time Maurice Sendak arrived on the scene less than a generation later, the situation in America had changed dramatically. Exhausted by years of depression and war, parents of the 1950s baby boom era were determined to give their children a happier, more opportunity-rich childhood than the one they themselves had experienced. They bought large numbers of books for their youngsters and supported the funding of public schools and libraries — the two institutions that between them purchased the lion's share of American children's books. As the field flourished, the status of illustrators rose. In 1963, when Sendak's Caldecott Medal–winning *Where the Wild Things Are* first appeared, an appreciative public was prepared to hail it as a masterpiece (albeit a somewhat controversial one, with its young tantrum-throwing boy and half-scary, half-goofy alter egos) and its creator as a pop-cultural hero.

Sendak's triumph added immeasurably to the forward momentum of the picture book as an art form. On both sides of the Atlantic, more and more talented young people entered the field, among them England's Quentin Blake and John Burningham, soon to be joined by the latter's wife, Helen Oxenbury, and by a brilliant young Austrian artist named Lisbeth Zwerger. American publishers were belatedly coming to grips with the multicultural and multiracial makeup of American society—and with their responsibility to publish for underserved minorities. Catalyzed by the civil rights movement, the new awareness of those years opened unprecedented opportunities to artists of color such as Ashley Bryan and Jerry Pinkney.

Such was the excitement and prestige surrounding picture books that even highly accomplished illustrators like Eric Carle (then a successful advertising artist) and *New Yorker* cartoonist William Steig might decide, in mid-career, to turn to the picture book as a worthy outlet for their talents. Carle took the leap in reaction to his growing disenchantment with the world of selling. To supplement his magazine income, Steig too had been designing ads, and he too had come to long for more satisfying work. In 1969, Steig's *Sylvester and the Magic Pebble* (which received the Caldecott Medal for 1970) and Carle's *The Very Hungry Caterpillar* both were published—landmark picture books that have not only delighted countless children but also inspired new generations of illustrators.

Carle's name became synonymous with a type of picture book for which there were few historical precedents: books for children even younger than those of the traditional "picture-book ages" of four to eight; books that often had built-in novelty or "toylike" elements. His relatively brief, read-aloud stories introduced basic concepts such as counting and the days of the week in a playful way, as much by "showing" as by "telling." At first, America's public libraries, which had not yet committed themselves to serving the needs of toddlers and preschoolers, had no use for Carle's books. But a new generation of parents quickly discovered them for themselves, as did educators at the preschools and day-care centers that were opening everywhere. As the growing demand for such "young" picture books became increasingly clear, more artists began to create them — including one American photographer who earlier in her career had specialized in making photographic portraits of children, Tana Hoban. So too did an energetic young book designer at a Boston educational publishing house named Rosemary Wells. During the 1980s, Wells and Helen Oxenbury each produced memorable baby and toddler books salted with developmental insight, wry humor, and well-placed, knowing nods to the difficulties of being a good parent. Together, they popularized the board book as the ideal format for the youngest children, those who were as apt to yank and bite their books as look at them.

By then, children's-book publishing had become international in scope and flavor, with publishers from many countries sharing an eagerness to expose their children to books and ideas from other cultures. Japanese author and illustrator Mitsumasa Anno first became known to American readers in 1970 with the publication of *Topsy-Turvies: Pictures to Stretch the Imagination*. Throughout the 1970s and '80s, his extraordinary picture books attracted an ever wider international audience. Like Eric Carle, Anno won fans among educators and librarians for being a gentle teacher with a genius for transforming learning into an absorbing and seemingly effortless game.

It took American critics a long time to grasp the special achievement of picture books as "simple" as Carle's; not surprisingly, Carle has not won the Caldecott Medal. Another popular American artist whose picture books were long underrated by critics, in his case because the books were so funny, was James Marshall. A largely self-taught artist, Marshall was inspired to create children's books after discovering the work of Sendak, Tomi Ungerer, and Edward Gorey. Although less of a technical wizard than any of these role models, Marshall nonetheless mastered his own idiosyncratic approach to drawing and design, and developed a signature line that harmonized perfectly with his archly witty voice. Sendak himself would later express his envy of the lightness and mischief of Marshall's drawings. The endlessly amusing rogues' gallery of Marshall's characters — George and

Martha, Miss Nelson, Viola Swamp, Fox, and others—have the enduring distinction of being both funny and true. Awards committees recognized Marshall's worth later than children did. In 1992, with dozens of books to his credit, he finally received a Caldecott Honor (a runner-up prize to the medal) for *Goldilocks and the Three Bears.* In 2007 the American Library Association posthumously awarded him its Laura Ingalls Wilder Award for illustration in recognition of the entire body of his work.

As the millennium approached, the first generation of readers of *Where the Wild Things Are,* now parents themselves, made Max a popular name choice for a newborn boy; museum exhibitions of picture-book art, though still rare, were becoming less so, and a new wave of museums devoted entirely to children's-book art were opening their doors or were about to do so; art schools were introducing courses in children's-book illustration; and a whole generation of young artists were passionately committing themselves to the field, having themselves grown up on Sendak, Steig, Burningham, and company. The territory now being explored by such notable artists as Lois Ehlert and Vera B. Williams, the latter a painter and printmaker who had studied with Josef Albers, had fewer of the makeshift trappings of a frontier than had been the case a generation earlier, and more the look and substance of a thriving creative and commercial enterprise. Kevin Henkes, Chris Raschka, Yumi Heo (a Korean émigré), Peter Sís (a Czech artist who sought asylum in the United States during the last years of the Cold War), and animator Mo Willems all carved out unique niches for themselves in a world and marketplace that seemed more receptive than ever to whatever an artist with a talent for reaching one-, or three-, or seven-year-olds might have to offer. Meanwhile, as new technologies stood poised to supplant entire genres of traditional print-on-paper books with quicksilver screen equivalents, the future of the picture book remained comparatively secure—even as digitized picture books joined the mix. Artists seemed likelier than ever to devise new ways to tap the distinctive potential of the traditional picture book as an extraordinarily flexible and child-friendly format. Parents and caregivers seemed as likely as ever to prize the intimate tactile experience of holding an illustrated book in hand while perching a young child on their lap, the adult and child basking together in the magical yet familiar glow of a good story shared.

In each of these interviews, I am on a kind of mad quest for the vital thread that links an artist's life story to the stories and images for which he or she is known. How does a young person grow up to become an artist? What childhood experiences prepared these particular twenty-one men and women — or left them unprepared — for what was to come in their creative lives? What was it that inspired them, and where did they find the courage they required, and who gave them the help and guidance that sent them on their way? And why of all art forms did they choose the picture book to be their life's work and passion?

I hope these interviews, each of which is a honeycomb of memorable tales about growing up and coming into one's own, will inspire young people, especially those who like to paint and write and draw, as well as working artists at every stage of their career. I hope as well that teachers, librarians, parents, book collectors, and others who care about children and their books will find in these pages new insights into the mysterious process of artistic creation, and a fuller appreciation of an art form that is almost never as simple as it seems.

MITSUMASA ANNO

Born 1926, Tsuwano, Japan

W hen I was a child," Mitsumasa Anno has recalled, "I pictured the world-is-round concept as a rubber ball turned inside out with the people of the different continents living inside the ball. Of course it was a boy's way of imagining. . . . But this kind of imagination . . . is another sort of eye for perceiving what things really are. And it is the source of all [my] books."

A robust, barrel-chested man with an intense gaze and mischievous manner, Anno came of age in Japan in the 1970s, at a time when idealistic editors in the United States, Europe, and Japan were eager to publish picture books cooperatively. Hoping to instill a spirit of cultural open-mindedness and tolerance in young children from different parts of the world, the editors also saw an opportunity in such joint ventures to hold down the cost of color printing through the economies of scale to be gained from larger combined print runs. In order for the experiment to work, the picture books these editors championed naturally had to have broad-based appeal. Mitsumasa Anno, with his brilliant knack for visual narrative, his seasoned traveler's knowledge of the world's storied locales, and his nuanced appreciation of both cultural differences and universals, proved to be the ideal artist to meet the challenge.

Anno was teaching art to Tokyo schoolchildren when a publisher who was the father of one of his students suggested that he apply his talents to the making of children's books. His first picture book, *Topsy-Turvies: Pictures to Stretch the Imagination,* was published in 1970. *Anno's Alphabet* (1975), *Anno's Journey* (1978), *Anno's Medieval World* (1980), and *Anno's Mysterious Multiplying Jar* (1983) — the original Japanese titles do not incorporate the artist's name — all served to enhance his reputation as an innovator and latter-day Renaissance man. In 1984 Anno received children's literature's highest honor, the international Hans Christian Andersen Medal, in recognition of his "unique [gift for] communicating to both East and West."

In Japan, where nearly all youngsters grow up knowing his picture books, Anno is also celebrated for his books for adult readers on mathematics, philosophy, history, and travel, for his striking cover designs for the Japanese equivalent of *Scientific American* magazine, and for his lively television talks on art and art history.

I first became aware of Anno when I noticed copies of his early books for sale in museum shops around New York. I saw right away that he was an artist of extraordinary inventiveness and originality. I decided I wanted to meet him. The chance finally came more than ten years later. This interview was recorded between the lunch and dinner hours in the restaurant of the Hotel Kitano in New York City on April 22, 1989, with Akiko Kurita serving as interpreter. From time to time throughout our conversation, Anno reached for a pencil and sketched on a legal pad to illustrate his idea.

LEONARD S. MARCUS: Adults sometimes assume that young children don't think abstractly. Judging from your books, you don't agree.

MITSUMASA ANNO: A young child might not understand Picasso, but if I draw a circle and add a short line at the top for a stem, even a two-year-old will see that it's an apple. No color is needed, just the outline. This is one of a child's first steps toward abstract understanding. And if I make a simple drawing with circles for heads and rectangles for bodies and single lines for arms and legs, a child will understand me when I say, "This is Father. This is Mother." Adults take such leaps for granted. That a two-year-old can do so is a kind of miracle.

Q: Your books seem aimed at challenging preconceived ideas about the world and encouraging independent thinking. *Anno's Medieval World,* for instance, concerns the difficulty that people once had in accepting the notion that the world was round.

A: A child's mind, unlike an adult's, can absorb anything and accept any number of new ideas. For this reason, it is not always good to teach only "correct" ideas to children. Scientific understanding is important, but imagination should also be encouraged. When some adults see a rainbow, they think they must explain the color spectrum to a child. The sense of wonder at such things should come first.

Recently, I spoke to a group of schoolchildren in Sydney, Australia. I told them that I had been afraid to come "down under" to Sydney lest I fall off the earth on my way. They laughed and then explained to me that "the world is round but there are also some flat places where it is safe." These children did not yet know the difference between imagination and reality. It is important to let them imagine things in their own way for a while before teaching them differently.

Q: Your first book to become well known in the United States was *Anno's Alphabet.* Why did you make a book about the Roman alphabet — the alphabet of Western languages?

A: One day when I was tired I found myself looking at the corner of a table. Just then two converging sides of the tabletop and the leg below began to look to me like a letter *T.* I made a drawing of what I had seen, and began to wonder whether Westerners, who were used to thinking of a *T* as a flat, printed symbol, would realize that my drawing of the table corner and leg was also a *T.* The book evolved from there.

Q: In your *Alphabet,* as well as in *Topsy-Turvies,* you seem fascinated by visual paradoxes and illusions.

A: In 1960 or 1961, after having taught school for ten years, I went to Paris. I did not as yet have any intention of making children's books. I wanted to paint. It was during that time that I first saw the illusionist prints and drawings of the Dutch graphic artist M. C. Escher. Escher's work greatly excited me. Unlike some modern art, his style is easily understood. I began to think that his images might please children as much as they pleased me, and I realized that no one had done an alphabet using that technique before. At first I thought the letters would make a good picture book by themselves, but my Japanese publisher asked me to add companion pictures for each letter.

Q: *Anno's Alphabet* doesn't simply begin with the letter *A,* as do most alphabet books. You first show a question mark carved out of wood, then a tree . . . and finally, a carving in the form of a book — an alphabet book. That initial sequence of pages reminds me of the opening credits of a film.

A: That is exactly what I wanted. I think of all my books as films.

Q: *Anno's Alphabet* was published both in Japan and in the West. Did creating a book for such a diverse audience influence your choice of imagery?

A: Very definitely. I drew an angel, for example, to illustrate the letter *A.* It looked rather like a baby with swan's wings. But when the American and British editors saw my drawing, they said, "This is not an angel! It's a cupid." I replied that it looked like an angel to me. My drawing, you see, was similar to the angel trademark of a well-known Japanese confectioner. The incident underscored for me the fact that pictorial images do not necessarily carry the same associations from culture to culture. I had to give up my angel and replace it with a picture of an anvil.

Then, in the decorative border for the letter *B,* I drew a type of bean that I thought would surely be recognizable to everyone in the West. I had checked it in an encyclopedia! I knew we had the same type of bean in Japan, so I proceeded to do my drawing. Nevertheless, my American editor objected, "That bean is too short. Make it longer!" Whereupon, I produced my encyclopedia. My editor would still have none of it. "We don't see our beans in books," she said. "We see them in the supermarket." So I had to redraw the entire rather complicated border. Later I found that my book showed an older type of bean that was no longer widely available. Many such changes were necessary.

Q: The border drawings in your *Alphabet* contain small details that a young child might not notice at first, but that might very well intrigue him years later. Do you intentionally create drawings with different layers that, in a sense, run parallel to children's education and development?

A: In one of the scenes in *Anno's Journey,* I incorporated a rendering of *The Gleaners,* a well-known work by the nineteenth-century French painter [Jean] François Millet, in which peasant women are seen at work in a field. When a small child sees those women in the book, he doesn't know the source of that particular image but can make up his own story about them — who they are, what they are thinking about, in what kind of house each one lives, and so on. Later he may see the Millet painting and remember the women.

As a child, I would do much the same thing. I liked to observe people and make up stories about them. If a man walked by, I would decide that he must be a carpenter, or a doctor on his way to see a child in the hospital, or whatever.

Q: In the Journey books you have mixed together imaginary scenes with images from the real world — for instance, in *Anno's U.S.A.* (1983), a scene from *Shane* and landmarks such as the Empire State Building and Independence Hall. What do you want children to learn from this?

A: That imagination, which is about impossibility, and reality aren't opposites, but complement each other. One might say that reality and imagination differ from each other in the same way that the audience at a play is set apart from the actors. It's where the two meet that hope is to be found.

In my books, I don't want to teach. What I have done might better be described as "teaching without teaching" — providing the conditions that allow children to learn for themselves. I once heard about a little boy who excitedly showed the Superman picture in *Anno's U.S.A.* to his teacher. She acted surprised, even though she knew it was there. This teacher's response allowed the child to feel the joy of having made a personal discovery.

Q: In format, the Journey books resemble traditional Japanese picture scrolls, yet the countries depicted in your stories — Britain, Italy, the United States — are all Western.

A: When I made *Anno's Journey*, I did not intend to use the traditional picture-scroll form. It simply came out that way. What I had set out to do was to draw pictures from a certain distance — in terms of time as well as of space. You will find many historical details in my pictures. The reader's perspective on time is expanded as a result. The Journey books also show different portions of the world's geography, expanding the reader's sense of space, too.

Q: Why haven't you made a Journey book about your native Japan?

A: The essence of being human is the same everywhere. Many Westerners have told me, "You know more about Europe and the United States than we do." But everywhere in the world, if there is a road and a river, there is always a bridge. In making my books, I have been seeking archetypes that transcend any particular culture. I have looked for images that people everywhere would know.

Q: Have you also made some books on specifically Japanese themes?

A: At the moment, I am working on a historical picture book for older children and adults, *The Tale of the Heike.* It is a classic Japanese war story that was first written down in the thirteenth century. It tells of the powerful Heike clan, who enjoyed prosperity for a time but was then defeated in battle by the rival Genji clan, and faded away into the western sea. The story is a beautiful description of human destiny.

Q: Would you tell me something about the place where you were born?

A: I was born in Tsuwano, a village surrounded by mountains in the west of Japan, on the "sea side," as we say. Now it has become a tourist town, and is called "Little Kyoto." But when I was a boy, an airplane would fly over our village maybe once a year. We would catch a brief glimpse of it between the mountains. That, for us, was very exciting.

Because of all the mountains, we could not see the ocean, which to me as a small boy seemed very far away. I couldn't believe that seawater was salty. I was ten years old when I first saw the ocean for myself, and when no one was looking, I reached down to taste the water.

My parents kept an inn, where I helped out as a child. From that experience, I determined that I would never keep an inn myself!

Q: Did you like to draw as a child?

A: Yes, I began on my own as a small boy, drawing mountains, houses, and ghosts.

Q: How did you know what a ghost looked like?

A: Years later, when I was doing the illustrations for *Anno's Alphabet,* I drew a devil to illustrate the letter *D.* My British editor looked at it and said, "That's not a devil!" And so I asked this person, "Have you seen a devil yourself?" He replied that he had not, but that in his own mind he was sure how a devil would look. He proceeded to make all kinds of gestures in order to show me his idea of a devil. From that exchange I realized that there are many invisible things that have never actually existed, but which nonetheless exist in people's minds as quite specific images.

Q: What pictures and images influenced you as a young artist?

A: It was thanks to my parents' inn that as a child I saw all kinds of magazines that were left around for the guests. Looking through those magazines, I was exposed to all sorts of pictures, from classical to modern in style. Even as a child I thought that an artist should be free to work in any number of styles to suit his purposes. Now I have my own style, but I still think it is important for an artist to feel that freedom.

Q: Did the art teachers you went on to study with feel the same way?

A: Not at all. But then later, when I myself taught drawing and painting to children, I realized that, aside from technique, drawing and painting cannot be taught. Most people think that the technique *is* the art. That is a great misunderstanding.

Q: Were there books you especially liked as a child?

A: Lots of books. I had no picture books, though — only the magazines. I read Mark Twain in Japanese.

Q: Did you find that teaching children was more or less what you expected it would be like?

A: School did not totally prepare me for what lay ahead, but in any case I wanted to experiment in my teaching. On the first day of class, the cherry blossoms were all out, and I asked each child to bring a flower into the classroom. When I was a child of eleven, my teacher had shown me how to draw this flower. So now I sketched the same drawing on the blackboard for my students. I showed them the stamens and pistils — the female and male parts of the flower. I explained that everything in nature is made up of female and male parts. In my drawing — *my* teacher hadn't done this — I added a bee heading straight for the flower.

In the classroom there was also a camellia, which has a great many petals. The children said, "This camellia has no pistils!" To which I replied, "No, you are not correct." Then in order to prove it, I opened all the petals — and found no pistils, just stamens.

Q: At least you taught them well. They had really looked.

A: Yes, but I was vexed because what I said had not been true!

Q: That's often the case with teachers. [*Laughter.*]

A: Later when I was visiting a museum in Tokyo I asked someone why this was so and was told that the pistils *become* the camellia's petals. That's why camellias have so many.

Q: What else did you do to engage their interest?

A: One day I had planned to take the children outdoors to draw in the wheat fields. I was thinking of a particular painting by Van Gogh with crows flying over a wheat field, and wondered how the children would draw such a scene. Suddenly, however, it began to pour, and so the children had to stay indoors. Abandoning our original plan, I went outdoors myself and picked a single stalk of wheat from the field and brought it back to the classroom, where I drew a picture of it on the blackboard. I explained that the wheat field was really just a collection of stalks like the one I had brought in, and that they could draw the whole field by seeing only a single stalk. And so they did.

The next day I had another group of children. This time the weather was fine, so we went outdoors to sketch in the fields. When you look at such a field, it's like looking at a toothbrush. You can't see each individual bristle or stalk, and so you can't draw it effectively that way, either. But that is exactly what those children tried to do — with so many upright strokes that their pictures were all black! Their pictures didn't look at all like the field. The children who stayed indoors produced pictures that were more abstract, that picked out only the important details. Ironically, the children who stayed indoors were the ones who could draw the real field.

Q: The drawings in your books are beautiful, as well as imaginative. What role does beauty play in children's books?

A: All beautiful things encourage a child's sense of wonder — and everything that encourages a child's sense of wonder is beautiful. In my three Math Games books and several others, I have tried to show that mathematics is beautiful and not necessarily difficult — that math is primarily a way of thinking about things.

Q: One of the unusual aspects of *Anno's Counting Book* is that you start not with the number one, as is typical, but with zero. Did you have a hard time deciding how to express the concept of zero pictorially?

A: Zero is not simply "nothing" but "something missing." A boy with a severe learning impairment was once looking at the book. He started at the end, where the number twelve is illustrated in a scene with twelve houses, twelve trees, twelve reindeer, and so on. "Oh, there are many houses," he said. Then as he turned the pages and there were fewer and fewer of everything, he said, "Getting lonely." When he turned from the picture for the number three, with three houses, to the picture for two, he said, "House disappeared." Finally, when the boy came to the picture for zero, which is just a snowy field through which a river is running, he sighed and said, "Now we have nothing." I was very moved by this child.

Q: In your Math Games you present a series of mathematical ideas, starting with simple ones and progressing to more challenging concepts. Are these books to be read through all at once?

A: There may well be some concepts that a younger child will not be ready to understand, and in that case the parent should skip those pages and wait until the child is ready. But, as I show in those books, there are many real-life illustrations of mathematical ideas in a child's own world, and all one has to do is point them out to the child and he will understand — without having to be taught.

Q: So the world can itself be viewed as a kind of picture book, as a series of illustrations from which a child will learn?

A: Yes. For instance, if you have two brothers at home, and one of them is a "bigger quantity" and the other is a "smaller quantity," a child immediately knows the difference. That is mathematics. Children can of course be taught such things in the traditional manner. But their joy is always much greater when they make the discovery for themselves.

QUENTIN BLAKE

Born 1932, Sidcup, Kent, England

I n Quentin Blake's opinion, "If someone is asleep in bed dreaming, you don't necessarily want to see [the] bed, but you might want to look at the dreams." Blake approaches his work as an illustrator with very much this same idea in mind. It's not important to him that he show every bump on a frog's back or every hair on the head of a precocious schoolgirl named Matilda. What does matter is capturing the essence of things: a character's pose and expression, the core drama (and comedy) of a scene. Equally key is maintaining the lightness and liveliness of his scribbly drawing line.

At first glance, Blake's illustrations look more than a bit like doodles that couldn't possibly have taken anyone very long to draw. Risking the appearance of effortlessness seems not to have hurt his reputation any, while the world of good it has probably done young readers would be hard to measure. A madcap, unfussy Blake illustration is, as countless children have recognized, an open invitation to read.

Blake has long played an informal public role in England as an advocate for children's books. In 1999 this aspect of his work — which harks back to his early days as a teacher — was made official with his appointment as Britain's first Children's Laureate, a post he held through 2001. Blake has won every major prize for illustration and has even been knighted by the Queen. When I spoke with him by phone on November 11, 2009, he was in the thick of laying plans for a major new project: a museum of children's-book art to be located in the heart of his adopted city of London.

~~~~~~~~~~~~~~~~~~~~~~~~~~~~~~~~

LEONARD S. MARCUS: What kind of child were you?

QUENTIN BLAKE: Probably rather quiet, maybe a bit shy. Having been born eleven years after my brother, it was a bit like being an only child. I didn't talk a great deal, though I've talked a great deal since then! I did a lot of drawing.

Q: Did people encourage you?

A: I had a drawing printed in my secondary-school magazine almost as soon as I got there. It was a drawing of some boys changing after a game of football — a game I hated, by the way! I was eleven or twelve. At about that same time I was introduced to a man who was both a painter and a cartoonist, and I had some visits to him for what I later would have called tutorials. He would go through my drawings and talk with me about them. He would also talk about the drawings in *Punch* that week and about Michelangelo — a very broad spread of references!

Q: You then went to Cambridge.

A: Before I decided to go there, I thought, *If I go to an art school I might stop reading, whereas if I go to university I know I won't stop drawing.* There were times when I wondered whether I had done the right thing. But as an illustrator, reading is an important part of what I do, so I think it turned out to be good training.

At Cambridge, I studied with F. R. Leavis, who was one of the great literature scholars of the day. Leavis was a powerful presence and some people felt overwhelmed by him. I didn't feel that way and found the experience of his teaching rather liberating. Leavis was a man who never wore a tie, which was unusual in those days, and he was famous for disagreeing with a lot of people. I came away thinking, *Well, I can disagree if I feel like it, too.* There's an idea to hold on to! I later had the same feeling about the illustrator André François, who illustrated children's books and designed a lot of advertising. I would look at one of his drawings and think, *Oh, you don't have to be so well-behaved!* There was a story that he would go around Paris post offices and steal the worst pens to use for his drawings, so as to get a scratchier line. There was the sense that he could draw with anything.

Q: Do you remember reading *Lord of the Flies,* which was published in 1954, while you were still at Cambridge? It must have caused quite a sensation.

A: Yes, I read it. What was interesting about *Lord of the Flies* was that it took the conventions of children's books and inverted them. It starts off as a boy's adventure yarn and then shows how much worse things really are. The other aspect of it that interested me was its being a symbolic story — a kind of metaphor. You are not meant to quite believe it. In that sense it is like the picture books I have done on my own. Michael Rosen's books are based on his memories of childhood, and when I illustrate them I try to make them look almost as if I am drawing from life. But any idea for a book that I might have is apt to be some kind of fable. It's not about everyday life, even though it refers back to it — the way that *Zagazoo* (1998) does, for example.

Q: *Zagazoo* is a little bit like *Lord of the Flies* in that it presents children as wild beasts.

A: Sometimes they are! I had noticed that you could have terribly badly behaved children who then, after a time, come out quite different. When I first showed the book to my editor, he thought it ought to be more realistic, that more background should be provided about the characters. But I said, "No, it's like a Eugene Ionesco play"—theater of the absurd. He liked that analogy, so the story stayed as it was! There was a certain amount of experiment in choosing the animals that the child became and I had to work out the sequence. And I had a huge list of titles before I finally settled on *Zagazoo*. The original working title was *Orinoco*. When the book was published, some critics said it was really for the parents, and it is partly for them. But young children can cope with it. They know what's happening.

Q: What did you do after leaving Cambridge?

A: When I completed my degree in English literature, I got a teacher's certificate, and then at last I went to Chelsea Art School. I was already drawing for magazines but I had found that I couldn't draw some of the things I wanted to draw. So I became a part-time art student, taking life classes two days a week for the next two years. Life drawing wasn't very fashionable then — any more than it is now — but it was something I needed, so I was very motivated. My wonderful teacher, Brian Robb, also taught a course in illustration, which he advised me *not* to take. He thought it was too late or something! But he continued to advise me and eventually he gave me a job at the Royal College of Art — teaching illustration!

It was after I stopped being a student that I got into illustration in a serious way. It was then that *Punch* magazine, for which I had already been doing drawings, gave me a regular job of doing two small drawings every week. As I wasn't being paid all that much money, I went on living at home. My parents, without discouraging my interest in drawing, had already made it clear to me that they thought art was no way to make a living. The *Punch* assignment at least gave a small kind of professional authenticity.

Q: Did you work at creating the drawing style that you have long since become so identified with? Or did it somehow just "happen"?

A: It sort of happened. It was before I was doing books and was working for *Punch* and other magazines. If you wanted to do gag illustrations for a magazine, you would send in a rough version first. If it was accepted, you were then commissioned to do the finished drawing. An art director I was working with told me one day that my roughs were a bit better than my finished art. That comment led me to be more relaxed about my drawing, and that feeling in turn released the movement of the hand. My handwriting and drawing became more alike.

Q: Once you found your more relaxed style, was it hard not to become self-conscious about being unself-conscious?

A: You train yourself to do it. I draw my finished art very fast, but by then I've already done roughs in which I have worked out the overall structure of the drawing I want. I know where everything is going to go. With all that in mind, I try to draw the picture as though for the first time.

Q: How did you become interested in children's books?

A: Initially, all I knew was that I wanted to draw and that I liked being funny. It took me some time to get to the idea that it was a good thing to do a picture book. When I finally did get there, it was partly because I had trained as a teacher: in a very small way I see making children's books as being like teaching a class. I am interested in that relationship, even though I didn't go on to make teaching my career. It became even more appealing when full-color printing became readily available to illustrators. I had become known as an illustrator who worked in black and white and was fed up with that reputation. So when I wrote my first picture book, I deliberately made *Patrick* (1969) a story that *had* to be illustrated in color.

Q: It seems that drawing for an audience really matters to you.

A: Yes, I would say it does. Some artists insist, "I draw for myself!" I think it's possible to draw for an audience *and* to draw for oneself. That's one of the things that has always interested me about making children's books. You're thinking about the young audience while also thinking about the drawing you want to do — about questions that the child who sees it won't ever think about.

Q: What do you especially admire in the work of the French artist [Honoré] Daumier?

A: You can't see it in my drawing, but Daumier has been a major influence on me, even though my drawings are much lighter in feeling than his. What interests me most is the way his people react to each other. It's a kind of theater. The theater aspect of illustration is very important to me, too.

Q: His faces are very animated.

A: Yes, and when I'm drawing I feel in a sense that I'm acting out whatever it is that the characters are doing. Michael Rosen, the poet with whom I've collaborated on several books, said of me once, "You're a mime, really."

Q: In Roald Dahl's *The Magic Finger,* the character William Gregg says: "Oh isn't it lovely! I've always wanted to know what it feels like to be a bird." Do you wonder about that, too? You've said that you especially like to draw birds, and in your drawings it often feels as if everything in them is about to take flight.

A: I was an enthusiastic bird-watcher as a schoolboy and I think I'm attracted to birds as subjects because you can make them move like humans to some extent. They have two legs, they stand up, and so on. Many of my characters *do* fly through the air — generally, because they're thrown! But yes, a lot of flying goes on.

Q: How did you come to be Roald Dahl's illustrator?

A: That was thanks to my publisher, Tom Maschler, who brought out my first picture books as well as Roald Dahl's first picture book, *The Enormous Crocodile* (1978), which I illustrated. Then I illustrated *The Twits* (1980) and *The BFG* (1982), at which point the relationship matured because *The BFG* is a book with quite a lot of richness of feeling in it and so Roald and I had to talk about it.

Q: Did you and he become friends?

A: Oh, yes, and when I went down to visit him, I met his family and I got to know them, too. I'd go and we'd talk about the illustrations, and then we'd have dinner and relax together. I got to know him quite slowly because we were such very different kinds of people. Fundamentally, he was a man of action who had been quite a sportsman as a young man, whereas I have always hated any kind of game! He was much more confrontational than I've ever been. Still, we found plenty of common ground.

Q: How did you arrive at your image of the Oompa-Loompas? Did you try different versions of them?

A: Some, but not a huge number. That book had been illustrated a few times before I took it on. I wanted them to look a bit mischievous and I wanted to do something with their hair that was different from what had been done before. I had two students at the Royal College of Art at the time, two young women who had cut their hair short in such a way that it stood on end. I admired it tremendously and then I found out how nice it was to draw! I think that's where my Oompa-Loompas came from.

Q: Your Willy Wonka looks like a music hall performer or street musician.

A: Yes, well the drawings are themselves a kind of performance. Occasionally, Willy Wonka speaks to the audience. He even *winks* at the audience.

Q: How did you approach making your *ABC* (1990) book, knowing as you did how very many alphabet books had come before it?

A: It was a mixture of finding images that fit the letters and organizing the drawings so that I could draw things I wanted to draw anyway. I knew it had to be fairly crazy. That was what I felt about it. I thought of it as an excuse for entertainment more than a way of learning the alphabet. I particularly like the little girl jumping into the mud (*M*). There's a drawing with a strangely shaped parcel in it (*P*) and you don't ever find out what's in the parcel, which gives the reader something to wonder about.

Q: Was there a real Mrs. Armitage?

A: I don't think I know a Mrs. Armitage, although several people have written to me subsequently saying they are like that — including one named Mrs. Armitage! In creating that character, I never once thought about who Mr. Armitage might have been. Maybe he died or the marriage had foundered. She has the spirit of someone who is carrying on regardless. We may crash but we'll carry on.

Q: Do you ever draw models?

A: No, and I don't use sketchbooks either. If I need to know what a certain car or tree looks like, I may get reference material, but ninety percent of the time I'm just making it up. I seem to be able to make up anatomy: I have a sense of how people stand and how they move. I did do a lot of drawing from life in the past and so now I live out of that, in a sense.

Q: Is there anything you can't draw?

A: I'm not good at drawing any smooth piece of equipment. I wouldn't be very good at drawing a Ferrari! For some reason, I'm only good at machines if they're breaking up.

Q: Tell me about the experience of illustrating *Michael Rosen's Sad Book* (2005), which deals with the author's son's death and is such a heart-wrenching book.

A: I talked to Michael on the phone from time to time, but I wouldn't say we worked especially closely together on the book. I had already known Michael for a long time by then. It's a gloomy book, of course, but it's not just gloomy — and it has a wonderful text. It's about such a sensitive subject that one felt slightly guilty wanting to do it so much. The problems in it were so interesting that illustrating it became pleasurable. There would be a line like: "I think about people looking out of windows" — and it was only when I came to draw it that I discovered what it meant, that the book was about looking back but also about looking ahead. Books like that are needed, and by a tragic coincidence Michael was perfectly equipped to write it.

Q: What do you think of the advent of museums devoted to picture-book art?

A: I'm very glad about that. People enjoy the art in picture books but they're not often aware of the history behind it or of the richness of the field. The strange thing is that when a picture is hanging in a museum, people will look at it as art, but if a picture is printed on paper, they may look at it as "ephemeral." To take a picture out of a book and put it on the wall invites people, in a sense, to hold up a magnifying glass to it. It's a way of saying, "Why not stop and have a good look at this." In fact we are at present attempting to set up such a museum, a center for illustration, in London, and if we can raise the money for the building we have in view, it will become the House of Illustration.

ASHLEY BRYAN

Born 1923, New York, New York

As an illustrator, painter, printmaker, writer, folklorist, and story-teller, Ashley Bryan has crafted a vibrant and amazingly var-ied body of work for both children and adults. Bryan's African-American heritage has inspired much of this remarkable output, including the lion's share of the more than thirty children's books he has written and/or illustrated since the late 1960s. Throughout his career, how-ever, Bryan has also remained open to all sorts of other creative influences, including Japanese brush painting, medieval woodblock art, Mother Goose nonsense, and the thoughtful comments of his Maine schoolchild friends. Time and again, he has borne out the truth of the Tuscan proverb that "the story is not beautiful if nothing is added to it." Something, that is, of the storyteller's own deeply felt personal experience.

Perhaps no other living artist can claim to have both taught painting to kindergartners and chaired the art department of a major American institution of higher learning — Dartmouth College. To Bryan, however, there is nothing incongruous about his "range." A wiry, tall man with a warm, booming voice and ready laugh, he approaches every aspect of his work as a learning experience and has therefore always felt a genuine sense of comradeship with his students and readers, whatever their age. Although Bryan no longer teaches, he spends half of each year on the road, giving poetry readings and storytelling performances for schoolchildren and other audiences throughout the world.

Bryan and I have been crossing paths at conferences, and catching occasional meals together, for years. For this interview, he spoke with me by telephone from his studio in Maine on October 30, 1999.

~~~~~~~~~~~~~~~~~~~~~~~~~

LEONARD S. MARCUS: How did you get started making books?

ASHLEY BRYAN: In the public school I attended in the South Bronx during the Great Depression years, we began early on making books about whatever we learned. As we learned the alphabet, for instance, we did pictures for the letters and then sewed them together, and our teacher would say, "You've just published an alphabet book!" That was the beginning. There was a lot of fun and play associated with our bookmaking. Our teacher would say, "You're the author, you're the illustrator, you're the publisher. Take it home. You're the distributor!" I got such a warm response at home from my parents and brothers and sisters and the cousins who were growing up with us that I just kept making books as gifts. I never stopped, and it was that initial satisfaction that sustained me later, when there was no commercial interest in my work. It took over fifteen years before my work was finally picked up on.

Q: Despite the Depression, you seem to have had a wonderful introduction to art and learning.

A: Thanks to the Works Progress Administration, there were free art and music classes in the community where we lived and throughout the country. My parents sent us children out to whatever was free. They said, "Learn to entertain yourselves." That idea was behind it all. So my brothers, my sisters, and I were all painting, drawing, and playing instruments. The WPA teachers were very exciting for me as a nine-, ten-, and eleven-year-old. I might paint an apple red or green, for instance, and then the instructor would show us work of the Impressionists and explain how a fruit could be explored in many different colors while still giving the impression of *its* color. I was fascinated and would play around with these ideas.

Q: What was it like growing up in the Bronx during those years?

A: Our neighborhood and my public school were ethnically and racially quite mixed, with German, Irish, Italian, Jewish, and black people living on the same streets. There was a fairly tolerant atmosphere. Next to our school was a German Lutheran church, and it was so big and so pretty that we children said to our parents, "We want to go to that great big pretty church." So my mother did take us. Services were both in German and in English. And we grew up in that church, which was always active in the community.

Q: Did you go to the public library in your neighborhood?

A: Oh, yes. Although we children could not afford to buy books, we borrowed books from the library and felt that they were our books for the time that we had them out. We used to clip coupons from the daily newspaper, and at a certain point, when you had enough coupons, you could trade them in for a book. It meant so much to me to have a book of my own. I can remember seeing listed among the books to send in for *The Sketch Book,* by Washington Irving, and thinking it was a book of drawings. So I did send in for it and was surprised to find a drawing only on the title page. At home we had orange crates on which to set our books. That was our library.

Q: Were certain books special to you then?

A: Oh, yes. Basically, it was poetry and folktales and fairy tales, which I read quite exhaustively. Poetry, from Mother Goose to Robert Louis Stevenson's *A Child's Garden of Verses* to Eugene Field's *Poems of Childhood* to Christina Rossetti's *Sing-Song* poems. I loved poetry and I began to explore poetry myself. I didn't take to novels until later because I didn't go for the long reading of a book. I loved stories that could be told within a brief span of pages. I relished the language and would go back over words that seemed nicely placed. I would read a paragraph that thrilled me with a sense of adventure or the beauty of words, and would stop, go back, and read it again.

Q: Were you a good student?

A: I was a very good student academically all the way through. I was in high school wondering whether I would be a doctor or lawyer or what-ever when I decided that, having always drawn and painted, I wanted to study art. And so during my senior year, I put together a portfolio with the help of my teachers, all of whom were white and were very supportive of me.

Q: Did your parents encourage you, too?

A: I was very fortunate in that it never occurred to them that I would not go on doing what I loved to do. The point my parents always made was that if you are doing something creative and constructive, there is no reason not to continue. And so, as a teacher, I found a way to keep doing what I enjoyed while also continuing to make art. Now when I speak to schoolchildren, I tell them, "You need encouragement. If you can't get it at home, knock on the door next door and keep on knocking all the way down until you come to someone who will encourage you in the constructive, creative work that you are doing."

Q: Tell me about your grandmother, the one who spent time with your family when you were growing up.

A: She was such a wonderful person. Granny Sarah Bryan was my father's mother. Both my parents had left Antigua at the end of World War I and settled in New York City. My grandmother had not seen my father, or all but one of her other children, in many years when she came to visit us in the Bronx. I just loved being with her and got to talking with her and asking her questions. I would sit with her, drawing all the time. I can even remember once drawing her when it was evening and she was in her nightgown sitting on her bed. I was sitting in a nearby chair when a friend walked in and my grandmother, who was very quick, looked up and said, "Ee oh me husbend"—"He is my husband." She was so witty, and she loved to dance. My book *The Dancing Granny* (1977) is an African tale collected in Antigua and it has as one of its two main characters a spider called Anansi the trickster. I did that book to bring out the spirit of the dance that my grandmother had in her. She would outdance the great-grandchildren. She used to say, "The music sweet me so!" I used that phrase in retelling the story. In the original, the spider continually gets away with his tricks. That, of course, is generally the point of trickster tales — that the trickster gets away with mischief. But when I was basing my story on the motif, I thought, *Well, he might trick my grandma a few times, but she's eventually going to figure out what he's up to, and she's going to get him!* So that is why in my version I worked it to the point where she waits for him and catches him before he can get up into that tree, and then they have to dance together, and "As the lead bends / The dance goes on, but the story ends."

Q: Is that your grandmother pictured in the drawings of *The Dancing Granny*?

A: Well, it's her spirit. Children ask: "Could your granny really do that?" And I say, "Listen, my friends, if you don't exaggerate, a story won't come true to life." I used swift brush paintings in the spirit of the Japanese brush painter [Katsushika] Hokusai, in his scenes of everyday life, to capture the swift spirit of the moving figure. When I look at those pictures I can still see my granny alive and spinning. She was about ninety-four when she died.

Q: You served in the army during World War II. Would you tell me about your experiences during those years?

A: I was in my third year in the Cooper Union Art School when I was drafted. It was a time of segregated armies and most blacks were in transportation corps. I was assigned to a stevedore battalion responsible for loading and unloading cargo at docks. I was first stationed in Boston, then sent to Scotland, where we were stationed in Glasgow. Then we went in as part of the Normandy invasion. The beaches were heavily mined, many lives were lost, and I was fortunate in having survived that experience.

Q: It must have been emotionally complicated to be fighting for freedom in a segregated army.

A: It was very difficult when you were finally in it because you went in with ideals but they were quickly weighed down by what you were experiencing. We were continually facing restrictions in both Boston and Glasgow because the army did not want the black soldiers to go out and meet with the white population.

Q: Were you able to continue to draw during those years?

A: I always had drawing materials with me, which I stuffed into my gas mask. Whenever I had an opportunity, I would take out my drawing materials and sketch whatever was going on. In Glasgow, I went to the battalion commander and got permission to attend the Glasgow School of Art. The other fellows, who were faced with the usual restrictions, always supported me when I went off to class because they thought I was putting something over on the officers. I thought I was fighting for my right to keep growing as an artist.

When I returned to Cooper Union to complete my studies, I had an exhibition of the drawings and paintings I had done during the war. But because of the experiences of the army and the war, I found I could not go on directly in art. So instead I did my undergraduate work all over again, as a philosophy major at Columbia University. I was trying to get some understanding of why it is that we continually choose war. Of course there were no answers but I became very caught up in the way the mind works, how man constructs philosophical systems of ethics and politics and aesthetics. Summers, I would come up to Maine, to the Cranberry Isles, which I had discovered while at Cooper Union. I was awarded a scholarship to the Skowhegan School of Painting and Sculpture in Maine in its founding year of 1946. I would paint through summer and when I returned to my studies in New York I would always keep a sketchbook at hand. Sketchbooks for me are always the connection to the mystery and wonder of marking a blank space and seeing something emerge from it. And so I would draw but was not able to go more deeply into the work. But as soon as I completed my work at Columbia I went to Aix-en-Provence, in the south of France, where, under the G.I. Bill, I began to paint all day.

Q: Did your interest in philosophy merge with your early interest in folklore? Characters in folk stories so often represent universal types — the trickster, the fool — that add up to a kind of inventory and philosophy of human potential.

A: The mind tends to make connections, and I have always felt that whatever I learn becomes integrated with everything else. And yes, I came to feel that the stories of the world tend to bring us together. I speak of folk stories as a "tender bridge," as a way of connecting past cultures and times to the present.

Q: When did you begin telling stories before a live audience?

A: It was a natural extension of my work as a teacher. I have always been teaching — at universities, in after-school programs for elementary school children. At the Dalton School in New York I taught drawing and painting to kindergartners and first-graders. All of my work as a teacher has involved story. The most important aspect of story is the way one person speaks to another. Children pick up on story simply from all the things that other people say to them, the answers their parents give, for example, to their questions: "What was it like when you were growing up?" "Would you tell me that story again about when you were on the boat coming over from your country to this country?" All of this is oral tradition to the child. It becomes a part of their lives. If they become writers, they will draw upon those sources. If they don't become writers, they will still pass those stories along, with their own additions to them. In that sense, story is always going on. When I'm teaching a class in painting and drawing, there's a kind of storytelling that plays an active part in it as well. I'm not talking now about the literal sense of working from a story in a book, of interpreting visually a tale about a king or queen or a princess. It is also a kind of storytelling when a student, coming to terms with an exercise, finds an inventive way, for instance, of relating a series of straight lines marked across a page to the trunks of trees.

Q: What did you like best about teaching?

A: When I have taught college students, I have loved in particular to work in the introductory courses, teaching basics. Students who had not been drawing or painting for years would begin to make discoveries through the exercises offered. So, for instance, if we worked with straight lines — with divisions between one straight line and another, with questions of spacing and rhythm — we would then go outdoors and draw the trunks of trees. Our goal would be to relate the reality of the trees to the abstraction of lines on a page. I have always tried to connect up with the essentially abstract nature of any art, whether it be dance or painting or poetry.

I would always give my college students set exercises and set limits. I would say, "This is an 8 × 10 paper. This is a pencil. The exercise is to draw these apples on the table. They're your challenge. When you understand their limits and work with all that you are, then you will be able to surpass those limits." I would tell them, "A Rembrandt drawing was done on a piece of paper of a certain size and shape and it was because Rembrandt gave of himself that he surpassed the limits of that paper and he was able to create something invaluable with it. That is what we are after."

Q: How did you approach teaching art to very young children? What did you like to do with them?

A: With the young children it was a question of what *they* did with me! I enjoyed their absorption in what they were doing. They would become so absorbed that it would be as if time no longer mattered. At the Dalton School, where I taught for many years, I would simply have materials ready for the children — brushes, paper, and a muffin tin for each two children with paints, the primary colors plus green, black, and white. I never said, "Today we'll do this or we'll do that." The children would come in and simply get to work. They would have their ideas. They would go on and on with what they were doing. If a child didn't have an idea, I might say, "Maybe there were some horses . . ." or some such thing, and right away the child would say, "Don't tell me, don't tell me. I know what I want to do!" And they'd go right ahead. My goal was to create a situation in which the children would not be dependent on me but would rather come with a tremendous sense of excitement about whatever it was that they had to offer. I remember one child who day after day painted columns of starlike forms in different colors. The other children said to him, "You're always painting stars!" And the child kept on painting stars. After a while some of the other children began painting stars, too. But I never said to him, "You've already done that," which is so often what happens to a child. You let the child go to the limit, the exhaustion of possibility, which is what art is about. Any motif is absolutely endless in its possibilities of exploration, and you don't know beforehand how far a child might like to go with an idea.

Q: Tell me about meeting Jean Karl, the editor with whom you have worked now at Atheneum for more than thirty years.

A: Jean, who founded the children's-book department at Atheneum, came up to my studio one day in the Bronx. I wasn't sure what she was interested in, so I brought out paintings to show her of my family and other subjects. She went over to the table where I did my book projects, however, and when she saw the things of that kind that I was doing, she simply decided to send me a contract to illustrate Richard Lewis's anthology of poems by Rabindranath Tagore, *Moon, For What Do You Wait?* (1967). Then she asked if she could publish some illustrations I had done for African folktales. I had originally done these paintings, which are often mistaken for block prints or silkscreen paints, for a folklore research project for Pantheon Books. Later the project was bought by the Bollingen Foundation, but my illustrations had, in the end, not been used. I had done the paintings in red, yellow, black, and white — the colors of the ancient rock paintings. I painted them so strictly that I almost felt I was carving an African mask or sculpture as I did them. I then wrote my own retellings of the stories, based on the ethnographers' summaries. As I did my own research, I realized that I wanted to do what storytellers have always done, to flesh out the story motifs by bringing into them any connections from my own life that I felt might help make the stories, when printed, approach the spirit of the oral tradition. That has been my challenge in all that I have done. The stories of *The Ox of the Wonderful Horns and Other African Folktales* (1971), for example, follow that pattern. I research the background of the tribe from which the African tale comes. I always acknowledge the source of the story and then set out to make the story my own.

Q: How, more specifically, have you gone about trying to capture a sense of the spoken word on paper?

A: I work from poetry. I use the devices of poetry — close rhyme, rhythm, onomatopoeia, alliteration — to slow the reader and make the reader feel that he or she is hearing a storyteller.

Q: How do you go about deciding on your visual approach to a given book?

A: The art that I have drawn upon comes from many different sources depending on the text. In the case of my books of spirituals, for instance, starting with *Walk Together Children* (1974), I used block prints in the spirit of medieval European religious block-printed books. I worked from that tradition in order to connect up the spirituals — which a great many people sing but which very few people realize were the creation of black slaves — and the European tradition of religious music and art. I was stirred by the realization that the slaves had created these songs as a way of being free. The slaves were in chains, they suffered, but they had to give forth something rich and beautiful of themselves. There are thousands of these songs, and they are considered our finest contribution to world music. And yet they were completely overlooked in introductory books for children, which is why I began my series.

Q: As a child, did you meet older people living in your neighborhood who remembered the days of slavery?

A: No, and I'm not sure to what extent that history would have been a part of my knowing, and of my asking of questions as a child. You see, in our studies anything about the black world had to come from family or from the community. It wasn't taught at school. What I got to know of any of the black writers and artists or of black history came from a special reach for it. It was when I was in junior high school or in high school, searching out through my love of poetry, that I first became aware of the poetry of Paul Laurence Dunbar, Countee Cullen, and others. Today as I travel around I find that, even though some books are more readily available, a special reach is still needed. Teachers generally still seem unaware of most of the black poets I talk about when I visit schools. They may know of Langston Hughes. My point has always been: They are writing in English; their work is accessible. I illustrated a book of Nikki Giovanni's poems, *The Sun Is So Quiet* (1996), which is firmly in the tradition of the childhood poems of Stevenson and Field. Her poems are so fresh and unaffected and yet they are not all that well known.

Q: Tell me more about your interest in the poetry of Paul Laurence Dunbar. You edited a book of his work, *I Greet the Dawn: Poems* (1978).

A: He was pursued constantly for the poems he wrote in black dialect. Those are the poems for which he became well known, but they represent only a small percentage of his work, the rest of which is in standard English, in the tradition of Keats and Shelley. I compiled my collection in order to help bring that other work, which is so very touching, and so accessible, to young peoples' attention.

Q: Would you talk about the illustration style you have used in recent years for full-color books such as *Turtle Knows Your Name* (1989) and *The Night Has Ears* (1999)?

A: I am a trained artist, but a strong feeling for the untrained artist has always endured in me. So I am a sophisticated artist working, at times, within the folk tradition. Working in that way, there is a sort of lessening of ambition, of wanting to be good. You just know it's going to *be* — and what is done is going to be right. It's wonderful to lose yourself in that kind of approach.

Q: Why did you dedicate *Turtle Knows Your Name* in part to your editor Jean Karl?

A: It was her persistence, I suppose, in keeping after me to do my books, in much the same way that that grandma keeps after the little child in the story to learn his name. Jean has been so wonderful over the years. I doubt that my work would have reached a wider audience than family or friends without her. The book is also dedicated to a little boy who was living on my island here in Maine, where I myself have lived now for over fifty years, and seen whole generations grow up. In some ways, the community atmosphere on the island reminds me very much of the neighborhood in which I was raised.

Q: I've read that you like to paint by day and illustrate by night. Why do you divide up your time in that way?

A: Painting is at the center of what I do. As a painter, I love to work directly from the landscape. In Maine, from spring until late October I can be outdoors painting in my garden or down by the ocean. My books are a natural outgrowth of my love of painting. You'll find that throughout the history of art, painters have loved working from texts. Much of the art in museums comes from books, whether it is the Bible or mythology or history. Everyone who reads is seeing images. The artist wants to draw them down. So I have always to find my balance between painting and books.

Q: Have you ever revisited your old South Bronx neighborhood?

A: On visits to New York, I do. I have family and friends still living there. About ten years ago, there was a fire at St. John's Evangelical Lutheran

Church, where I spent so much of my childhood — that beautiful big church we talked about earlier, with the high vaulted ceilings and stained-glass windows from Germany or Italy with their depictions of Bible stories acted out by blondes and brunettes. In that fire a major window, a resurrection panel over the altar, was destroyed. I have always supported the church from a distance and after the fire the church contacted me about designing the replacement window. I had been working for years with beach glass that I pick up here, making my own little windows, but had never done a stained-glass window before. I was thrilled to have this opportunity. I designed a black Christ rising from the tomb with the three Marys — each a different shade of black, to indicate the range of colors of black people in the United States — bearing their ointments. And so my window is up there in the church now, glowing along with all the others.

JOHN BURNINGHAM

Born 1936, Farnham, Surrey, England

M y true interest," John Burningham once wrote of himself as an artist, "is in landscape and light." Wild landscapes were among his first playgrounds he ever knew as the financially strapped Burninghams adopted a strangely nomadic life during World War II, renting out their modest house southwest of London and wandering the English countryside in a trailer. Amid all their comings and goings, and with both his parents attracted to offbeat theories of education that emphasized a child's creative potential, John attended nine experimental schools before he was eighteen, boarding at several of them. Wherever he was, he drew.

As a young man, Burningham registered as a conscientious objector and ventured farther afield, performing alternative service in Scotland, Italy, and Israel. He then enrolled at a London art school where he honed his craft as a painter and draftsman and met his future wife, a theater design student named Helen Oxenbury.

London during the early 1960s was the red-hot center of a worldwide youth-culture explosion — home to the Beatles and the Rolling Stones, mod Carnaby Street fashion, and a hip new approach to graphic art that viewed life through rainbow-colored glasses. Burningham had come to London with no thought of pursuing a career in children's-book art. But a chance encounter with an enterprising and warmly encouraging editor tilted him, provisionally, in that direction, and the prizes and high praise that greeted his first efforts quickly sealed his fate.

He and I spoke by phone on December 21, 2009, nearly twenty years after I visited him and his wife (whom I had recently interviewed in New York) in their rambling, delightfully overstuffed Victorian home in Hampstead. When we spoke this time, *John Burningham,* his illustrated memoir (which concludes: "End of Part One: to be continued . . .") had just been published and an exhibition surveying the whole of his career had recently been on view at Dovecot Studios, Edinburgh. Burningham, not surprisingly, was in a reflective if quite wistful mood as he looked back at a lifetime of art making and storytelling.

LEONARD S. MARCUS: Did you like to draw as a child?

JOHN BURNINGHAM: I did a lot of drawing and was lucky in that I was given the facilities. In a lot of cases, particularly at school, kids are not that lucky: they're just given a rotten small piece of paper and a couple of hard crayons, and are told what to do. That's not going to inspire them to do very much.

Q: Did both your parents encourage you?

A: Yes, and my mother was pretty good at drawing. She should have been an artist, but it was thought at the time that women were meant to be mothers and not have a career too, which is sad.

Q: Your family moved a great deal and even lived for a time in a mobile home. Do you think your nomadic childhood had something to do with your love, in more recent years, of collecting old objects, including even bits and pieces of old buildings?

A: It could well be. I am always finding things of that kind. Just recently I bought four rather nice stone heads on eBay, four nice young ladies representing the arts. I want to try and find out who the sculptor was, because he was obviously a very talented man.

Q: In addition to moving often as a child, you attended many different schools, including the famous experimental English boarding school called Summerhill. Did you like Summerhill's founder, A. S. Neill?

A: Yes, I did. He was a very impressive man.

Q: Once during your time there, you stole the key to the pantry, where all the food was stored. Neill did not react in the way most teachers or adults generally would have reacted, did he?

A: His idea was that you get results through love rather than authoritarianism and punishment. I think he was right. He wanted the key back but he was very kind about it and saw no need for a punishment. He was also the sort of man who could look straight through you. It would have been very difficult to tell him a lie: he would have sussed you out. One respected that — and one never took the key again.

Q: Neill's handling of the incident reminds me of Mr. Gumpy's reaction to the calamity of the boat tipping over in *Mr. Gumpy's Outing* (1970). Even though he warned every one of the passengers not to rock the boat, he doesn't scold them when they do so anyway. He doesn't even seem to think twice about having gotten drenched. Instead, he invites them all to tea. Could there be something of A. S. Neill in Mr. Gumpy?

A: Well, there could be.

Q: Did you have books at home as a child?

A: I had Randolph Caldecott picture books and books illustrated by Cecil Aldin, who was one of my heroes. He was such a great draftsman! My mother used to read to me. We didn't have television, thank God.

Q: Once you became an illustrator, did you take a closer look at the Caldecott books or other childhood favorites?

A: No, I wouldn't say that I did. Helen and I have some of Caldecott's prints on the wall now, and I admire his draftsmanship. But I don't look at anybody's work in particular and then put it away and think, *Now I'm going to draw like that.*

Q: Did you have a teacher who influenced or inspired you?

A: There were some good teachers at the Central School of Art in London, where both Helen and I studied. We had a lot of part-time teachers who were working artists. That was good because they weren't stale from doing nothing but teaching all day. Teaching art is never easy because unlike mathematics, say, there are no rules.

Q: Was there the feeling in England during the years after World War II of wanting to start things over again — to find new ways of making art?

A: Yes. I think I was very lucky to be getting going in the 1960s. We were throwing off the very depressing shackles of World War II and the 1950s, which in this country was such a grim time of continued rationing. Suddenly we had the Beatles! The whole scene came alive and it felt like anything was possible. That was a good feeling and I was lucky to be part of that.

Q: You expressed that feeling in part through color.

A: *Borka* (1963), my first picture book, was one of the first four-color picture books published in the U.K.

Q: You must have felt a little bit like the title character of that book: a strange bird who had gone to London, where it was absolutely fine to be a strange bird.

A: Again, that *could* be. When *Borka* won the [Kate] Greenaway Medal and proved to be a great success, the publisher said, "Can we have another one?" I would have had no reason to say no, and so I carried on as a picture-book artist. Fairly soon after that I got the assignment of illustrating Ian Fleming's *Chitty Chitty Bang Bang,* which was quite a coup for a comparatively unknown illustrator.

Q: By then you had designed some posters for the London Transit Authority. Was creating poster art good training for picture-book making?

A: Not especially. The people who commission posters are usually quite timid. They know that, if it's a success, they will get all the accolades, but if it doesn't work, they're for the chop. So nobody wants to be the first person to commission you to do something original. It's rather sad that it's like that.

The editor with whom I began to work on books, on the other hand, was a very clever man who would take on anything. He — Tom Maschler of Jonathan Cape — would say, "Let's do a book." When I did *Granpa* (1985) he immediately rang up John Coates, the producer of the animated film based on *The Snowman* by Raymond Briggs, and he said, "Look, I've got your next film lying on the floor. Do you want to come round now and see it?" John, who was working around the corner, did come round and said, "Yup, you're right!" And he went from there. Tom has that kind of vision. He got John Lennon to write poetry. I was lucky to work with somebody like that.

Q: You visited New York in the 1960s. Was that an eye-opening experience?

A: I was there only briefly and I wish I could have stayed longer. But I didn't want to live on the sixteenth floor of an apartment building. I like to be able to step out into a garden! Maurice Sendak was just getting going then, and Push Pin Studios was doing amazing graphic design work. Really good stuff was coming out of New York then. New York seemed more exciting than London.

Q: Few illustrators have worked in as many media as you have. Do you experiment at the start of a project in order to decide how you want the pictures for that story to look?

A: I try not to repeat something unless it has a purpose. It becomes a challenge to use different media, a way to make illustration more interesting, I suppose.

Q: Sometimes — as in the Shirley books — you'll show what the parent is saying in one medium and what the child is imagining in a different one.

A: Oh, yes. There, of course, the purpose is to show the juxtaposition between the two worlds.

Q: In the Mr. Gumpy books, you rendered the animals in such a painterly, sensuous way. Then for the illustrations across the page, you chose to have line drawings.

A: I think I started by having all the illustrations in *Mr. Gumpy's Outing* in color and then decided it would be more powerful to have one side of each page be monotone. This makes me want to go have a look and see. Making pictures is like making a conversation: you can use hundreds and hundreds of different colors and patterns and things but it will be completely meaningless unless it accomplishes what you set out to do. Some people can't stop talking. It's a sign of insecurity, usually. They fear the silence. They can't have a pause. And there's this awful idea about illustration that if you have lots and lots of color, then you have given children what they want. I think that that is a way to make kids bored. The wonderful thing about kids is that when they're bored, they let you know.

Q: Do you receive lots of letters from children?

A: I do get letters from children, but mercifully the age group I tend to make books for are not the letter writers. If I wrote for twelve- or thirteen-year-olds, I would have to employ three secretaries. I have met people who find themselves in that situation. It's very endearing, but — my God! I get a lot of letters from teachers, too.

Q: What about parents? In your Shirley books and others, you sometimes show the parents' point of view as well as the child's. In *The Magic Bed* (2003), you have a moment where you offer an amusing, tension-breaking explanation for why a child's bed might be wet in the morning. You are being as reassuring, I think, to the parent as to the child that bed-wetting isn't something to get overly worried about.

A: Well, it's very difficult being a parent.

Q: Looking at one of your early books, *Humbert* (1965), brought me back to your interest in collecting old, discarded things. The hero of that book is someone who collects and carts scrap for a living. You must feel that in some ways people in general are very wasteful.

A: Well, I suppose I do, but that book was simply about someone — a scrap dealer with a horse and cart — whom I would see in the street where I was living at the time. In that sense, the book just happened.

Q: In your memoir you talk fondly about your very old wooden dining-room table, and about the stories that such an old table could tell. For you, collecting old things is connected to storytelling, isn't it?

A: Well, that's the attraction of things that are handed down: the stories that are attached to them.

Q: And *The Magic Bed* is about an old bed that is found in a junkyard, and which turns out to be a far better place to dream up stories than a new, store-bought bed could ever possibly be.

A: Yes, I suppose that's true!

Q: In *Whaddayamean* (1999), you suggest that children should consider speaking up to their elders about matters of general importance like the fate of the environment. You seem to be saying that children have a role to play. Yet it's always a bit tricky, isn't it, to make that kind of statement in a children's book without it becoming prescriptive or too heavy?

A: It's a very tricky business. Many people have tried it, and I think *The Lorax,* which was a very early comment on pollution and the destruction of the environment, is the most successful book of its kind and a brilliant book. It's a hard one to tackle. The problem I had with *Whaddayamean* was, first, talking about God at all and, second, my not wanting to indicate that God was either a he or a she. It was all such a lot of trouble! Still, I quite like that book.

Q: You have said your work has always been strongly affected by the landscapes in which you have lived. Was that true for the making of *Hey! Get Off Our Train* (1989)?

A: I was commissioned to do that book for Expo 90, a world's fair in Osaka, Japan. In preparation for my work on it, I was taken out on a river through an incredibly beautiful national park in southern Japan, and many of my pictures for the book are based on the things that I saw there.

Q: Do you spend much time looking at landscapes in museums?

A: I don't go to museums much because they're always full of people! I become terribly conscious of the people and then I can't focus on the art.

Q: You have had a museum exhibition of your own artwork recently. How did that go?

A: I thought it was time and I wanted to include my posters and illustrations from my so-called adult books — which always sounds a bit iffy! — as well as from my picture books.

Q: Do you think an illustration changes when it's taken out of the framework of a book and framed instead on a museum wall?

A: Well, it should do because as an illustrator you are usually building up to some sort of visual climax. Illustrating a book is not about just making one loud noise on every page. The quiet "movements," if one can describe illustration in musical terms, are not necessarily going to stand out when you take them out of their intended context and frame them up — though it's surprising how by and large they do seem to work.

Q: You have also recently collaborated with Helen on a picture book for the first time ever.

A: What is wonderful about that is that she battled away with the drawings and I only had to battle away with the text, though like so many projects that end up with what appears to be a minimal text, it went through a number of drafts.

Q: Some of the illustrations for *It's a Secret!* (2009) look like drawings from a sketchbook. They are among the most relaxed and casual-seeming illustrations you have published.

A: I'm fond of that book, but one regret I have about the illustrations has to do with those dogs. I quite like the dogs, but I wanted to change one of them. I had had them all smoking and was told that that was absolutely forbidden now. Then I wanted to have one of them just staring into a mobile phone. But I was so fed up with doing the drawings that I couldn't get round to making the effort to change it. It seems such a tiny detail now. But still I'm sad I didn't do the dog with the mobile phone.

Eric Carle

Born 1929, Syracuse, New York

A t first glance, the lemon-yellow sun that shines down benevolently in every one of Eric Carle's picture books might easily be mistaken for an image from a kindergartner's drawing. It is not by chance that this is so. The childlike simplicity of Carle's illustrations is a deftly managed fiction aimed, as is every element of his meticulously crafted work, toward the goal of making books that young children feel to be entirely their own.

As a design student in Germany, Carle received his initiation into the traditions and practices of the modernist applied arts, an aesthetic tendency that, during the decades that bracketed World War II, set out to streamline everything man-made, from type fonts to flatware to architecture. Seen purely in design terms, the airy expanses of white space and sleek layouts of Carle's picture books have more in common with the look of a contemporary art gallery than they do with *The Little Engine That Could*. Carle, however, also reaches out to his young audience through the life lessons his gentle fables pass down to them. Stories such as his — about the value of work, the importance of friendship, and the everyday miracle of a caterpillar's metamorphosis — have special meaning, Carle believes, for children just making their own life-altering transition from home to school.

Carle is a precise and energetic man whose large studio hums and clatters at one end with the high-tech whir of computers and scanners, and at the other with the old-fashioned rustling and scratching sounds that artists working with papers, pens, and brushes have generated for centuries. On July 28, 1994, the day this interview was recorded at the artist's summer home in the Berkshire Mountains of western Massachusetts, Carle was busy gathering material for the autobiographical essay that was subsequently published in *The Art of Eric Carle* (1996), a book for which I wrote the introduction. A far more ambitious project lay just ahead: the founding of the Eric Carle Museum of Picture Book Art, in Amherst, Massachusetts, an institution aimed at giving the picture book its due as an art form.

LEONARD S. MARCUS: You have written that your father liked to draw. What kinds of drawings did he make?

ERIC CARLE: To entertain me as a child, he would do what I'm doing today — tell stories while drawing pictures of trees and animals, and sometimes people. He might say of a queen bee, "Oh, she's a little bigger than the others." Then he would draw a number of bees, point to the largest one, and say, "That's the queen."

Q: Did he ever say to you that he had wanted to become an artist?

A: Yes, he did. His father had not let him.

Q: Was it after your first-grade teacher told your mother that you had artistic talent that you first began to think of yourself in that way?

A: At that age I did not think in those terms. But even before then, I knew that I enjoyed drawing and that it gave me a lot of satisfaction.

I only have vague feelings about that period of my life. Some time ago, I gave a talk in Syracuse, and the nephew of my teacher came to hear me. The following day, we visited my old school building — it's now condominiums!

I've written about my memory of the light streaming in through the windows of my classroom, as a sort of first memory of the experience of beauty. Well, during this last visit I realized, for the first time, why the light made such an impression. The building is set on a knoll. It has no trees or houses around it, and so the light coming in through the windows is strong. You walk up the street with all its houses and trees, and all of a sudden you get to this building which is not surrounded by anything. I am still amazed that a five-year-old could have had so vivid a response to such an experience.

Q: What else do you remember about your first year of school?

A: I still remember the walk there, and the brushes and the papers and the paints and the large colorful paintings I did. I know I had a woman for a teacher, but I don't recall what she looked like, whether she was young or old. Yet to this day I sense her influence and her being, somehow.

From that time onward, I always knew that I would be an artist. I wouldn't have said "artist" then. I only knew that when I grew up I would have to work for a living, and that I was going to work with a brush and a pencil and papers and do pictures. That's how I would have put it then.

Q: Did you speak German at home?

A: My parents spoke German to me, but I answered in English. When we came to Germany, I could understand my relatives, but I couldn't answer them.

Q: Oh, I see! [*Both laugh.*]

A: Quite quickly, though, within a short time, I was speaking German.

Q: Was it following your first-grade year that you and your family went over to Germany?

A: Actually, as it turned out, I went to first grade for about half of the year in Syracuse. I didn't know that until just recently, when we found my first-grade report card and the name of my teacher, Miss Frickey.

Q: Did you have many children's books at home?

A: No, we didn't. I had a Mickey Mouse book, I remember, and I loved Flash Gordon comic books. You know those fat, small books, which are now collectors' items. I was terribly intrigued by Flash Gordon, and even more so by the beautiful women in these stories! He was always rescuing some damsel in distress. I remember certain pages as vividly as when I first looked at them.

In one scene, Flash Gordon is traveling in an airplane, and a meteorite slashes through the wings. There is also a beautiful woman in the plane, and because only he has a parachute, he holds her tight so that they can parachute down together to safety. There I was, only four, five years old, and I liked such things!

Q: Did you go to the movies?

A: Yes. My father would take me to see any movie about nature. He loved animals. He also liked to take me for walks in the woods. In Syracuse my parents belonged to a nature club, and on the weekends we'd all go out to the Finger Lakes, where there were log cabins and boats. I remember on one such outing catching a snake that scared the other adults. But then my father stepped in and explained that it was only a harmless garter snake.

Q: You sometimes put snakes in your books. Yours are never too frightening, but they usually come as a surprise.

A: Yes, I suppose that's true.

Q: It struck me just now as you described that incident with the snake that you had enjoyed getting a rise out of the grown-ups.

A: Could be! [*Both laugh.*] All children like to do that.

In Germany, where the forests are more cultivated than here, with paths winding through the woods and then opening onto beautiful meadows, we would go hiking every weekend until I was ten, when my father was drafted into the army at the beginning of World War II. Even if we just walked down behind our own house we came to a brook, which we could follow out into the meadows and then on into the forest. If we kept on going, we eventually came out at a castle.

Q: It all sounds like a dream — or a German fairy tale. Was there a spiritual quality to the love of nature shared by your parents and their friends?

A: My mother was the more practical, realistic type, but, yes, I think my father was a very spiritual man, though I didn't know it at the time. I would also describe him as a very intelligent, nonambitious man.

Q: He was content with the kind of work that he was doing?

A: He was a clerk with the City Health Department — and I don't think he particularly enjoyed it. It was a dumb job, really. But he liked people, and they liked him, so that made it bearable. The rest was routine. It paid the rent.

Q: Were your parents religious in the traditional sense?

A: No. We were of Protestant background, but no one in my family went to church, not even my grandparents. In fact, I wasn't even baptized. Religion meant nothing to us. On the other hand, we didn't look down on it either, any more than up. It was just meaningless to us.

As it happened, we lived next door to the church, and often the preacher would pass by and he and my mother would chat with each other. My mother would always slip him five marks for the church [*both laugh*] to pay off her guilt, I think, for not going!

Q: At the time you went to Germany, there were many Germans living here in this country, and there were people in Germany who had recently come from America. So, in a sense, as the war approached and then began, the two countries were more closely linked than one might have thought.

A: Yes, that's very true. In the suburb of Stuttgart where we lived, there were a number of people with relatives who had come back to Germany from America. My father hadn't wanted to return to Germany. But my mother had become homesick after my Carle grandmother had visited in Syracuse in 1934. And so it was decided to go. Of course they later regretted it.

Q: You've written about your new school as being very different from the one you attended in Syracuse.

A: Yes, I hated the school in my new country.

Q: How did you cope?

A: By blending in — so well, in fact, that my teachers barely noticed me. I have described the corporal punishment aspect of that school's philosophy of education. I think I turned off in the face of that, and decided to just get by.

Q: As a child, did you know the classic German children's picture book *Struwwelpeter*? Readers have always had such extreme reactions to the book, finding it either utterly terrifying or hilariously funny.

A: I loved it. Most child psychologists and psychiatrists who work with children, educators — the official people — reject that book. Kids love it. It's outrageous, often cruel and fear-inducing, and full of exaggeration. A child's thumb gets cut off, another child burns to death, and yet another one starves himself to death! I find that you cannot be very subtle in your humor with children. Children often seem to enjoy these spine-tingling "cheap thrills" because deep down they know that these stories are invented, that the humor, depiction of cruelty, and the fierce creatures are only in our imagination. Subtlety, on the other hand, may confuse the child. It has to be slapstick, and *Struwwelpeter* is slapstick — as are Mickey Mouse and Flash Gordon. It's so exaggerated that children know it's not true. Exaggeration takes the edge off. The same can be said of *Where the Wild Things Are.*

Q: In *Rooster's Off to See the World* (1972) you provided a note saying that as a child you were more of a philosopher than a mathematician. Do you remember that?

A: Yes, it had to do with my teacher trying to explain subtraction by speaking of "taking away an apple." My response at the time was that you cannot really take an apple away. You can hide it, you can put it behind your back, but then everyone knows it's behind your back.

Q: Was there a hint of rebelliousness in your not wanting subtraction to work in the prescribed way?

A: I don't know. I think my rebellion was an internal one. I had had this wonderful gentle teacher in Syracuse who formed the foundation, and when I came to Germany an old-fashioned disciplinarian teacher tried to tear it down. At some point, I must have decided that he was not going to win against me. That is my nature. I'm stubborn on certain issues.

Q: You continued to draw and paint?

A: Yes, always, and my parents were very supportive. When my relatives came visiting, they brought me pencils and watercolors and brushes. My mother would proudly show my work to visitors, and they would praise it.

Q: She had taken to heart what your first teacher had told her.

A: Absolutely. Otherwise, however, my mother was Germanic—somewhat dictatorial and domineering. In Germany at that time, the idea was that a child had to be broken in by the time he or she was six years old. It was terrible. It's how the teachers thought, why mine felt justified in administering corporal punishment. He decided this free-spirited little American kid had to be broken in. He saw it as his duty.

Q: Was there a certain point when you realized your family would not be returning to America?

A: Yes, and that is when I decided I would become an engineer and build a bridge across the Atlantic. Looking back at my life, I think I have done so through my books. I say many critical things about Germany, but I also love Germany. But there are certain facts about Germany's history that one cannot overlook.

Q: As a child who was visually oriented, did you notice the Nazi propaganda posters? They must have been posted everywhere.

A: I did. In Europe, newspapers were publicly displayed in glass cases for all to read. I remember looking at those, too. I also remember Herr Heller's shop being destroyed on Kristallnacht, in November 1938, when I was nine years old. As I walked past it on my way to school, I saw that the shopwindows were bashed in and that a policeman was standing guard, who told me to move on and go to school. And, I suppose, I forgot about it. But did I? We are talking about it. I feel ashamed that it didn't make more of an impression on me, that I wasn't outraged. I have discussed this with my wife, who is a childhood specialist, and she says that it might be too much to expect from a child of that age.

Q: When you first moved to Germany, it would seem from what you have written that the other children took a special interest in you because you were an American. Did those same children turn against you when America became the enemy?

A: America never really became the enemy.

Q: What do you mean?

A: Even during the war, the Germans, I think, always looked up to the English and the Americans, especially the Americans. I know people won't believe that. The German propaganda of that time depicted the Russians as subhuman beings, the Poles as having no class, the Balkan peoples as primitive peasants, and the French as degenerates. But they admired the English and the Americans. America was about jazz and chewing gum and Hollywood. But it was also about big power, industrial might. They respected power. The sun never set on the British empire, and so on. In school we learned English and studied English history, culture, and literature — Shakespeare, for example.

Q: How did you meet the first of the German teachers to have a great positive influence on you, Herr Krauss?

A: In Germany children went to grammar school for four years, until the age of ten. Then a choice was made — whether you would go on to higher education or become, say, an apprentice mason, or railroad worker, or whatever. If you and your family chose a more advanced education, you would go eight more years to Gymnasium, or high school, which is what I did. That's where I met Herr Krauss. He was my art teacher, and he was a fabulous guy.

Q: You have written that he spoke to you about your "free and sketchy style" of drawing.

A: Yes, he pointed it out to me.

Q: So you evidently had an artistic style by the time you were ten! You have also written that Herr Krauss expressed his distaste for the propagandistic and naturalistic styles of art that were dominant in Germany during the Nazi period.

A: It was all so heavy: the flag, the raised fist and the raised hand, and the soldiers and the workers and the farmers and the proud Germans. On a more sentimental level, there might also be an image of the sun setting on a farm. There was this strange combination of images of sentiment and images of power. Herr Krauss, however, had hung out and studied with the German Expressionists, whose art the Nazis condemned as "degenerate," and was forbidden to be shown or exhibited. On top of that, he had belonged to the Socialist Youth Movement. He must have been a pretty bohemian intellectual artist type in his youth. Later, he had a family to support and so he became an art teacher. He did not agree with what was going on, but like many people, he felt he had to shut up about it.

I don't remember art classes in grammar school, but in Gymnasium, art classes were organized, and I was happy making pictures. Herr Krauss sensed some potential in me; he knew more about me than I knew about myself. That is why he asked me to come to his house, where he showed me reproductions of Expressionist and abstract paintings. That was when he pointed out the loose and sketchy quality of my work, and when I heard him call the Nazis "charlatans" and *"Schweine,"* which was utterly amazing, a very dangerous thing for him to do. These so-called degenerate paintings didn't make that much of an impression on me at the time — but I did come away with a certain strange feeling that I would not have been able to put into words.

Q: Yet you still remember his exact words now!

A: Yes, that's true. At the time, I must have thought he was crazy: *What does he know?*

Q: Would you say that he risked his life that day he invited you over?

A: I certainly think so. As a Socialist and an Expressionist, he already had two strikes against him. If I had turned him in, something I didn't even think of, he would have been interviewed by some horrible official person, who would have brought out his past, his mistakes, and next thing you know, he'd have been sent to a concentration camp. Those things happened, as I now know. After all, he didn't know me well. I was just one of his students, and we were all so idealistic: we thought we were *good* people. For Herr Krauss to contradict our reality was definitely a very dangerous move.

Now, when I visit my sister in Germany, I always have to drive through the village where he lived, and say, "Oh, Herr Krauss lived around the corner." I visited him often in later years, long after I had returned to live in the States. The last time I saw him he was retired and had gone senile. He didn't recognize me. His housekeeper had prepared for him a little basket with his medicine and an apple in it and his pipe and tobacco, and he just shuffled around with it. He was painting a very neat and conventional little painting of sunflowers and — this is the funny part — he raged against abstract artists. In his senility, he considered *them* total charlatans.

Q: You enrolled in art school after the war?

A: In '45, immediately after the war. Germany was in chaos. All of the schools had been closed down. They had either been bombed out or could no longer be heated because of coal or oil shortages, or the teachers had to undergo the de-Nazification process. For the first six months after the war, I worked as a filing clerk for the American military government to earn some money. After that, I returned to school and disliked it more than ever. So, I went to Herr Krauss for advice about my future, which I knew had to be in an art-related field. He made a list of the possibilities: window decorator, painter, theater designer, all the artistic professions. Then he added "graphic designer" to the list and said, "These people make the most money." That sealed my fate! [*Both laugh.*] He then recommended that I go see Professor Ernst Schneidler, head of the Graphic Arts Department of the *Akademie der Bildenden Künste* (Academy of Art and Design) in Stuttgart. My family, you see, wouldn't let me go to school to become just an artist. They were very practical. But graphic design was another matter. *That* was a profession, and it was fine with me, too. So off I went. I was sixteen years old. Here in the United States, it could be said that I dropped out of high school.

I studied with a man who was considered one of Germany's finest teachers in the field. Professor Ernst Schneidler was also known by connoisseurs of the graphic arts as the designer of several well-known typefaces, among other things. My father was still away, in a prisoner-of-war camp in the Soviet Union, from which he didn't return until late 1947. In Herr Schneidler I finally found someone I could look up to, someone who understood me.

After my conference with Herr Krauss about my future, my mother and I decided that I would enroll in the academy. In 1946, my mother accompanied me to go see Professor Schneidler. I was accepted at an exceptionally early age. Professor Schneidler looked at my portfolio and accepted me without requiring that I take the usual test. He also waived most of the other standard requirements — all of which went to my head. I thought I was this hot shit. [*Both laugh.*] I became an *artiste*. I was insufferable, and my work suffered as a result. So at the end of the first semester, he asked to see me in his office. He called me on the carpet, saying that he wanted to kick me out of the school. But the next day I went back to talk to him, asking that he change his mind. He then told me that for the next three semesters I would be assigned to the typesetting shop as an apprentice.

The typesetting shop was part of the Graphic Arts Department. Herr Veith would be my teacher. He was an old traditionalist who could have come straight from the typesetting shop of Gutenberg. He lived and breathed type, typesetting, and typography. And I would be an apprentice and set type by hand for the next three semesters.

Q: You make it sound like the equivalent of digging ditches.

A: It *was* like digging ditches — and it was a stroke of genius on Professor Schneidler's part. That kind of disciplined training was just what I needed if I was going to go on developing my talent.

Q: Did Professor Schneidler warm up to you later?

A: I would see him in the hallway, and of course we Germans were always very formal about addressing our professors. I would say, "Professor Schneidler, how are you?" "Oh, fine. How's your mother?" "Good." For the next year and a half, that was the extent of our relationship. Finally, however, I went to see him and said, "Herr Professor, my three semesters are up. I hope you will critique my work again, and that I will be admitted again to the art classes." He agreed to do so, and from that moment onward we had a wonderful relationship.

He was a difficult man. We called him the *Meister* — and he *was* the master. He only came in once or twice a week for an hour or two, and in fact said very little. He would look at a piece of work and say, "Dumb" or

"Not dumb." Yet for forty years he produced most of Germany's leading graphic artists, type designers, poster and book designers, illustrators, and art teachers. He somehow made us want to please him.

He would speak about "our cause," by which he meant our responsibility as designers to create better surroundings for people: a pleasing fabric for a jacket, a striking poster for a public space, a good typeface for reading, a satisfying design for a cup. This was our cause. I remember him saying that we were not going to change the world, but that we should think of ourselves as a link in a chain — an important link in society. That was his first message. After that, it was all about composition and color and design. He'd always spoken of being "decent" in our approach to design — that is, about being sure that we had aesthetic integrity — and about the ends to which we applied our talent.

Q: That is fascinating to consider as a reaction or postscript to the legacy of the Nazi era.

A: I still feel that I learned my most basic professional values from him. That is what made him a master. His students still occasionally meet to talk about him. It's almost like a knighthood to have been his student. I taught one year at Pratt in '63 as a guest lecturer, and the attitude then was that the students expected the professor to please, to entertain them. When I went to school, it was the other way around: I was there to please Professor Schneidler, to gain *his* respect.

Q: Did he give exercises or assignments?

A: Not many.

Q: What exactly did he do, then?

A: He discovered each student's talent and nurtured it. Some students were good in calligraphy and others in poster design, and he would channel those talents. But most of all he somehow instilled a spirit in us. This will sound crazy, but it was almost a religious experience.

It was during this period of my life that I finally separated from my family, who were tradespeople, clerks, laborers, bakers, butchers, tinsmiths. We didn't have many books. My mother went to one opera when she was eighteen years old, a performance of *La Bohème* — and talked about it for the rest of her life. My parents read little. And then there I was in Schneidler's class with, first of all, Schneidler himself, this magnificent man, as my mentor, and with all my fellow students, and with the knowledge of those who had come before us and gone on to do great things. A new world had opened up to me. They became my family. Even now the spirit of Schneidler is with me: The Force is with me! [*Both laugh.*]

Q: What kinds of artwork were you doing at that time?

A: Remember, we were engaged in graphic design and applied arts. Art per se was not the goal. We started out with exercises in "dividing space," or composition. For that part of our work, we would make up our own colored papers. For instance, we'd take a pot of red paint and a pot of yellow paint. Then we'd do a sheet of pure red, followed by a sheet of red with one or maybe two drops of yellow, gradually increasing the yellow until we arrived at a sheet of almost pure yellow. Then we would work with green and black, blue and orange, and so forth. In this way, we accumulated a great many different colored papers, which we then would cut or tear into pieces and arrange in mostly abstract patterns and designs. We then placed a mat around our compositions and put a piece of glass over them to hold them in place for Schneidler to view and critique. We didn't glue the papers down: the idea was just to train our sense of shape and color and composition, not to create something permanent. We regularly practiced this particular exercise throughout the four years. It was the equivalent I suppose of a pianist's scales.

From there it was on to calligraphy, bookbinding, lithography, photography, typography, printing, etching, woodcut and linoleum block engraving, poster design, illustration. After my stint at the typesetting shop, I did some linoleum cuts that Professor Schneidler looked at — and you know what he said? "Good!" Usually, as I told you earlier, it was either "Dumb" or "Not dumb." "Good" meant exceptional! Right away, however, he tempered his high praise. He said, in his precise Prussian accent, "That's good, all right. But, ah! You don't even understand *why* it's good. Try to find out why." [*Both laugh.*] That, I think, was good advice.

Q: So he kept you on edge.

A: Yes, and then I did several etchings, and it did not turn out so good. I was not so good with the thin lines. My strength has always been in big, bold shapes. So with the etchings, it was back to "Not so good, not so good. Dumb, dumb." When we did calligraphy, he watched me for three months and finally he said, "Herr Carle, not so good. Dumb. Don't do that anymore. We don't need more calligraphers!"

Q: And so he pointed you in a certain direction.

A: Yes, and with his guidance a great many of us became strong and capable at one specialty or another.

Q: Did you feel as though you were being initiated into a tradition?

A: Yes, I did. For instance, when my typography teacher was a young man, there were still journeymen in Germany, as there had been since the Middle Ages. First, there would be a three-year apprenticeship, and then you became a journeyman. A journeyman would walk, say, from Stuttgart to the next town, and to the next town, looking for work in the shop of a master, wearing a certain scarf or hat, or carrying a walking stick that identified his trade. And then finally, after many years, if he qualified, he might become a master himself. This system of training hardly existed by the time I was growing up, but through my typography teacher I had contact with the last generation of these journeymen. I think that a little of that tradition was passed on to me.

Q: The term "international style" is often applied to the postwar developments in architecture and design. Did you feel a part of that emerging tradition, too?

A: Yes. For us in Germany it was very exciting because for twelve years, during the Nazi regime, so much had been repressed in art and design. I remember seeing experimental movies, for instance, some consisting strictly of abstract shapes, and thinking they were *wild*. I hadn't known such things could be done.

Having experienced that horrible war, we also realized what nationalism could lead to, and so we became internationalists — at least, the artists, the designers, and the thinkers did. We felt very much like pioneers.

Q: Then, in 1952, you returned to the United States.

A: I always knew I would come back to America, but I felt I needed some professional experience first. So I worked for one year as a freelance poster designer for the United States Information Agency, and a second year as art director at a fashion magazine. By then, I had my portfolio and felt confident enough to return.

When as a greenhorn I arrived in New York City, I wanted to find a job as a graphic designer, preferably in advertising. Someone suggested that I go see the New York Art Directors' Show, which was on exhibit at the time. There I discovered the beautiful designs for *Fortune* magazine, for which Leo Lionni was the art director. Immediately after I left the exhibit, I called him on the telephone and asked if I could show him my work. He told me to come the next day at eleven o'clock. Mr. Lionni looked through my portfolio and arranged a meeting for me with George Krikorian, the art director for the Promotion Department of the *New York Times,* where Mr. Lionni knew of a job opening. I got the job! Leo Lionni became the next in the line of people who helped me professionally. Several years later, after he had created his own picture books, he encouraged me to do picture books, too. In two successive years, he set up appointments for me to see his editor. But both times, nothing came of it. It was much later, through Bill Martin Jr., that my career as a picture-book artist began.

Q: On leaving Europe for America, did you feel you were coming to a less cultured part of the world?

A: Not at all. When the war broke out, and for some time after the war ended, there was no opportunity for me as a young man to absorb the famous European culture, the magnificent cathedrals and the art, to visit the great museums. But then when I came to New York, I went to the Museum of Modern Art, the Metropolitan Museum of Art, and this was more culture than I had ever experienced.

Q: Soon after your return, however, you were drafted into the United States Army. When you returned to civilian life, you went to work for the *Times* and then for an advertising agency specializing in pharmaceutical advertising. Did your experience as an advertising artist serve you well when you later turned to children's-book illustration?

A: In advertising, you try to surprise, be different. If everyone uses big type, you use small type. If everybody uses red, you use green, not because green is better than red, but because it will stand apart. In advertising, surprise and shock are important. In advertising, you can shock or you can be extremely tasteful, or you can combine the two!

Q: You've never been shocking in your books, though, have you?

A: Not I suppose until *Draw Me a Star* (1992), in which I painted Adam and Eve as a nude couple. I got a little flak for that, but I still don't consider it daring. One teacher wrote to say, "Your grandmother would be ashamed of you." [*Both laugh.*] But it really was so mild.

Q: Why did you leave advertising?

A: Advertising is a profession for young men and women. At the age of forty you ought to be a partner or own your own business or be the manager or executive or something, and that's exactly what happened with me. I had started out as a designer at the agency, and frankly I was doing fine work there. Then I got the very glamorous title of international art director. We had overseas offices, and it became my job to set up our art departments in them all. I was still in my early thirties, and all that travel seemed very exciting to me. Then, one day, I found I did not want to do it anymore. All too often I had to go out with clients, have dinner and drinks with them, attend meetings, and there was all the backstabbing and office intrigue. It just hit me one day that I wanted to make pictures.

Q: You remind me now of your book *A House for Hermit Crab* (1987). You knew it was time to move on.

A: I suppose that's true. I'm a Cancer, born in June: that's the sign of the crab. And I myself am somewhat of a hermit. In general, I'd much rather stay at home and work in my garden than travel. Also, I suppose, the message of that book is the lesson that Professor Schneidler gave his students: start anew, move on, keep surprising.

Q: You met Bill Martin Jr. around the time you left the advertising agency, did you not?

A: I illustrated his *Brown Bear, Brown Bear, What Do You See?* (1967) before I quit my job. I had already been thinking of quitting when I met Bill, who was employed at the time as an editor and writer at Henry Holt, where he created a line of books for the school market, not for the trade.

Bill's version of how we met is that he was at his doctor's office leafing through one of the medical magazines when he saw an ad I had designed featuring a collage image of a lobster. He told his art director to find the artist who had done that ad. In my version, I was getting ready to freelance and left my portfolio one day with his art director, who showed it to Bill. His story's more colorful than mine, but I think mine is the truth!

In any case, that was a lucky combination — Bill Martin Jr. and Eric Carle. A few years ago we traveled together on a book-signing tour and got to know each other better. One morning he came down from his hotel room to breakfast and said, "Eric, what do you think of this? *'Da da da da da DAH.'* Or should it be: *'Da da DAH da da DAH?'*" "Bill, what are you talking about?" I said. "Oh, my next book. I usually do the rhythm first, before I do the words." Isn't that wonderful? Therein lies the secret of his success. His books are *all* rhythm — heartbeat!

Q: What else did you learn about writing picture books from him?

A: Bill opened up the world of picture books for me when I illustrated *Brown Bear, Brown Bear, What Do You See?* For one thing, I learned the value of repetition and rhythm. That lesson stood me in good stead when I came to write the text of *The Very Hungry Caterpillar* (1969).

Before I met Bill, I had been given a freelance assignment by an educational publisher for which I was asked, in essence, to illustrate thirty-two good ideas on a single page. My reaction was that I would rather take one good idea and illustrate it across thirty-two pages. Bill's idea about picture books was the same as mine.

Q: Then you met Ann Beneduce, who remained your editor for all these years.

A: The first book I brought her was *1, 2, 3 to the Zoo* (1968). I was being very careful. It was like dipping my big toe in the water. It was a wordless book; I had stayed away from language because I didn't yet trust myself to write. It was a conventional counting book; you know the kind, with one elephant, two giraffes, and so forth. Ann looked it over and said, "There are many children's counting books. We have to give this something extra to take it out of the ordinary. You can do it!" That was *all* she said.

So I went home and added the little train on the bottom in the gatefold. That was the next lesson I learned: have something extra. When it came to *The Very Hungry Caterpillar,* Ann didn't have to say, "Add holes." I had done a dummy for that book, with holes and all, before I met her. It originally was going to be called *A Week With Willi Worm!* I worked on it with Ann, who first suggested a caterpillar instead of a worm, and who of course published it.

Q: Children aren't supposed to punch holes in their books. Did you feel that by adding the die-cut holes to *The Very Hungry Caterpillar* you were introducing an element of mischief into your work?

A: Perhaps, without realizing it. But I thought of the holes primarily as a design element. I always try to squeeze as much as possible out of the paper. I don't want just a plain sheet of paper. I often want to have a fold or a hole or other device. I want to change that flat sheet any way I can. That is how the designer in me came to do holes.

Q: You have also talked about wanting to make books that are also toys.

A: That impulse comes from the observation that up to a point a child is more tactile than verbal: holding hands, holding his or her bottle or rattle, and being held is what matters to them at first. School comes later, and with school comes sitting still and focusing on the words in books. So I thought there should be something between the warmth of being held and of holding on to a toy, and the more abstract experience of book learning. There should be a bridge between — and that is what I've tried to create in the form of a book with holes in it, for example, a book that is partly also a toy. It is a toy you can read, and a book you can touch.

Q: Why do you choose to illustrate your children's books in collage?

A: In thinking about my books, I don't put too much emphasis on collage per se. It's just a technique. Some paint in oils; others draw in pen and ink. At least, that's how I see it. The reason I happen to do collage *may* of course go back to my art school experiences with Professor Schneidler, "dividing spaces" with our colorful papers, which I created as an art student. That could be so.

Q: Collage seems to be such a free-form medium.

A: Well, yes and no. It's very free in that you can shift the papers around. But the shapes are very defined, and once they are glued down, their relationship to each other is also defined.

Q: The article about your work in *Graphis* [volume 15, November 1959] refers to your interest in chance elements. Does that, too, go back to your classes with Professor Schneidler?

A: Yes. Sometimes you have to listen to chance. You have to look at the crack in the wall. You might follow the crack and be surprised to find a picture in it. It's like the children's game of looking at a cloud and seeing an image, say, of a sheep, in the shape of the cloud.

In my studio, I have files full of my papers, hundreds and hundreds of tissue papers, all filed by color. I may take one that happens to be on the top: it will look good, and so I'll glue it down. That's the way it goes, often. Other times, it won't look good to me, and so I'll take out another paper and another. But often one that pleases me just happens to be in the top of my drawer. I believe in chance. You carry a cup of coffee across a room. You look at it and it spills, or you don't look at it, and it doesn't spill. It's that type of chance event that I have in mind.

For instance, consider how this illustration emerged as the image of a porcupine in *Today Is Monday* (1993). I started by thinking, how am I going to do a porcupine? You see the gray paper here, the grayish paper? First I took a gray paper, then I went over it with black-and-white brush-strokes. From this I cut out the pieces for the quills. At that point, I didn't know what the quills would look like. It was unpredictable. I then cut out a dark blue shape for the porcupine's body and glued it down on a white board, and over the dark blue shape I glued the quills. I didn't know what would happen. I just had an idea it was going to work, and I was right in my assessment.

Other times it doesn't work. I'll have the same sort of impulse — that I should do this, this, and this, and then this, this, and this is going to happen. Only it doesn't happen at all. That's the chance of it.

In my picture of a porcupine, there must be a hundred quills, each individually pasted down. That takes a long time, but I enjoy doing it. I'm sort of *suspended* as I work. That's the most satisfying part of my work, I think, simply being in that state.

Q: In the video you have made about your working methods, it looks as if making the papers is almost a meditation for you, to be putting the colors down and observing the patterns and effects as they play themselves out.

A: Yes, it is. It's like being in an alpha state: total peace. Other artists must have the same sort of experience.

Q: You have said that often the idea for a book forms in your mind rather quickly, and that it then often takes you another couple of years to work the idea out to your satisfaction.

A: That's true, in general. I'll have a rough idea, just a seed, a beginning. In the case of *The Very Quiet Cricket* (1990), I simply decided that I wanted to do a book about a cricket. That was all I had, at the beginning. In the case of *The Very Hungry Caterpillar,* all I knew was that I had the holes punched into a stack of papers. All I needed now was a "hero."

That doesn't mean I toil daily on a book. I might put an idea I've worked on away for two weeks or six months or a year or more, and then take it out again. The first dummies I make are quite rough, then they get neater and neater. Finally, I make one in color, in crayon maybe, for myself and to show my editor.

As I work on the book, I love it. I hate it. I think it's awful — and I think it's wonderful. I discuss it some more with my editor. Then there comes a time when I feel it's right: I don't *know,* but I feel it to be so. That's when I consider the book done.

Q: Recently, you have started to do books that are more directly autobiographical.

A: I tried to write a longer book, without pictures, about my boyhood in Germany during the war. I started to write it, but I found it very disturbing. I had nightmares about the war and tanks and people shooting at me. So I stopped and instead wrote *Flora and Tiger: 19 Very Short Stories from My Life* (1997). They're simple autobiographical stories, each somehow concerned with animals, a relative or a friend, and me.

Q: Would you tell me about your experiences visiting children in schools?

A: I used to do a lot of that. After a while I could tell almost from the moment I entered a school what kind of principal it had. I found that the principal's spirit pervaded everything. I would walk in and say to myself, *This is a rigid school.* Then I would actually meet the principal, and sure enough he or she would turn out to be a rigid person. Other schools would be just the reverse.

But let me tell you about the presentation I made. The children and I would pretend to do an illustration for a book together. I'd say, "What is your favorite animal?" Someone would answer, "Cats," so I would draw a cat's head. Then, another child would say, "Giraffes," so I would put a giraffe's neck on, and then as others spoke up asking for a turtle, I would add a shell, and so on. That presentation of mine in fact was the beginning of *The Mixed-Up Chameleon* (1975).

Here is another exercise that I did with children in their classroom. I would ask, "Do you think I can fool your eyes?" What happened next depended on how they answered. If they said, "No!" I'd know I hadn't made contact with them. But if the children shouted, "Yes, yes you can fool our eyes!" This would mean that I had gained their confidence. I would then say, "What's the opposite of black?" They'd shout, "White!" Then I would ask, "What's the opposite of red?" After a brief pause, they would always say, with confusion in their voices, "What do you mean, what's the opposite of red?" That's when I would hold up a big red dot in front of a white wall, and say, "Now stare at the red dot, and stare at it, and stare at it. Don't let your eyes wander at all, and watch what happens when I pull away the red dot. Watch carefully. Another color will appear, and *that* is the opposite — or complementary — color of red." When I pulled the dot away, they continued to look and look and, finally, very tentatively, someone would always say, "Green?" After that, the other children felt confident that they too had seen the green afterimage. By the way, this exercise is based on Goethe's color theory. It became the basis for my book *Hello, Red Fox* (1998).

Q: Ann Beneduce was also the first American editor to publish the work of Mitsumasa Anno. Do you know his books?

A: Oh, I love his work. He's one of my absolute favorites. Ann introduced me to him once in London. His books and mine are very different, yet our goals are the same.

Q: Anno said something to me that I thought summed up a lot about his work. He said that he wanted his books to "teach without teaching."

A: That is what I do, too. I would put it a little differently. I would say that I camouflage my teaching. Yes, I camouflage mine.

Q: I also wonder whether you are acquainted with Margaret Wise Brown's books?

A: I had seen *Goodnight Moon* before I began doing my own books. As an adult who was not particularly interested in picture books, I didn't quite understand the appeal of *Goodnight Moon.* It seems to me that adults don't always appreciate the artistry of picture books, especially the picture books for preschoolers and just-about readers. And early on, I, too thought, *What's so great about that?* Later as I began to do my own books, I realized the depth of mastery of Margaret Wise Brown's work. I now know why children respond to her work with all their heart and soul. And that brings me to an interesting point. It was the children who embraced my work to begin with, not the adults. I still feel that teachers and librarians would not be aware of my work were it not for the many children who wanted to look at and read my books and take them out of the library. That's what Margaret Wise Brown and I have in common: children have chosen us, not the professionals, not the librarians, or the teachers, or the grandmothers. I don't just think that, I *know* it to be so.

Q: How has your work changed over the years?

A: It has become more painterly — and after so many years I would think it also should be better. When I visit museums now, I look less at a painting as a whole. Instead, I get intrigued by the textures created by the brushstrokes on the canvas or by the patterns in the grass or in the leaves or brickwork or water. Seen that way, a painting becomes an abstraction. I'm especially fascinated by the brushstrokes, dots, and patterns of the impressionists — Renoir, Seurat, Monet, Degas, and don't forget Van Gogh. I focus entirely on the brushstrokes or, say, on a certain pattern of dots. Inspired, I return to my studio and paint more of my papers.

LEONARD S. MARCUS: Since we first talked, you founded a museum — the Eric Carle Museum of Picture Book Art, in Amherst, Massachusetts. What got you started on that extremely ambitious project, and how did your thoughts about it evolve?

ERIC CARLE: The seed was sown many years ago, in the early 1980s, when my wife, Bobbie, and I visited Japan and were shown the Chihiro Art Museum, which is the home of the work of the children's-book artist Iwasaki Chihiro. The story was that, after she died, the neighbors came to her son Takashi and asked if they could look at her originals, and he thumbtacked them to the walls, and that was how the museum started. First he opened a small museum in Tokyo, then a much larger, gorgeous one in Azumino. That experience influenced us very much.

At first our museum was just going to be a single large room. You would go in one door, look at the pictures, exit by the other door, and maybe buy some postcards. That was going to be it! But then we thought: it will need a library; it will need an art studio; it will need an auditorium and food and some gifts. So then the question became, how big a building? The architect didn't know, so he said, "How many school buses would you like to provide parking for?" I said, "How about two?" And from that it grew.

I use white a lot in my picture books, and our architect, Earl Pope, wanted to do the same with the museum. We also wanted to light up the lobby somehow, and so I decided to paint four large panels featuring complementary colors: a red panel next to a green one and a yellow panel next to a blue one. I did not think of them as paintings but rather more like decorations, like endpapers in a book. I painted the panels on the floor of my studio on Tyvec, the durable, lightweight material that is used for wrapping buildings under construction. I used janitor's brooms for paintbrushes and did one panel a day, with no plan in mind. All I knew was the color! I had a really good time.

Q: Do you recall the first time you walked in the front door?

A: I had been very interested in the construction process all along, so my first time inside the finished building was not a surprise. Still, it was a wonderful feeling. Bobbie and I felt so proud. There had been nights along the way when I had woken up in a sweat, thinking, what was I doing? But I have discovered that a lot of things get done in this world by people who don't know what they're doing, things that if they *did* know better, they might not even try.

Q: What kinds of art interests you these days?

A: Robert Rauschenberg, Richard Diebenkorn, Cy Twombly. I don't know why, exactly, but as a friend once said, "If you have a good meal set in front of you, you can analyze it or you can eat it."

Q: You are such a perfectionist about design. When you pass a sign or poster in the street, do you mentally redesign it on the spot?

A: All the time! When we go out for dinner, I redesign the menu as I'm ordering. The same for everything I look at: it's a curse, an absolute curse! We'll be out on the highway, a road sign will being coming up ahead of us, and I'll say, "Why didn't they make that lettering a little bigger?"

My latest project is making what I call "street art." I'm photographing traffic lines, the arrows they paint on the blacktop, cracks in the pavement. The idea is to put a little twist on everyday things, to find the beauty in them. Interestingly enough, it can be done.

LOIS EHLERT

Born 1934, Beaver Dam, Wisconsin

A rt supplies," Lois Ehlert once pointed out, "are really all around us." Leaves, feathers, buttons, corn kernels, sticks, and plastic forks, to her way of thinking, count as art supplies every bit as much as paint pots and stacks of brightly colored papers. Looking closely at how these and other building blocks of her art — some store-bought, others foraged for at home or outdoors — come together as an image or scene in one of Ehlert's collages can feel like an adventure in seeing. But Ehlert usually has another story to tell as well, whether it be about cats or birds or a child building a snow family or making vegetable soup.

With a woodworker father and a seamstress mother, Ehlert grew up knowing all about the routines and rewards of making things by hand. With her parents' encouragement, she soon got into the act herself. Art and craft supplies were her favorite childhood playthings. Later, when she trained as a graphic designer, Ehlert became intrigued with books as physical — even sculptural — objects. More than most picture books, hers tell their stories in part by means of the changing sizes and shapes of their pages and with the addition of die-cut holes that serve as windows between pages, linking their images in all sorts of ingenious ways.

We first met in 1993 when I moderated a daylong program about picture-book making at the Corcoran Gallery, in Washington, D.C., and Ehlert was one of twenty-three illustrators who sat at drawing tables and gave visitors a demonstration of how picture books are made. For this interview, she spoke with me by telephone from her home in Milwaukee, Wisconsin.

∿ ∿ ∿ ∿ ∿ ∿ ∿ ∿ ∿ ∿ ∿ ∿ ∿ ∿ ∿

LEONARD S. MARCUS: What kind of child were you?

LOIS EHLERT: I was a quiet child. I was not in the big pack — and I didn't have a desire to be popular either. I didn't have the same interests as the other children. I was in my own world. I have taught children who were in their own world, too, and that is wonderful to see and to be able to encourage.

Q: Both your parents encouraged you to be an artist from an early age, didn't they? That is fairly unusual.

A: I didn't realize it was unusual at the time. Both my parents made things with their hands. I thought everybody did. It may have been partly a matter of necessity. My parents had lived through the Depression, when people often had to make things for themselves. I was the youngest of three children, and my mother made a lot of our clothes. My father did woodworking. When I was in art school, he built some cabinets for me. Growing up,

I had a special folding table at home on which I did my art. My father put a special plywood top on it, which made it special. I still have it. The other thing that made it special was that I didn't have to clean it up every day when I was done. My brother and sister were not that lucky. I think my parents must have sensed that I was a different sort of child! Now when I speak to young people, I say to them, "Find a spot that's your own. It doesn't have to be big. But find a place where you can create, whether it's drawing or writing or whatever." One of the main ways that my parents encouraged me was simply by not discouraging me — by letting me have that spot in our house.

Q: What is your earliest memory of making art?

A: I made a pot holder for my mother that she happened to save. I found it later and I have it now. You can see a picture of it in my book *Hands* (1997). It has flowers at the top, which were sewn by me, and a piece of brown fabric lower down that is meant to be a flowerpot. I had taken the word *pot holder* rather literally!

Now when I make art for a book, I try to make it in such a way that some kids, seeing it, will say, "Well, I could do that." As you know I like to use buttons and ribbons and fabrics — things that children are apt to find at home. As a child, the colors of the fabrics I got from my mom were much better than the wimpy colors of the colored construction paper of the time. I never gave up on cutting and pasting.

Q: What art did you see as a child apart from what you yourself were making?

A: I didn't go to an art museum when I was a child, because we didn't have one nearby. The only art I saw was reproduced in art history books and in picture books. We didn't own many books, but we did have a very good public library, which my brother and sister and I visited with our mother every week. We could each take out five books at a time. One picture book I remember is *Millions of Cats*. Later I liked the Laura Ingalls Wilder books, not so much for the pictures as for the descriptions of the way things looked.

Q: Were you the class artist?

A: Yes, and I always knew I wanted to be an artist. The only problem was that I didn't know how I was going to do it. I had no idea.

When I got out of high school I was lucky enough to have won a scholarship to art school, because I had no money and my parents didn't either. By then I had realized that I loved books, and I figured that if I could do artwork for books, it would be just about like going to heaven.

Q: So you studied illustration?

A: No, because art schools didn't offer illustration courses the way they do now. I studied color theory, drawing from life — all the basics. When I graduated, my goal was to illustrate books, but that didn't happen, so I got a job as an apprentice in a commercial art studio in Milwaukee. I might have thought of going to Chicago or New York, but I loved Wisconsin so much that I didn't want to leave. I knew, of course, that most of the publishers were in New York, but I thought that my work could get there without me. When I was twenty-two, I got an art agent, which helped.

Q: You became a published illustrator during the 1960s, but about twenty years elapsed between those early efforts and the first of the many picture books you are known for now. Why did you wait so long?

A: I had been very disappointed with the quality of art reproduction, and in the earlier time it had not occurred to me that I might have any say in how the printing of my work was done. During that in-between time I visited Europe, where color reproduction was of much better quality, and I brought home copies of the European children's books I admired — picture books by the great Italian illustrator Bruno Munari and others. That experience showed me that good reproduction was possible. In a way it also rekindled my interest in making books, though I don't think I had ever lost interest.

I began showing my portfolio again. I was making illustrations involving die-cuts. Publishers at first didn't know what to do with art like that, which was much less common then than it is now.

I did *Color Zoo* (1989) originally as an artist's book. Because of all the production-related challenges it posed, I didn't think it would ever be published. But it *was* published, and by the time it came around to being done as a board book, those die-cuts were made with a laser. New ways of doing things have continued to appear throughout my career.

Q: Tell me about your experiences working with children.

A: I taught art classes to children while I was still in college. I still do it occasionally at the Milwaukee Art Museum. I just love it. I could very easily have become an art teacher. I like preschoolers, kindergarteners, and first graders best. It's such an exciting time for them. I've had children make fish aquariums in conjunction with my book *Fish Eyes* (1990). We might take a recycled plastic box, the kind you might find at a salad bar, and stand it on end and make two-sided fish that will comfortably fit inside. You could do many fish or one big fish. And you would hold the fish in place by suspending them from the top of the container with thread. If you shake the box, the fish swim! The kids always come up with some good-looking fish.

Q: What got you started on *Fish Eyes*? Did you simply want to make a long, narrow book for a change?

A: What I knew when I started *Fish Eyes* was that I wanted to make a counting book and I wanted to do it with fish. I went to the Shedd Aquarium in

Chicago to do the research. Of course the tropical fish are generally the most colorful ones. I brought along a sketchbook, though other times I might just look with my eyes. I have a very good memory for what I see. Because I did the art for *Waiting for Wings* (2001) in wintertime and because it's not easy to find blooming flowers around here at that time of year, I had to rely on photographs.

When I was working on *Eating the Alphabet* (1989), I would go to a local fruit and vegetable market each week and shop for one letter of the alphabet: dates for *D*, endive and eggplant for *E*, and so on. I would take everything home and make a painting of each of the fruits and vegetables I had purchased, and then I would eat them. I think Cézanne probably did the same with those apples, don't you?

Q: You must have had fun — or did you? — choosing the perfect orange and banana and so forth.

A: Yes, I did. I thought that someone at the store would eventually catch on to what I was doing, but no one ever did.

Q: You came up with an unusual solution for the letter *X*—*Xigua,* the Chinese word for "watermelon." It comes as a surprise at the end of the book and it adds another layer to the book, showing young children that a thing can have more than one name.

A: A China scholar at the University of Wisconsin helped me out with that. I did the book at the time when kiwifruit was just becoming popular. I included kiwis, star fruit, and a few other exotic fruits and vegetables. There was some discussion with the publisher about whether it was a good idea to have things in the book that readers wouldn't recognize immediately, but I thought, *Why not? They can go out and look for them and learn about something new.*

Q: Do you have favorite typefaces?

A: Oh, yes. The type in all my Harcourt books is Century Schoolbook. For the books I have done for HarperCollins, I have used a typeface called Avant Garde. Century Schoolbook is a very readable typeface, and it is a very beautiful one, too. I don't see any reason not to use it. The clearer the better is my idea — especially in a book for children who are perhaps just learning to read. Avant Garde is what's known as a compass-generated typeface. It's very close to the way a child would learn to print letters. It made sense to use it for a book like *Color Zoo*, which is about geometric shapes. It seemed compatible.

Q: Did it surprise you that you could be a writer as well as a visual artist?

A: Yes, it did. I originally did *Color Zoo* and *Hands* for the course I was taking at the University of Wisconsin on making artist's books. It was then that I realized that if I was going to make books, most likely they weren't going to be wordless books — and that I would therefore have to write some sort of text for them. So I gave it a try. I have always started with a visual idea and I still do, even when I know what the writing *might* be about. I always do a painting first to establish the mood.

Q: I want to ask you about your book *Market Day* (2000). Have you been collecting folk art for a long time?

A: Probably since I got out of art school — for as long, that is, as I've had the money to buy it. A lot of the things I have are not particularly costly. They're just very inventive, and I thought *Market Day* would be an interesting way to introduce folk art to young people.

Q: You managed to combine so many different objects and to weave a narrative around them.

A: I used color photocopies to design the compositions, and I then had a photographer take the photos for the finished art. I used the photocopy machine to great advantage for *Leaf Man* (2005), too, I think.

Q: Some of your books — *Waiting for Wings,* for example — are so complex in design. Did it take a long time to figure out how to size the various pages in that book, how much complication might be too much, and how to make it all come together?

A: Yes, I spent a lot more time on the conception of the book — the layout or dummy — than I did on the finished art. It went through several stages. By the time I had worked out the design, *Waiting for Wings* had to be the way it was or not at all.

KEVIN HENKES

Born 1960, Racine, Wisconsin

I n the life of a young child," Kevin Henkes has observed, "there are many firsts, one right after the next, in a row that seems to stretch to eternity." In his picture books, Henkes often focuses on these early milestones: a child's first experiences of sibling relationships, friendship, and school. In doing so, he brings to bear uncommon powers of empathy and a gentle way of pointing out the humor in ticklish situations that nearly everybody has at some time faced. It's the psychological truth of Henkes's books that gives them their staying power: a child and adult reading one together are both reminded what it is like to go out on an emotional limb and come back again, a little sturdier and wiser for the effort.

In *Kitten's First Full Moon* (2004), the book for which Henkes won the 2005 Caldecott Medal, a young feline's climb in the higher reaches of a tree is an actual plot point, and Henkes himself took a chance by completely reinventing his illustration style, even temporarily jettisoning color in favor of rounded, lyrical black-line graphics of classic simplicity. In his more recent books, he has set out in yet another direction, painting like someone who just discovered color: and so his remarkable career continues to unfold.

I had been reviewing Henkes's books at *Parenting* magazine since the late 1980s, but this was our first interview. Henkes was at home, in Madison, Wisconsin, when we spoke by phone on November 25, 2009.

LEONARD S. MARCUS: What kind of child were you?

KEVIN HENKES: I was shy. I loved to read. I loved to draw. I think I had a rich interior life. I was one of five children, so often there was a lot going on in the house. For me there was nothing better than to curl up with a book or take a notebook and snuggle into the corner by the heat register in the winter and draw.

Q: Where did you fall in the birth order?

A: I was the fourth, which I think was a good position to be in for my art. I knew what it felt like to be the youngest, and then I learned what it was like to have a younger sibling. There is a pretty big age gap between my younger brother and me, so what I most remember about his arrival is a feeling of excitement.

Q: Were there artists in your family?

A: My grandfather was a photographer. He owned a photography store in downtown Racine, Wisconsin, my hometown. He had a darkroom in his basement, which he loved to share with his grandchildren. The photography business was amazing to me. It's interesting that I had all that at my disposal and yet chose to draw. Looking back, it was probably because drawing gave me more control. With photography it seemed there were too many variables, but with drawing it was just me and the paper and the pencil.

Q: In *Lilly's Purple Plastic Purse* (1996), Lilly loves her pencils and other school supplies. Did you, too?

A: Yes, absolutely. I also loved the physical details of some books. Golden Books were published in Racine, and I thought the gold-foil bindings of those books were beautiful. Several fathers in my neighborhood worked for Western Publishing Company, so Golden Books were very much around. I even visited the printing plant once, probably with one of our neighbors.

Q: What other books did you know as a boy?

A: We didn't have a lot of books at home other than Scholastic Book Club books, but the Racine Public Library was wonderful and we went there regularly. I loved choosing books and then feeling as if they were truly mine. That was something my mother believed in and made sure happened. One of my most vivid childhood memories concerning the library is of the big retirement party for my first children's librarian, Mrs. Schowalter. There was a big cake in the form of an open book with little statues of storybook characters on top. I thought it was the most glorious thing.

Q: Can you recall learning to read?

A: I remember taking an edition of *Hansel and Gretel* to kindergarten and reading it to my class, although I don't know if I was really reading or if I had memorized it. It was one of those books in which the illustrations were photographs of cloth dolls. I felt very proud about that, and whenever I think about reading, that memory comes back to me.

Q: In *Lilly's Purple Plastic Purse,* Lilly says she wants an illustrated encyclopedia. Did you have *The Golden Book Encyclopedia* as a child?

A: We did not, and our neighbors did.

Q: So you wanted one, too.

A: Absolutely. We had it at school, and I can still picture the covers.

Q: You started drawing when you were very young, didn't you?

A: I can't remember a time when I didn't draw.

Q: Were you the class artist?

A: Yes, I was. It was a big part of my identity. My oldest brother was a very good artist, and because he was five years older, he had a level of expertise that I had not yet reached. If we were painting together at home, he would get the nice thin brushes and I would be left with the fat bristly ones. Once, my parents had a watercolor painting of his framed and they hung it on the living room wall. I'd stare at it and think, *What could be better than that?*

Q: It sounds as if your parents were very supportive.

A: Yes, and we lived very near an art museum where I took lessons as a boy, which I loved.

Q: What did you dress up as for Halloween?

A: I remember being a clown and a lumberjack. For the lumberjack I put Vaseline and coffee grounds on my face to make a beard. It looked great, but because I was so shy, it made me feel self-conscious. Other years I tried to blend in more by dressing up as a Green Bay Packer!

Q: You made your first picture book while you were still in high school. Of all the kinds of art there were to do, why did you choose to make picture books?

A: As a junior in high school, I had an English teacher who encouraged my writing. She said, "One day I think I'll see a book with your name on it." That was a very powerful experience for me. Drawing and painting were still my favorite things to do. I had begun to think about what I might do with my life, what kind of job I might want to have. Somehow, the combination of my love of art and my newfound love of writing made me realize that making picture books would be a great career for me.

I was always drawn to picture books, even when I was older than a typical picture-book reader. Judging from the handwriting in it, I must have gotten my Scholastic Book Club copy of *Where the Wild Things Are* as an older child. I would study the pictures in books like that. I also went through a *Peanuts* phase, in which I'd copy Charles Schulz's drawings. I have a notebook that is filled with newspaper cartoon characters I had copied.

Q: Schulz's drawings look simple yet they are so expressive.

A: Yes, and I learned that just because something looks simple, it doesn't mean that it was easy to draw.

Q: It's unusual to be an undergraduate at college and to have already published a book. What was that like for you?

A: There were great art teachers I wanted to learn from at college, so I was glad to have the chance to continue learning. Gradually picture-book making took over more and more of my time. I would take a semester off to do a book and then go back to college. This back-and-forth became a pattern I repeated for a while.

Q: You've said your favorite childhood book was one by Ruth Krauss and Crockett Johnson called *Is This You?* What did you like so much about it?

A: One reason I loved it is that it is essentially an instructional manual on how to make a book about oneself. I made many little booklets based on the formula presented in it. Also, my copy of the book had a phonetic text that looked like a foreign language, though one I could somehow read! It made the book seem very exotic to me. And I loved Crockett Johnson's artwork in the same way that I did Charles Shulz's drawings.

Q: How did you get from your first book, *All Alone* (1981), to *A Weekend With Wendell* (1986), which is so different in both its pictures and text?

A: Because I began publishing so young, I grew up, in a sense, trying to figure out on paper who I was as an artist. At nineteen, I was idealistic and I wanted to be profound. Hence, *All Alone*. With time, my texts became more humorous. There's already a hint of that in my second book, *Clean Enough* (1982). I got to the point where I thought that because the texts were becoming more humorous, the way I was drawing my characters — as realistic humans — no longer fit. I thought I could better tap the humor in the text by drawing more loosely and by trying to draw animals.

Q: Do you think that becoming a parent influenced the way you make picture books?

A: I don't think it has, particularly. Before I was a parent, people assumed I was one. Then when I became parent, people said, "Now you'll have unlimited ideas!" I don't think that happened either. The only way that being a father influenced my books early on is that it made me look at very young picture books again, because that is what was filling up our house, and I grew to love that kind of book again. But before I became a parent, I was an uncle. It was a niece with a blanket who was the inspiration for *Owen* (1993), and two of my nieces were the inspiration for *Julius, the Baby of the World* (1990).

Q: By then you were putting in more and more bits of satire for the parents' amusement: the comment in *Owen* about the parents having never learned to say no to their child, and the parodies in various illustrations of Picasso and Edvard Munch's *The Scream.*

A: I love having something for the adult who is reading to the child. But I try to keep in mind at all times that the book is for the child. I don't want any of that extra layer to interfere with the main objective, which is to make an entertaining book for a kid.

Q: Your illustrations were getting more layered, with more decorative patterns, more highly developed backgrounds, more interest in spatial depth. Then with *Kitten's First Full Moon,* you completely changed your style. Do you set specific technical challenges for yourself as you start a new book? Is that one of the ways you keep bookmaking interesting for yourself?

A: I wanted *Kitten's First Full Moon* to be different. I wanted to illustrate the book in black and white, and I wanted it to be bold. I had been used to using a certain kind of paper, certain kinds of pen nibs, a certain kind of ink. I had been working with the same materials for years and years, and it felt very comfortable because I knew what I was doing. I knew what to expect. I'm a creature of habit, so setting all that aside felt very scary.

But the text for *Kitten* begged for something different. The words pulled me in a different direction. Besides limiting the color, I tried to keep anything out of the pictures that I didn't need.

The early sketches included several background elements. I eliminated most of them. J. M. Barrie said something like, "Cut it down by half and leave nothing out." I think that's the ideal to strive for in picture books.

I experimented a lot before showing anything to anyone. Originally, I thought I would do the art all in gouache or all in ink. But the velvety look I wanted was best achieved with colored pencil.

Q: What are some of the picture books you consider touchstones now?

A: There are so many. *A Child's Good Night Book* by Margaret Wise Brown and Jean Charlot is one. I love *Harry the Dirty Dog.* It tells a real story and it surprises the reader. It's all so right. I would also choose M. B. Goffstein's *Me and My Captain.* It conveys such a beautiful sense of longing.

Q: In *Chrysanthemum* (1991), you tell a story about a child who has strong feelings about her name. As a child, did you have strong feelings about yours?

A: No, I didn't really think about it one way or the other. Although there was a book I loved when I was a boy called *Patrick Michael Kevin,* and the only reason I loved it was that my name was in the title of the book.

Q: In recent books, you have gotten more involved with color.

A: That evolved over time. In *Old Bear* (2008), when I realized I could give each dream a double-page spread, I thought, *How can I expand and enrich the dream sequences using color?* One thing often leads to another when you are scribbling on paper. The first idea that came to me was to draw the dreams in a different-colored ink from the brown of the rest of the book. Then I thought, *I can do each dream in a different color and have the type printed in the corresponding color.* That seemed right — a little window opened up and I felt a rush of excitement.

Q: Has making picture books become easier for you with time?

A: No, I think it has become harder. I worry more than before about whether I am going to have another idea for a book. I also worry about when my eyes feel tired at the end of the workday — things like that.

Q: Do you identify with one of your characters more than all the others?

A: I must like Lilly best because I have returned to her so often. But Lilly is not like me at all.

Q: Lilly is so outgoing. She's such a character. Do you perhaps wish you were more like her?

A: That could be. *She* wouldn't be embarrassed about her Halloween costume.

YUMI HEO

Born 1964, Seoul, Korea

Although illustrators are routinely asked to say where they "get" their ideas, the truth is that they often don't know. Yumi Heo recalls: "When I was making sample drawings for my first picture book, a Korean folktale called *The Green Frogs* (1996), I drew a picture of a plant with hanging bell-shaped flowers. I thought I had simply made up the flower in my head. But years later, on a return trip to Korea, I happened to see that very same kind of flower, and it was then that I realized that my memories of childhood had actually played an important part in the making of my first children's book."

Heo's talent for art was clear from the start, and as a schoolchild she was fortunate enough to receive steady encouragement and special training. The old-fashioned, formal approach to art education that guided her

Korean teachers, however, soon came to feel stifling, and Heo jumped at the chance to study art in New York City. More than twenty-five years later, she seems to have no regrets that she chose to build her career and make her life in the United States.

Heo is a sprightly, reed-thin woman with an intense gaze and a lively, joking manner. We had spoken on two or three previous occasions when we sat down together before opening time at the suburban New York ceramics shop that she and her husband own and where young children and their parents come to do craft projects together. The cheerful signage and other wall decorations are all the artist's work, and copies of her picture books perched on nearby shelves as I took advantage of the quiet of the early morning and recorded this conversation on September 18, 2009.

LEONARD S. MARCUS: Tell me about growing up in Korea.

YUMI HEO: My parents were not artists, but I always liked to draw and my mom knew it. When we went on a family picnic, she would ask me to bring a sketch pad. I would always have to make a drawing of whatever we were doing. My dad was in the army, and we moved every year as he was transferred from place to place. As a result, I did not have many friends, and when I was in junior high, my mom enrolled me at an art studio where I could draw after school.

Q: Were you aware of Korean art traditions then?

A: No. In the art studio, we drew statues of Greek gods! That was how you learned to draw in Korea. It's not that way there now.

Q: What about children's books?

A: I didn't have many books. I had one collection of Korean folktales that when I was in fifth grade I carried around everywhere with me. I would sit by a pond and read that book every day after school. That's where I found the story on which I based *The Green Frogs: A Korean Folktale.* The stories in my book were similar to Aesop, though some were very gruesome. There was one about a Snail Lady, another about a Half Man who has only one eye and half a nose! There were just a few black-and-white drawings. I also read a series of biographies of famous people, which were illustrated comics-style. There just wasn't much being published for children in Korea at that time. I grew up in the country, but had we lived in a big city, I doubt I would have had more books.

Q: When did you leave Korea for the United States?

A: I was twenty-four. I came by myself. In Korea, I had not gotten into the college where I wanted to study fine art, and so I had gone instead to a college where I could only study graphic design. Then I found a job working as a graphic designer at an amusement park. I designed uniforms for the people who worked at the park and created a big sign for the front gate — which I was proud last year to see they still have! But I always had the thought that I wanted to study fine art, and when I saw a magazine ad for the School of Visual Arts, in New York, I decided to apply, and was accepted.

When I got to SVA, I entered the masters program, and I thought I would study graphic design. But SVA didn't offer a masters in a graphic design, and illustration was the closest thing, so I became an illustrator by chance. That is when I began to have the time of my life. One day I was walking down the street and suddenly I felt great. I thought, *Here I am, in one of the world's biggest cities, surrounded by so many people, and so excited to be learning!* That was in 1989. My curiosity was all about America.

Q: What type of illustration did you specialize in?

A: Not children's-book illustration at first. For my second-year project,

I thought I would make an animation using stick-figure dolls that I had made myself. It was going to be about the racial disharmony in New York. I made Korean American dolls, Hasidic dolls, African-American dolls! In 1990, there had been an incident in the news involving a small Korean grocery store in Brooklyn, which was boycotted by African Americans from the community. Then an African-American high-school teacher decided to bring his students to the store to try to make peace with the store owner. He became a hero to the city's Korean-American community. The only problem was that I didn't know how to make animations, and time was running out! My teacher suggested that I tell the story by making a book instead. So that's how I started.

I made a book dummy that I also sent to editors in New York, Boston, and California. They liked my art and the way I had put my book together, but they weren't sure how to deal with a story about such a sensitive topic. One editor sent me a Korean folktale collection and suggested I make a picture book based on one of the stories. That is how my first picture book, *The Rabbit's Judgment* (1994) by Suzanne Crowder Han, came about.

Q: Once you became interested in making picture books, did you look at other illustrators' books?

A: I began looking at picture books in the library. I never knew about Maurice Sendak or Dr. Seuss before I got here. One of the first picture books I liked was *The Bomb and the General,* written by Umberto Eco and illustrated by Eugenio Carmi. It's about a bad general who makes atomic bombs. The collage art is very simple, but it has a lot of meaning. Henrik Drescher visited one of my classes at SVA. He brought his sketchbooks to show us. When I saw his work, I thought, *This is what I want to do, too.* I also liked the work of Maira Kalman. One of my editors showed me books by Ezra Jack Keats.

Q: You have such a distinctive style. How did it develop?

A: I found my style during my second year at SVA. The art I had done in Korea was very realistic. I'm very good at rendering. I can render anything! In Korea, we were trained in art school to draw things exactly as they appear. But my Korean drawings expressed none of my feelings. At SVA I spent a lot of time drawing in the studio. I also drew in train stations and on the train. I would go to Chinatown to draw the fish markets. I experimented with acrylics, pastels.

One day it just came together. I covered a piece of paper with gesso, which has texture, and when it dried I painted on it with oils. I also doodled on it. I love to doodle when I talk on the phone. Suddenly, my doodle habit became my art! I love spirals — don't ask me why! — and there are lots of floating things in my illustrations. More doodling influence. I need to fill out my page, even if it's just by smudging with the pencil. I am obsessed with these small details.

Q: You'll sometimes leave a little empty white space around the outline of a character.

A: I paint the background first with oil, and then remove some of the paint. When the turpentine hits the oil, it leaves those white spaces, which I like.

Q: It makes the viewer aware of the hand of the artist.

A: Yes, it shows that what I'm doing is on purpose! I also love patterns and textiles. I collect things with patterns on them — handmade papers, even shopping bags. I have a big flat file full of samples.

The sketches I show my editors have just the main figures, with no backgrounds indicated whatsoever. Even I don't know what will be in the background until I sit down and paint it spontaneously. It's like an improvisation, and usually I am happy with the first version. But sometimes it can be painful to work that way. I have friends who plan every detail of an illustration in advance, whereas for me it's only when I sit down to do the finished painting that the real work begins.

Q: Do you write your stories in English? Do you think you have thoughts in English that you might not have had in Korean?

A: I always write in English. When I came to America, I did everything I could to learn English well. For me, part of the process was avoiding speaking Korean and seeing Korean movies and TV. I trained myself. Now I don't think that being Korean affects the way I write at all, except of course for what I sometimes write about. *Father's Rubber Shoes* (1995) is a story my mother used to tell me. It relates to why all the Korean immigrants came here, for a better life for themselves or for the next generation. Now five of my books are translated into Korean.

Q: Would you say there is something Korean about your art?

A: That's interesting. When my first book was published, my Korean friends all said, "Oh, it looks so American!" and my American friends all said, "Oh, it looks so Asian!" I often put the bugs and frogs I played with as child in my illustrations. But it terms of the style, I couldn't say for sure. My illustrations are certainly far from the kind of art I learned to make in Korea.

Q: Western art is often about materiality, the solidity of things, with a hero at the center, whereas your characters sometimes float in space. Lots of things in your paintings seem to defy gravity. In that sense, they remind me of some Japanese screen paintings I've seen.

A: I see what you mean, though Japanese paintings are very calm and subtle. They're very muted, not colorful or full of energy. My way of painting may be more a reflection of my personality and of being in such a very crowded city.

Q: How does it feel to be called on now to illustrate books with Asian themes?

A: I'm glad because I think that maybe I understand a little more about the culture than would an illustrator who grew up here. Even so, I often have to do research. When I was illustrating Lenore Look's *Uncle Peter's Amazing Chinese Wedding,* I went to Chinatown and got fabric swatches to use when I painted the wedding party's clothes. I made the mother's dress black with a very beautiful floral design, but when I handed in my art, the editor told me that a dress worn at a wedding could not be black because black meant bad luck. And so I did those illustrations over again.

Q: How would you compare your childhood in Korea to your own children's lives here?

A: It's a completely different life! Children growing up in America now have everything materially — food, clothing, computer games. What they don't have is much time for themselves, time to sit and think or to experience nature. Their time is too scheduled. When I was growing up, we didn't have a TV until I was in sixth grade. In the small towns where we lived, there wasn't even a library.

At the art studio I went to every day, the training was very rigid. I learned all about light and shadow and reflections, and I'm glad I did. But they didn't teach us how to express ourselves. They taught us to draw exactly what we saw. The same was true for education in general. We were taught not to talk back, not to ask questions. I was always a good student. I learned to listen to my teachers well, and to do what they asked.

Q: What did your teachers at SVA do that helped you to become more spontaneous?

A: They made us think. One of my teachers would give us an 11 × 17 inch paper divided into nine boxes, and a list of nine sounds — the sound of a dog barking, for example. We would then have to come up with a visual equivalent for each sound. You could use color, or pattern, or whatever you wanted. This kind of assignment was very hard for me at first, because I was so used to doing what I was told. I would think, if only you would tell me what to do! Gradually, I learned to have my own ideas.

TANA HOBAN

Born 1917, Philadelphia, Pennsylvania; Died 2006, Louveciennes, France

ana Hoban grew up in and around Philadelphia, the eldest of three children of Russian and Ukrainian Jewish immigrants. She enrolled in art school intending to draw and paint but found herself drawn increasingly to photography. On graduation, she pursued her interest in both the fine-art and the commercial sides of camera work. By the 1940s, Hoban's photographs were appearing in *Good Housekeeping, Ladies' Home Journal,* and other important national magazines. During the following decade, a meeting with legendary photographer and curator Edward Steichen led to Hoban's photographs being selected for two exhibitions at the Museum of Modern Art, including the groundbreaking "Family of Man" show of 1955.

In 1970, the year Hoban published her first children's picture-book, *Shapes and Things* (1970), books for the youngest ages were receiving increased attention from critics, but many critics still viewed photography as a literal-minded medium of illustration that was ill suited to stimulating a child's imagination. Against this mixed background, Hoban's visually striking, thought-provoking "concept books" came as a revelation. *Shapes and Things* and her many subsequent books proved decisively that photographs had the power not only to "copy" reality but also to encourage in young viewers a heightened awareness of their everyday world.

Hoban, whose brother, Russell, is the author of the Frances books and *The Mouse and His Child* for children and such novels as *Riddley Walker,* lived in Paris for many years. She was visiting New York to deliver the dummy of her picture book *More, Fewer, Less* (1998) when we recorded this interview at the offices of her longtime publisher, Greenwillow Books, on August 27, 1997.

LEONARD S. MARCUS: When you go out with your camera on a walk, what do you hope to find?

TANA HOBAN: I used to carry a camera everywhere. Now it's gotten heavier — so I carry a smaller one! More often than not, I go out now specifically looking for pictures for a book I'm working on. Many times I'm working on two books simultaneously and will be shooting for both. I'll go down the streets and visit the kinds of places that I think children can identify with, and sometimes the same scene will be good, say, for shapes and for colors. Maybe one time I'll be counting everything; another time I'll be looking for circles and squares.

I'm *always* looking for images for my Look book series. It's exciting to find subjects that work for one of those books.

Q: Do you test the Look book photographs by putting them behind a small opening, to see whether it's possible to readily identify the subject?

A: Yes. That's how I started on those books. I happened to have a cutout of a circle or a square in my studio, and by chance left it lying on top of a picture. Then I looked at it, also by chance, and thought, *Oh, here's an idea for a book!*

Q: *Look Again!* (1971) was one of your earliest children's books.

A: When I showed my dummy for *Look Again!* to Susan Hirschman, who was then the editor at Macmillan, her first response was that it might be too gimmicky. She said, "See what else you can do," and gave me a definite date by which to call her. So the following week I showed her a dummy for *Shapes and Things*, a book of photograms, which Macmillan published first.

A photogram is made by putting an object on the paper, shining the light on it, and then printing the resulting image as you would an ordinary enlargement. Photograms are so easy to make that I thought for sure someone else would have the same idea. So I worked night and day to get the book done.

Q: You photographed your first books in black and white. Was working in color an option for you then?

A: No, it wasn't. I don't know whether it was the expense of printing in color or what. Later, when I was told I could use color in books, I began to do so. Black and white can be richer than color, because it's so graphic. But color of course is the way we see.

Q: Do you still recall taking the photographs for *Look Again!*?

A: Absolutely. I was living in Philadelphia at the time. I found the little zebra at the Philadelphia Zoo. I think that that must have been the first image I did for the book. Those stripes are so strong graphically.

I did the photograph of the pear in my studio. My mother always cut an apple across so that we would see the star shape inside. As a child *I* would cut pears for my younger sister just as you see the one in my photograph: I would take the top, the cone shape, and she would get the bottom.

Q: Do you often feel as you work that you are photographing images remembered from your childhood?

A: Yes, often. We lived in the country, and my early love of nature is certainly reflected in my books. Growing up, we had lots of animals — dogs and cats and pigeons and squirrels. I always have animals in my books. My father and mother raised white pigeons — at one time we had five thousand of them — and since then I have always been fascinated by the pigeons I see in the park because of the beautiful designs on their backs. I photographed a group of pigeons for *Look Book* (1997).

I love doing the Look books. Children are so pleased that they know the answers. I have found that they also enjoy repeating going through the pictures, to see if anything has changed!

Q: Were there books that you considered special when you were a child?

A: No, but my father told us many traditional Russian stories, such as the one about it being so cold outside that birds dropped frozen from the sky. I think all Russian Jewish children knew that story. My father was a Socialist, and he also told us the one about the heroic engineer who sees something up ahead on the tracks, stops the train, then cuts his arm to make his shirt turn red, so he'll be able to stop the next train!

My brother, Russell, recalls that at dinner, my father had a glassful of nickels that he would give us children for clever remarks. Talking with my sister at the dinner table one evening, I apparently said, "N'est-ce pas?" And when she asked, "What's that?" I replied, "An old French general." Then my brother chimed in with, "Tecumseh!" And when I asked, "What's *that*?" he answered, "An old Indian chief!" He got a nickel for that remark. We both got nickels.

Q: Did you have a camera when you were young?

A: Not as a child, though my father had a large Graflex. There was flash powder, and there would be a big boom. Very dramatic! My father wasn't a photographer, however. He was advertising manager at *The Jewish Daily Forward.*

As a child I liked to draw and decided early on to become an artist. Later, when I went to art school, I studied photography and, in what felt like a strange coincidence, was given a Graflex like my father's to work with.

Q: Were there certain photographers whose work you felt influenced by or admired early on?

A: Of course there were Edward Weston and Edward Steichen, whose photographs had a poetic quality I liked. I showed Steichen my photographs and was included in a group show of women photographers that he curated at the Museum of Modern Art in 1949, as well as in the Museum's "Family of Man" exhibition of 1955.

Q: Did you know the two books that Steichen photographed for young children, *The First Picture Book* and *The Second Picture Book*?

A: Yes, but I couldn't say whether I saw them before or after I began doing my own books.

Q: Certainly your picture books have an affinity with the Steichen books as attempts to offer the very young compelling images of everyday objects and activities.

A: Yes, it has been my idea, too, to photograph everyday things that a child can relate to, as a vehicle for learning. Simple, generic things. Not Mickey Mouse!

Q: How did the children's-book world strike you as compared with the world of advertising, in which you were then still immersed?

A: I continued to work in advertising until I had published ten or so books. It was *very* different. The stress level in advertising was so much higher. You would get an assignment. You agreed on a price. Then you went and shot the assignment — and it might not come out at all right.

When I started out in photography after art school, I took pictures mainly for myself. I specialized in photographing children. I would find children I thought were photogenic and take them to the park, a natural setting, and try to get a spontaneous response. Instead of the typical Eastman Kodak look of the time, where the child was always blond, and not Jewish, and not black, not Italian, and not Chinese, and always smiling at the camera, I photographed a variety of children in more thoughtful, introspective moods. I wanted to show that childhood is not always the happy time it appears to be. Maybe the timing was right. My pictures were noticed, and became known. Even the J. Walter Thompson advertising agency, which had such a big part in creating the visual stereotypes of that period through their various advertising campaigns, gave me a big show in their gallery. Then, I myself worked on the Kodak and Polaroid accounts.

Q: Kodak, which you just mentioned in connection with the stereotyped images of childhood, became willing to try something different?

A: Yes. They saw my pictures and liked what I did. But I always did photographs to please myself as well.

Q: Your brother also worked in advertising, did he not?

A: Yes, writing copy. He began doing children's books long before I did, but there has never been any connection between his work in the field and mine. For me, there was simply the natural progression of going from photographing children to photographing images for children and, in a sense, from the child's point of view.

Q: What more specifically prompted you to try your hand at making children's picture books?

A: I had read an article about an experiment at the Bank Street School in New York. When the teachers first asked the children what they saw every day on their way to school, the children replied, "Nothing." Then the children were all given cameras, and they suddenly discovered the rivers, the construction sites, the food stands they passed every day. Having a camera opened their eyes. Reading about that experiment prompted me to wonder what things *I* was not seeing in the course of a day. I began to look at my surroundings differently.

Q: Have ideas for other books come to you in the same way?

A: The idea for *26 Letters & 99 Cents* (1987) did. I had read somewhere that children should know the alphabet by such-and-such age and be able by then to make a certain amount of change — thirty-nine cents, I think it was. When I discussed my idea for a book based on this premise with Susan Hirschman, we decided to make it ninety-nine cents, a less arbitrary-sounding number that, even with inflation, would never make the book seem out-of-date.

Q: You used a great many toys as subjects for the book. Do you collect toys?

A: When I see something that isn't associated with a particular trade name or character or designer, something that can't be pinned down, I usually buy it. I had, for instance, bought a set of the lowercase letters that I used for *26 Letters.* I also wanted a matching set of capital letters, but found that there was none. So I tracked down the people who designed and manufactured the letters I already had — they were a young couple living in Bath, England — and commissioned them to make the capital letters for me. I felt that it was important to have the letters look as they do.

As for the other objects I photographed for the book, I simply chose things that I thought children would like: toy dinosaurs, dragons, robots, and cars. An egg. A goldfish. Jellybeans are pretty universal. The quilt I photographed was given to me as a wedding present by Greenwillow when I married the second time. I found the sea horse that I photographed on the beach years ago.

Q: Do you spend much time arranging the objects in your photographs?

A: Not a lot of time. The objects in my pictures for *Of Colors and Things* (1989), for example, are casually arranged. I don't want them to look perfectly styled as in an ad.

Q: Do you take a great many pictures to produce a thirty-two-page picture book?

A: That depends. Take the cover photographs for *The Moon Was the Best* by Charlotte Zolotow (1993). On the front cover I have a picture of a girl running away from the viewer. On the back I have exactly the same scene, with the girl running toward you. To get that pair of pictures took two whole days. I wanted it to look fresh and spontaneous! And I had to make sure no one else had wandered into the picture, and so on. In that case, I started out with a preconceived notion of what I wanted.

Other times, I'll have some such idea, but it will turn out not to be the picture I take, or eventually use. Something will turn up in a picture by chance that will be better than what I had imagined. For instance, when I was photographing *Look Again!* and first saw the peacock at the Philadelphia Zoo, his back was to me and I thought I would just wait until he turned around. It had not occurred to me that I might want to photograph him from the back. But peacocks turn very slowly. They make a little dance of it. And as I continued to look at the outspread feathers from the back, I suddenly thought, Ah! *That's* the picture.

Q: Do you take all the pictures for a book at the same time of day, or in the same kind of light, for the sake of visual continuity? Is lighting a part of a book's formal design?

A: No, I don't worry about that. Most of my pictures are done in natural daylight, and if I use artificial light I do it in such a way as to imitate natural light.

Q: How involved do you become in the design of your books?

A: Very. My dummies look very much like the books that come out of them. Ava Weiss, the art director at Greenwillow, works out the precise details.

When I prepare my spreads, I put all the pictures on the floor and then pick them out two at a time and see how they look together. But I don't look for the S-curve, or the "center of interest" that graphic designers talk about. It's all intuitive, and very often the first choice I make turns out to be right.

Q: When your books are published abroad, do you sometimes have to replace photographs with others of subjects more familiar to the children of that country or part of the world?

A: For the French edition of *26 Letters & 99 Cents* (*Des Sous et des Lettres,* 1996), I photographed French coins. In the German edition of another book, I had to replace a photograph of a fire hydrant, because German children would have found it unrecognizable. There have been a few instances of that kind.

Q: Except for *The Moon Was the Best*, with its views of Paris, your photographs don't generally call attention to the locales where they were taken.

A: That's right. They could be anywhere. That's because I want them to be not so much about places as about seeing.

Q: How did *Little Elephant* by Miela Ford (1994), the first book written by your daughter, come about?

A: I often go to the Paris Zoo to photograph animals, and one day the baby elephant seemed to be acting exactly like a little child. I had never seen it behave that way before. I photographed as fast as I could! Usually the baby elephant would just be walking around, curling its trunk, doing the usual things. But that day, it took so many poses that it almost *wrote* the book for me. I went back the next day, and the elephant just stood around. It didn't do anything!

I say "almost wrote the book" because when I showed the photographs to Susan, she said that she loved the book but that this time my pictures would need words to accompany them. She tried several writers who didn't work out. Then my daughter, who was already grown by the time I began making my first books, and who had never written before, said that she would like to try—and she did. Now she both writes and photographs her own books. I loved it that we had done a book together.

Q: How has your work changed over the years?

A: I used to photograph children. But in my picture books, I don't often include children in the photographs. That is because I don't want to pin down just who the child of the book is; I want readers to put *themselves* in the book.

Q: Your books relate so directly to the theories about developmental learning that originated at Bank Street and at some of the other centers of progressive education. Have you ever had a more formal association with any of those schools, or studied the work of, say, John Dewey or Lucy Sprague Mitchell?

A: No. As I said earlier, I work very much by intuition. I don't test my books on children. I ask myself, *Is it childlike?* I do my work, and know when it's right.

Q: I have read that your books have been used by children with learning disabilities.

A: My books apparently work well with children with learning disabilities because there is no threat of the word on the page. If a picture comes with a caption, if a book says, "This is a such-and-such," there's a chance that the child may get it wrong. But if there is no word or caption, then a "car" can be an "auto," or a "means of transportation," or whatever the child thinks to call it. Having no words liberates a child to a certain extent. A picture by itself will elicit a personal response that will get him going. I like to think that my books provoke young children to talk and to express themselves.

JAMES MARSHALL

Born 1942, San Antonio, Texas; Died 1992, New York, New York

A s a writer, James Marshall specialized in sly comic tales high-
lighting life's little surprises—friendship's unending complica-
tions, the consequences of biting off more than one can chew.
As an illustrator, he favored drawings sporting a look of devil-may-care
abandon, a quicksilver effect he was generally prepared to sweat bullets to
achieve. Despite all appearances, Marshall was in fact, as Maurice Sendak
has observed, "a notorious perfectionist." With the publication of *George
and Martha* (1972), the first of many picture books he both wrote and
illustrated, Marshall established himself as a master of tongue-in-cheek
understatement, true-to-type characterization, and dead-on comic timing. During a hugely prolific career, he created (at times in collaboration

with the writer Harry Allard) a parade of freshly imagined, over-the-top characters: Fox, the Cut-Ups, Miss Nelson, Viola Swamp, and the Stupids, among others. Marshall heroes usually come out all right in the end, but just by the seat of their pants.

Marshall himself was a compulsively funny, extravagant, outgoing man who wore his vulnerabilities on his sleeve, alongside his heart. While accepting slapstick and light satire as his natural modes of expression, he regretted the lack of serious attention these tendencies all but guaranteed his creative efforts. "Zany," Marshall once said, "[is] a word I'd like to have wiped off every dust jacket of every book I've ever done."

Marshall's retelling of *Goldilocks and the Three Bears* (1988) garnered the artist his first major award, a Caldecott Honor, in 1989, at a time when he already had scores of books to his credit. In 2007, the American Library Association honored him posthumously with the Laura Ingalls Wilder Award for the entire body of his work.

Marshall loved to talk and socialize, and the afternoon of May 24, 1989, which we spent together in his Manhattan apartment to record this interview, was nothing if not fun.

~~~~~~~~~~~~~~~~~~~~~~~~~~~~~~~~

LEONARD S. MARCUS: Tell me about your first memories of books. Do you remember learning to read?

JAMES MARSHALL: No, I can't remember that, but I do remember a few of the first books I knew, including *Tubby the Tugboat* and *The Little Engine That Could.* My mother, who is a great reader, had a Palmer Cox Brownies book. I can still sort of smell it. In fact, I still have it somewhere. Very early on I started reading adult books. My favorite when I was six was Stefan Zweig's *Marie Antoinette.* I don't know if I *could* read, but I got very interested, and then my mother gave me Charles Dickens's *A Child's History of England.* So that's the sort of thing I read, or pretended I was reading. I think I learned to read by osmosis.

Q: What other kinds of reading matter did you have at home?

A: Mostly my mother's old movie magazines from the 1920s. I may in fact have learned to read from *Silver Screen*. She was a great movie nut, who saw every new picture.

I didn't start paying attention to kids' books until I was in my mid-twenties. Maurice [Sendak]'s *Where the Wild Things Are* and a fabulous book by Domenico Gnoli called *The Art of Smiling*, which was also published in the 1960s, got me started. Like a fool I looked at those two picture books and said, "Well, I can do that." And so I started drawing.

Q: You hadn't drawn much as a child?

A: Probably not — just the way kids doodle when they're kids. There was a time when I was passionately interested in drawing, but then I quit, absolutely quit. I was ten or eleven. My father had decided that I would be a musician. That was what I was going to be. One day he brought home a violin and I started playing. I was aimed to be a musician. After that, I went to music school and spent summers at the Interlocken, Michigan, music camp. In high school I realized I would need a college scholarship and that I would have a better chance as a viola student than as a violinist, because violinists were in much better supply in the 1950s. So I switched over to the viola and got scholarships everywhere. I could pick and choose, and I chose to go to the New England Conservatory in Boston.

Q: Earlier on, while you were still living in Texas with your parents, were you known among your classmates as the school musician?

A: I was the school creep! A couple of my creepy friends and I were the artists of Beaumont High School. I love my hometown, San Antonio. But my father, who worked for the Southern Pacific Railroad, was transferred to Beaumont when I was in high school, and I did not like Beaumont nearly as well. Beaumont is below sea level. It's a swamp. And there I was, coming in in the ninth grade, not knowing anybody — and playing the violin. I knew I had to get out of there, and a scholarship was the only way. So I practiced fiendishly!

Q: Does the name Viola Swamp owe anything to your feelings about Beaumont?

A: Yes, exactly. It's the two put together. When Harry Allard and I do books together, we generally can't say who wrote what. But that one — she's mine! I think she's my favorite character, actually.

Q: If you practiced so diligently, you can't have been much of a cut-up.

A: I wasn't a cut-up, but I was a smart-ass kid. I was always trying to show off in school by getting good grades and so on. But I didn't have the courage to be a real brat.

Q: So you think of the Cut-Ups as being brave?

A: In a way. I was very timid. I was a coward. I remember once, when a kid fell and slashed his forehead badly, I ran the other way. I didn't help him. For years I was tortured with that. The Cut-Ups are just kids I know in my neighborhood in Connecticut. They're either going to end up doing time or . . . I think they're both geniuses. One of them is now becoming a little actor in local plays and summer stock, so I think he's going to be OK. But they're not me at all. I loved school. I was crazy about school.

Q: The Alamo is in San Antonio.

A: I was born across the street from the Alamo!

Q: Was it exciting for you to be growing up in a place with such a rich history?

A: Actually, I grew up out in the country, twenty miles out of town. So I really grew up alone. I had no friends after school.

We lived in San Antonio after I was about twelve. My baby sister was born there. But earlier on, I lived out on that farm. I think that's where all the imagination came from. I was passionately interested in English history, so I imagined the back forty as the site of the Battle of Bosworth Field. I had no sense of its being Texas. It was always someplace else.

Q: Texas wasn't historical enough, so to speak?

A: That's how it seemed for a time. But then I got very interested in my father's family, all of whom were from West Texas, and became passionately interested in the West. In the 1880s, when they settled in West Texas, they were still having Indian raids. At one point — this was about 1910 — Pancho Villa raided my grandmother's ranch and stole her cattle. As a ten-year-old hearing that stuff, my imagination went wild.

Q: Were there good storytellers in your family?

A: My grandfather, for one. I would pump him and the others for information. Once, I discovered boxes and boxes of old Brownie pictures and I asked my grandmother about them and she said, "Hon, out here that was all we could do." It was flat for miles, with nothing going on. So when they got their Brownie cameras, they took pictures of each other constantly. I found photographs of my grandparents in buckboards, with shotguns. It was the end of the frontier era, and I had certifiable proof that my family had lived through it. That seemed just wonderful to me.

Q: Do you still have those photographs?

A: I have many of them. I always come back from Texas with some album that nobody wants.

Q: There are Texas flags in the schoolrooms in your books. Is that because you are still fond of the state?

A: Yes. Really, my roots are there. I like the climate.

I'm especially fond of West Texas. I went to bury my grandmother two years ago in a little town called Marathon, named after Marathon in Greece. It's like a ghost town. There's nothing there, except for a windmill. And when I arrived in town, I noticed that the windmill — I always put windmills in my books, too — was being taken down. I said, "You can't do that." It was the only thing there. It was like the Eiffel Tower of Marathon, Texas. So they said, "Well, if you want it, you buy it." So I bought it.

Now I own a windmill in the middle of God-knows-where. I bought it with the stipulation that it stays — you know — on Grandma's grave! She had a fairly good sense of humor and was a pretty good storyteller herself.

Q: Was coming East to study in Boston a turning point in your life?

A: Yes. I knew that I had to get out of Beaumont and I wanted to come East. Someone said that Boston was the place to go.

Q: Had you been studying languages by then? I know that at some point you studied French and Italian. Both languages are so musical, and I wonder if the musical connection was part of their appeal for you?

A: No. It was snobbery. I have always gone into things from the wrong end, the superficial end. I think I became an artist because I wanted a studio, because I wanted to buy art supplies! Then came the time when I had to prove something. I always wanted to love opera, symphonies, classical music — to distinguish myself. Later I realized, I really like these things. I'm not alone in this. I know a lot of people who say they were little snobs at fifteen, then suddenly it took.

Q: I have read that while you were in music school you were in a plane crash and injured your hand.

A: I don't know why I said that. It's not true. I was in a slight accident that had nothing to do with a plane, and I did injure my hand. I suppose I decided to make a good story out of it.

But I did botch up my hand and got a condition of permanently inflamed muscles. I would practice, and it would only get worse and worse. At the age of eighteen, I had to stop playing. Suddenly, I had no career, no future — nothing. It was a horrible, horrible time. And so I had to go back to Beaumont, and with little towns like that, when you go back, you never get out again. But by the grace of God, my father was transferred back to San Antonio. This was when I was eighteen or nineteen and had had one year of the conservatory. So I went back to Beaumont for about a year and enrolled in Lamar State College of Technology, where, of all people, Janis Joplin was a fellow student. I was a year older than Janis. I don't know how many times I changed my major. But that was how I got out of Beaumont the second time. After Lamar State, I went back to school in the East, and then taught high school in Boston, which nearly killed me because I was teaching Spanish and I didn't speak a word of the language. It was very odd.

Q: How did you manage it?

A: I also lacked teaching credentials, which meant that I couldn't teach in the public schools. But I knew I still might be able to teach at a private school, and I did have a degree in French. So I called up a certain Mother Superior about a job, and her first question was, "Do you speak Spanish?" When I replied, "I spent two weeks in Mexico City once," she said, "Come right over!" If that wasn't bad enough — because you can always intimidate high-school students — half of kids in that school were Puerto Rican. I was really in a jam — so I blackmailed them. I said, "If you give me trouble, you'll never get into another Catholic school in the world." I'm not even a Catholic, but that's what I said. Their little eyes popped out. I said, "If you shut up, I'll give you a C. If you teach me some Spanish, I'll give you a B." So we worked this out as best we could. They were very impressed. I got through two years of that. I did teach the kids some French. But I quickly realized that I would die of a stroke if I had to teach high school for the rest of my life. That's when I started drawing. That's when the doodling began.

Q: As an escape?

A: Yes. Have you ever taught high school? You're constantly on, from eight in the morning until three. You get so few breaks, you're just about dead by the end of the day. I feel so sorry for schoolteachers. They somehow have to have more stamina than the rest of us. I think they become like cockroaches — after a certain point, *nothing can destroy them.* I knew I had to do something else. I would come home and draw late at night. And a friend of mine who was an editor at Houghton Mifflin said, "This is children's-book art." By then I sort of was trying to do children's-book art because I had seen *Where the Wild Things Are* and Gnoli's book and the work of Tomi Ungerer. And I was crazy about Edward Gorey's stuff. And then I saw Arnold Lobel's Frog and Toad books with their very short chapters. I thought, "I can do *that.*" God only knows how I did it. Doing two- or three-page stories is *the* hardest thing. I think I also got into doing children's books because I thought it would be easy. It's a lot of fun sometimes — but it ain't easy. That's basically how I got started. I brought in my portfolio on napkins and all sorts of things to Walter Lorraine. It was very nice. He called back the next day and said, "We have a book for you to illustrate." It was Byrd Baylor's *Plink, Plink, Plink* (1971). And so I was off and running.

Q: Going back for a moment to your teaching days, despite the difficulties, did you empathize with your students on some level? Did getting to know them take you back to childhood or teenage feelings of your own?

A: I liked the kids a lot. They were rotten kids, a lot of them, and very hard to discipline. I was teaching in the South End. Some of the kids had never been to downtown Boston. I became very, very fond of them. Oddly enough, it was when I learned to discipline them, to shut them up — it's that paradox: you can't be their pals — that I became very fond of them. And I find I'm very fond of kids now.

Q: Given the circumstances you described earlier, did you really think of yourself as a teacher?

A: It was complete role-playing. I knew that a lot of it was very false.

I think you have to act and role-play when you're sitting at the drawing board, too. You have to play the role of the artist at least long enough to get yourself to the drawing board, and then you get caught up in that wonderful trance, and then you forget yourself. I think the one thing that disturbed me the most about teaching was the fatigue. I don't know how good a teacher I was. It was the same, later, at the Parsons School of Design, where I took over Maurice's picture-book class and was accused of great favoritism. The problem was that there were two geniuses in the class and I would spend all my time with them. I was very inspired by them and I didn't pay any attention to the others, which I guess was not fair. So I gave up teaching. Teaching is fun, but you have to be very careful about what you're doing.

I did at least teach them all what a picture book is, that no matter what the style, there are certain principles that underlie the picture book as a genre. How to move it. When to stop it. How to pace it. What to leave out. All sorts of little tricks. Never to have the action going into the gutter. A picture book becomes a whole world if it's done properly. I'm very surprised that sometimes people don't understand this, or realize that the picture book is a true art form.

Q: When you were doodling on napkins, were you already creating animal characters like George and Martha?

A: Yes, but not George and Martha. They came along a little later. I quit teaching even before I got the job to illustrate Byrd Baylor's book, having decided I was going to make it in publishing — or at least to try to. Then I went home to Texas for a while. I was still living there when I started developing George and Martha in a sketchbook.

Q: So one day you just hit upon the idea of hippopotamuses as characters?

A: Somebody else told me they were hippos. I started out with two little dots on the page. They were imperfections in the paper. That's how I got started. And my mother was watching *Who's Afraid of Virginia Woolf?* on television. That was my inspiration for George and Martha's names. I usually don't tell kiddies that. I once was on a live radio show in Chicago, and when I arrived at the station I asked the woman, "Do you need any information about me?" "No," she said, "I've done my homework." We went on the air and suddenly she wants to know, "What's it like writing about the First Family?" So I say, "Well, it's not *that* George and Martha!" "Who *are* they, then?" "Well . . . they're hippos." From that moment on, she was completely lost! I had to take over.

Q: So you had those two dots to begin with, and the characters somehow emerged from them. The stories are so wonderfully compact. Did you try to write several stories at once in order to find out more about your new characters?

A: First I drew them in various situations. Out of a scene would come a story. The fun of writing, of course, is paring the story down, whittling it down to the right word. You can become so self-conscious, so precious. You have to be careful not to get too sculptured. If I've got a character that I'm interested in, I can trust that I'll soon have a story as well. The story comes from the character. The ending is always my problem. I've ruined so many books with not-good endings. I find that when you read a book or see a movie, if fabulous, wonderful things have gone on, and if the ending doesn't give that period to it, you come out or close the book feeling you've seen or read something second-rate. I'm always so grateful when I know what the ending will be.

Q: What is your idea of a good ending?

A: A good ending is inevitable, but it's also a surprise.

Q: George and Martha get into little moral dilemmas from time to time, yet the stories don't feel moralistic.

A: God, I hope not. But I think that when there is a moral dilemma, I'm usually doing it tongue-in-cheek. If there's "teaching," it comes out of their characters and not little sayings or whatever. For instance, "Always tell your friends the truth" is a great lie, and you wouldn't always do that.

Q: Many of the stories show that, when George and Martha disagree, there is usually some merit in both their points of view.

A: I hope it isn't self-conscious. Sometimes I'm afraid it is. The situation has to be there. It has to be organic. If you try to impose a little moral, it gets very sticky.

Q: How would you describe George and Martha?

A: I think innocent, crafty, courtly. They're very courtly with each other. They usually have exquisite manners in the best sense. I think they have a sense of fun. I had a dream about Martha. She had become very cross with me. She wanted better stories, better lines. And I distinctly remember her telling me that if she didn't get them, she was going to Maurice's house. I woke up in a cold sweat!

One of my favorite authors is Chekhov, and one of the reasons I love his stories and plays so much is that things are not spelled out in them. It's in the story, it's in the characters, it's in the setting, and it's all very intuitive. You don't have to dot the i's. At the same time you've got to have a sense of artifice, too. Because it's the real world filtered through one intelligence and point of view.

Q: Your George and Martha drawings are very elegant, yet there's also something artless about them.

A: Maurice said they were "raw." They have to be fresh and the line has to be alive. Sometimes it takes a long time to achieve that quality. At other times I can just do it.

Q: When you say that the line has to be alive, what exactly do you mean?

A: It has to tell a story. It has to be an interpretation of something. It's there for a meaning rather than for an absolute realistic reflection.

Q: In Edward Lear's drawings, for instance, there's an obsessive, crazily manic quality to the line that certainly suits his subject matter. Can you describe your line in comparable terms? In the George and Martha books, for instance, are you trying for a "heavy" line to emphasize the characters' massive physique?

A: It's heavy, but my hand shakes a little when I do it. I do it in pencil and then I trace. Sometimes I do a basic pencil drawing to establish an architecture for the drawing. I really cannot stand it if something in a picture is misplaced. Scale is very important. I think I learned a lot about scale from looking at Maurice's work, although he and I don't approach scale in the same way. For me, it is like focusing in and out. There is only one point where that character should be in relation to the frame and to the viewer and to the back wall, and I spend hours erasing, pulling it down, bringing it up, until it's absolutely perfect, the way I want it. And then I have to forget all of that and make the line come alive for the finished drawing. So often the line gets tight, and when I look at a drawing the next morning, I say, "This has got to go out. It doesn't have that spontaneous quality."

Edward Gorey's work has enormous thought behind it. Someone said once that Gorey has been doing the same book for twenty or thirty years. It's not true. He keeps perfecting, getting better and better. We all have bad books every so often. I think that when you have a highly recognizable style, it can read to some people as formula. It can of course become formula, too, and that's one of the worst things that can happen to an artist. I don't know how someone in that situation could stand himself.

Q: George and Martha are quite vulnerable in many ways. Would you relate the shakiness of the line to that quality of theirs?

A: No, I think the shakiness is just to keep it from becoming too tight. It's a technique, although anything you do on the page relates to psychology. They *are* vulnerable and I think that's why kids, at least, like them. And because they're not fools. My characters usually have their wits about them. And they have the gift of wit, which can be a saving grace. How many of us have gotten out of awful situations by falling back on our sense of humor?

Q: How do you see George and Martha in relation to each other?

A: They probably reflect two sides of my own personality. He bumbles into things through, I think, innocence, and she gets a little grand in places. It's so silly that these light little entertainments can spark people, but I've gotten outraged letters. I got one recently from a Presbyterian minister in Tennessee who was just furious with me! He said first of all I was *clearly* a woman writing under a man's name, that I was a rabid feminist because the female character was always dominating the male character; and second of all, that he had been to Africa and had heard that hippos kill people. How dare I! I thought, *Oh God, this might be the one letter I answer back!* Then I thought, *That's not really true.* Martha's really quite pretentious in many ways.

Q: When you put together a George and Martha book, do you think a great deal about the ordering of the stories? Is there an emotional arc or contour to their arrangement?

A: Very definitely. You've got to think about what that second story's going to be. It's very important. It's just the same with pacing any kind of book. When to let up. When to turn up the juice. When to give a rest. When not to betray the characters. And always doing something that is within the context of their lives and personalities. There are so many considerations.

Q: Did your musical training carry over into your children's-book work in any way?

A: It's very funny. I have some tapes of myself playing the viola — I was pretty good, actually — and I think the way I approached playing the viola is very much the way I approach drawing now. There is some correlation between sound and space. I don't understand it. But I know that as a violist I had a very fat sound. I can almost say that the musical line I created when I played the viola is the line with which I now draw. It has the same weight. The viola is the alto voice of the string family. That's the sort of tonality of my drawings. It sounds so pretentious to say it, but I know it's true.

Q: There's a clarity to your drawings that relates to what you said earlier about leaving things out. Do your drawings get less cluttered as you work on them?

A: Oh, yes. It's one of my major concerns. Concerns — but not problems. Speaking broadly, I almost never have major problems, or a crack-up, doing a drawing. I draw with a lot of confidence. I don't know if it's going to be a good drawing or not, but it's going to be what I want. The real hell is constructing a plot, doing the Miss Nelson books, for instance, and getting the story to finally come together in that satisfying way. I sometimes do a book in a few weeks. Other times it may take a year. If I have one book that's successful, I may sign a contract for a sequel. I've got the character, so I'm confident about that. But then I think, *How did I get into this? I'm going to go crazy! This is awful!* Then I start drawing and the solution comes out of that, and I say "Ah!" I don't know where I'd be if I didn't know how to draw.

Q: I like the half-title pages in the George and Martha books. They remind me of the titles in old-fashioned newsreels and silent pictures.

A: I have always thought of them as a way of introducing kids to books — books with chapters and chapter headings. And with a this-little-story-will-only-take-you-three-pages-to-get-through kind of feeling.

I have drawers and drawers of George and Martha stories. Some are finished, others not. I have always wanted to do a book — and I may do one — as a sort of scrapbook or sketchbook with bits of stories — maybe even a sort of funny, juiced-up workbook for kids. I have the beginnings, I guess, of a hundred stories that never went anywhere, which I know somebody could finish. I have one picture of cows dancing a tango-y dance and the caption reads, "From the day the Hoovers learned they could dance, their lives have never been the same." Then you turn the page and — NOTHING. I have lots of stories like that. Then I have middles of stories, and I think it might be fun just to put eight of them together and say, "Take it, kids — and send me the royalties!"

I have always thought my best stuff was in my sketchbooks. I have hundreds and hundreds of sketchbooks. I like to work at night, I suppose because that's when my defenses are sort of low. I have my most creative ideas at night. I'm less inhibited and I really let it rip.

Q: Going back to George and Martha. Unlike Edward Albee's *Who's Afraid of Virginia Woolf?*, your books present the world as a fundamentally gentle and hospitable place.

A: Maybe I'm just hoping it's an OK place. Somebody said to me on television in San Francisco that the books are very sunny. Maybe I hope the world is full of innocence. But this woman asked me the same question. She said, "You must have a sunny, happy, healthy outlook on the world." And I said, "Well, let me think about it. I think most people are selfish and venal and that we deserve the horrors that have come into the world." She looked at me as if she had this snake sitting across from her — a snake who writes George and Martha books! I think to do a sunny, happy book doesn't necessarily mean that you're a sunny, happy person.

Q: I wasn't suggesting the books are sentimental.

A: I don't mind being light. Max Beerbohm said that there are many charming talents that ruin themselves by taking themselves too seriously.

Q: In the George and Martha books, you nonetheless also show that life is always a little more complicated than one thought.

A: If that has comes across, I'm delighted. I think that is how I do feel. At the same time, just doing a well-made book is in a way profound, too. It gives people a great sense of well-being to look at a book that is put together well, and that operates on the level it set out to do. That alone — just to be able to do that — is an achievement. I'm often asked what's my favorite book, and I say I don't know because I haven't been able to do it yet.

But there are pages, and sometimes series of pages, where I feel I've got it right. The entrances of Viola Swamp, I think, are particularly successful. She is sort of Maria Callas with a fake nose on. "Here I am!" *Crash.* And I think *Red Riding Hood* (1987) was successful. Then again, it's happened to me a lot that I'll say, *Ah, I've really got something here. People are going to sit up and take notice, fall on the floor laughing.* And the next morning I think, "I ought to be hospitalized. This is terrible!" Often I've been surprised at stuff that was sheer drudgery — you know, you just feel nausea in every cell of your body — but then the book gets published and it's this light, fluffy piece that works, with some humor in it. And you think, *Where the hell did that come from?*

Q: George and Martha look more like adults than children. But it's not clear how old they are.

A: I think that's good. I must do it deliberately. They're not children. It's clear they're not kids. It's also not so clear that they're grown-ups. And I find it interesting when people ask, "Are they ever going to get married?" Things like that. Because that would never occur to me. "Childlike" and "innocent"—I wonder if they're the same? You never know how they make their money. You never know anything realistic about them. Their houses are as goofy as can be, yet I don't think they're cardboard cutouts. There is some dimension to them.

Q: You like to play with the margins. Often a character will step halfway off the page.

A: I got criticized for that somewhere. Obviously, it's something that I do deliberately. I've always loved Japanese prints, and anybody who is influenced by Japanese prints will start doing that sort of thing. It's a technique and it does wonderful things dramatically.

Q: Do you think of the page of a book as a sort of proscenium stage?

A: Sure. I *don't* think of it as a cartoon strip. Many times my stuff has been called "cartoony." I think that's just wrong. I think of books as theater. I love the opera. I love the theater. The more artificial the better. The more artificial it is, if it is done well, the truer it is.

Q: By "artificial" do you mean the more it calls attention to itself as a book?

A: Oftentimes I love backstage more than what's up front. But that's just a quirk. I do think of the page as a proscenium.

Q: George and Martha are always changing costumes. Part of the fun of those books is in seeing what they'll have on next. That in itself makes them a little like actors.

A: I'm beginning to like them all over again! I might do another.

Q: Why did you invent a "collaborator" for yourself named Edward Marshall?

A: Walter Lorraine at Houghton Mifflin absolutely killed me at one point because I had published under the name Edward Marshall with another publisher, Dial. But Houghton didn't do easy-to-read books, and Phyllis Fogelman at Dial did. So that was the beginning of Edward. One day somebody called me after I'd come back from a long publishing lunch — I was really quite tipsy — and said, "Mr. Marshall?" I said, "Yeeessss . . ." "Can you tell us where we can find Edward Marshall?" And I said, "Well, he's very difficult to find . . . living out there by the crematorium, with those fourteen children." I could hear his pencil scratching away! I made up this incredible tale — and it was published, I forget where. You know, "The Biography of Edward Marshall." But then finally Walter figured out that there was no Edward Marshall — my middle name is Edward — and Phyllis and I decided that it would be better for the reviews of the Fox books to appear under "James." So we were having lunch in midtown and Phyllis was saying, "Well, you know, I think he should die in a hang-gliding accident off Carmel." And I said, "No, Phyllis . . ." And I noticed these two at the next table looking *very* interested in our conversation. I think Edward just sort of faded away.

Q: What about Harry Allard? Does *he* exist?

A: Yes, *unfortunately.* Actually he's a very good friend of mine. He lives in Mexico and is the one who taught me French. We've done the Stupids books and the Miss Nelson books and a few others. Collaboration is not a lot of fun. But Harry has a wonderful sense of humor. He invented the Stupids.

You can imagine the kinds of letters we get about that series. "How dare you make fun of the mentally deficient?" "Oh, I've been trying to keep children from using the word 'stupid' all my life. . . ." People are just outraged.

I suspect that most adults who object to those books — nine times out of ten — have not looked at them with children. I find that the kids who read the books don't think the stories are stupid at all. They think maybe the jerk who wrote them is stupid because there's a cow on the wall. And I've noticed that when kids are first starting to read, and the word *doesn't* correspond to whatever the picture is, they find it screamingly funny.

Q: There again, it's showing that the world is a little more complicated than one thought, isn't it? Instead of words and pictures matching up, there are reversals of sense.

A: I think that runs all through my work, in a sort of benign way. The Stupids, for instance, always have a good time.

Q: They don't know enough not to.

A: Right. They have a certain joie de vivre. They're fun to do in part because the level of humor is right on the edge of stupidity itself.

Q: Do you do many school visits?

A: I used to. I quit because it was taking too much time. I loved it, though. It was terrifying at first, mainly I think because having gone through three years as a substitute teacher in ghetto schools (that was before I taught high school), and not having been able to discipline the kids, I was really scared to death of them. But I always loved grammar school, and once I got back in that atmosphere, I gave a sigh. I just loved it. And the kids — I was thunderstruck that I had a rapport with them. At first I thought, *I'm pulling the wool over these kids' eyes.* I was very surprised that they really liked me. They got the jokes. Fourth-graders are the ones for me. Third- and fourth-graders.

They can really scream with laughter because they have a little bit of sophistication. I think they catch on.

Q: Would you draw pictures for them?

A: Well, see, I can draw like the wind, so they would shut up immediately. That conquered the discipline problem right from the start. Their little eyes would pop out of their heads, so long as they could see. Some of these God-awful principals, on the other hand . . . I'd say, "A group of sixty is all I can handle"—and then suddenly I'd be shown into the auditorium or the cafeteria, where six hundred kids would file in. None of them can see. It's overheated. The teachers want a free hour. That's vaudeville hell—with the audience squirming and your voice just going.

Q: Is it true that kids would sometimes ask you about George and Martha stories that aren't actually in any of the books?

A: Yes. They write their own stories, of course. But often I'd have kids tell me things that they thought were in my books that weren't. We all do that to some extent, since we can't read the author's mind and must interpret every word of a book in our own way. But I think anybody who does the kind of open-ended book that I do must have similar experiences with readers.

Q: Can you think of an example of a story that some child imagined reading in one of your books?

A: "When Martha sank her boat" is one of them. I thought at first, *Well, I've forgotten about that one. I'd better go back and look.* Well, I did, and there's nothing about Martha sinking a boat. There's another one about George blowing up Martha with dynamite. I thought, *I'd better speak to the counselor on this one!*

I get lots and lots of fan mail. Arnold Lobel, who was a dear friend of mine, once told me, "Answer every one of those letters back." When I receive individual letters, I will answer the kid back. But when I get a class letter — and you can see the teacher wrote it on the blackboard — I usually answer the class.

Q: Have you had running correspondences with certain children over the years?

A: Quite a few. After about twelve, I lose them. They're very embarrassed to be even *seen* with me! Then when they're eighteen or nineteen and they take kiddie-book courses in college, they start writing me again.

Q: Really?

A: Quite a few. I think it's fun. It's one of the nicer aspects. Sometimes it's a chore, if you don't work on the letters at least a little bit each day. There's always a big stack.

Q: Do the children get very personal with you?

A: Oh, yes, though I don't get any real horror stories. I think that, because of the nature of my work, they're not going to tell me about awful things that happened to them.

Q: Do kids ask you about how books are made? Do you find that they have many misconceptions?

A: When I was a kid I didn't know that people made books. All kids now know that it comes from a person. I think when they're very little, they do not understand that there are multiple copies of a book and that surprises them. But they're very sophisticated as a rule. I don't think they understand what happens at a printing press, but then neither do I. There's still some basic step that I can't quite get. When it goes into the stripping room, I sort of lose it.

Q: Which of your characters do they like the best?

A: George and Martha and the Stupids and Miss Nelson. Teachers all over the country are dressing up as Viola Swamp. I had one come to a book-signing in California. She called me up at my apartment in San Francisco and said, "I've got this wonderful idea. I'm going to come dressed as Viola Swamp. While you're signing books I'm going to beat you with a ruler!" I thought to myself, *Oh, God, you know, I'm a grown man. Why did I get into this profession?* And so I said, "This is not a good idea. First of all, there are going to be people there who aren't going to know who Viola Swamp is. This could only work — possibly — in a school set-ting." And she said: "Oh I've got to do it, I've got to do it!" Finally, the day came. It was shaping up to be a very successful signing, with kids and adults all the way out the door. Then suddenly I heard this scream out on the street. I thought, *Well, she's arrived.* She came tearing in. She was very successful, too. She looked just like the character. A little Japanese girl, maybe five, had just come up to me. I had signed her book and somehow she was absolutely captured by the experience and was chewing on the tablecloth, looking up. And then she caught sight of this woman who had just come in and was hitting me over the head, you know, really pounding me with a ruler. And the little girl — well, they had to carry her out like a surfboard! She just froze. I think she's probably in therapy to this day. So I said to the teacher, "You see!" And the teacher said, "But isn't it *fun?*" It's great when a character catches on like that. We may do one more Miss Nelson book.

Q: Many of your characters spend time looking for work — Fox in *Fox on the Job* (1988), Rapscallion Jones, and others.

A: I've never thought about that. I guess I'm subconsciously afraid that my books will flop and I'll have to be out looking for a job. I'm sure of that. I've always been afraid of that. I have the same dream that I'm sure everybody has, the dream of being back in school. And you've got that one test to take in chemistry and you forgot to study. And I find that if I don't have that dream, I have a variant of it where I'm back teaching high school again and I'm back with the nuns and I have signed a fifty-year contract that I can't get out of and I'll be in Cathedral High School for the rest of my life. And I wake up in a cold sweat and I'm screaming, "But I want to publish books. I want to draw." And there's no one in the school, in the corridors. I'm probably living in the school. *That* will get me to the drawing table the next morning so fast! And I'll really do a good drawing. So it's probably a good thing, in a way.

Q: One of the things I like about the folktale books you've been doing recently is the lightness you bring to them. It takes some of the weight off the stories that Bruno Bettelheim, for one, made everyone feel.

A: The old fool! I think he's *wrong* half the time and I also think he's, well . . . That's a tricky thing, to do those books. Obviously I can't help trying to be funny. I don't know if I always am. I didn't want to distort the tales and lose the truth in them but I thought they could be funny and light. At the same time I didn't want to go as far as the Disney version. And so I had to work very hard on them. I'm doing one more, *Hansel and Gretel* (1990), which *may* be very tricky, from two points of view. You've got the horrid mother and I've decided to push her hard, I mean in Roald Dahl's direction. Why soft-pedal it? She's a monster who wants to let the her own children starve.

Q: So, she won't be a stepmother?

A: No. And I've got to push her to the hilt to make her grotesque. I'm not quite sure how I'm going to do that graphically.

Q: You make the mother sound a little like Viola Swamp.

A: Yes, but I don't want to do that, either. It's going to be hard work.

Q: And what about the father? What will he be doing?

A: He's going to be sort of not there. I had the same problem with the father in *Cinderella* (1989). I had him always sleeping. I didn't want him to be an active character. And I didn't want him obviously to be watching all these horrible things happening and not doing anything about it. So I just had him sleep all the time. Maybe that's chickening out.

Q: There's a lot more background detail in the fairy-tale books than, say, in the George and Martha ones.

A: There's more background but it's not realistic background. It's more like an elaborate stage set, I think. That forest in *Red Riding Hood* is supposed to look artificial. I don't know why I keep wanting things to look artificial. I guess because I can't draw naturalistically and also because the artificial has a more poetic resonance.

Q: They look so different from your sparer drawings. I wonder if it has something to do with the fact that they're such old stories with so much tradition behind them.

A: I'm sure.

Q: And yet, some of the characters you've done in the past are very like characters found in folktales — tricksters and fools.

A: I like the tricksters. I like the fools. I like the old fools, for instance, in Molière, who is one of my favorite writers. In *The Misanthrope*, for example. I love that kind of wily character. I think kids do, too.

Q: Why do you think that is?

A: Well, it's the fascination with masks. In the second Miss Nelson book, she changes God knows how many times. I think it's creating that face for the world. It's fun dressing up. Just for that alone. Turning the world into a play. They're very broad characters acting out very broad humor.

Q: Many of your stories are about nervous anticipation: George and Martha worrying about what a scary movie will be like; Portly McSwine worrying about whether his party will be a success.

A: I suppose that comes up from my own shabby character — as a sort of a parody of my own character, and of a lot people I know. Always projecting in the future. Gandhi said, "Never rehearse a tragedy." I must have rehearsed ten thousand. Only now, in my forties, have I learned to live in the present.

ROBERT MCCLOSKEY

Born 1914, Hamilton, Ohio; Died 2003, Deer Isle, Maine

Robert McCloskey's initial success as an illustrator came as the American picture book was riding the crest of its first golden age. His first book, *Lentil* (1940), appeared within a year of Ludwig Bemelmans's *Madeline* (1939), Hardie Gramatky's *Little Toot,* and H. A. Rey's *Curious George* (1941). With the publication of *Lentil,* McCloskey joined Viking editor May Massee's legendary corps of illustrators, a group that also included Bemelmans, Robert Lawson, Marjorie Flack, Kurt Wiese, James Daugherty, and Ingri and Edgar Parin d'Aulaire.

Massee's artists had an unrivaled knack for winning Caldecott Medals. McCloskey received his own first Caldecott for his second picture book, *Make Way for Ducklings* (1941), in 1942, and won again for *Time of Wonder*

141

(1957) sixteen years later. The recipient as well of three Caldecott Honors, he retired from illustration in 1970 as one of the most celebrated artists in the history of the field.

Like American film director Frank Capra and magazine artist Norman Rockwell, McCloskey specialized in wry, upbeat stories that expressed a deep-seated faith in the essential goodness of people. His books have endured in part because they reveal a timeless dimension in everyday experience: the childhood rite of passage played out around a little girl's lost tooth in *One Morning in Maine* (1952), the parents' quest for a secure home in which to raise their young in *Make Way for Ducklings*. In each of his books, the comforts of the familiar are greatly enriched by McCloskey's sense that the wonderful is always near at hand.

In the latter years of his long life, McCloskey painted for his own pleasure, supported wilderness preservation and other not-for-profit causes, and worked on the prototypes for a new kind of articulated wood puppet intended for use in animated children's films. He rarely made public appearances, but when he did venture out, people lined up around the block to express their gratitude to him. We first met in 1990 when we both spoke at a daylong program at the Boston Athenaeum. "Bob," as he liked to be called, was completely indifferent to publicity in all its forms, and it took some persuading before he would agree to be interviewed. We recorded most of the conversation that follows at our second meeting, which took place at the Weston Woods film studios, in Weston, Connecticut, where he maintained a small workshop, on February 11, 1991. We taped additional material by telephone on April 13th and November 4th of that year.

~~~~~~~~~~~~~~~~~~~~~~~~~~~~~~~~~~~~~~

LEONARD S. MARCUS: Was reading important to you as a child?

ROBERT McCLOSKEY: It's hard to remember a time when there weren't very many children's books. But in our public library in Hamilton, Ohio, for instance, when I was a boy, one shelf would accommodate all of the children's books that they had, and a lot of those were duplicates. The good ones I remember were the Dr. Dolittles and one *Winnie the Pooh*. Later, when I was writing *Homer Price* (1943), I was really writing down the stories that I thought kids would like that I didn't find there on the shelf when I was a child.

Q: I've heard you were something of a boy inventor.

A: My grandfather was a tinkerer, and as a child I made our Christmas tree revolve and tried to build a cotton candy machine out of a vacuum cleaner motor and a dishpan. I poured sugar into my device, thinking it would spin the sugar out as I'd seen it done at carnivals, but it didn't. Then I figured I had to melt the sugar and as I didn't have the know-how for that, I poured molasses into my machine as the equivalent of sugar already melted. But the molasses just spun out all over the kitchen and all over me. I must have been upwards of ten when I did that.

Going back earlier, I remember when electricity arrived in our house. I was about three then. I don't recall anything about switches, but I do remember the difference in the quality of the light.

I was very interested in any news item about Edison, and I went through a long period of building model airplanes. I taught other boys soap carving and model-plane building at the YMCA.

Later, in the army during the war, I invented a machine for folding sticky tape and a machine for flipping over field charts. But the army had no place for an artist, so they used to hide me. They'd put me on a truck and send me off into the hills.

Q: Did art interest you as a child?

A: Yes, but I couldn't make up my mind what I might end up being. I played the piano and oboe, and at one time thought of becoming a musician. I had a harmonica band, which performed at local lodge meetings and church socials. *Lentil,* my first published book, is a spin-off of that.

Q: Did your parents encourage your artistic side?

A: They did, but I think they would have been much happier if I had chosen a career in, say, engineering.

Hamilton was the center of the universe to me. I had been nowhere else except to a summer resort on Lake Erie for family vacations, and I'd spent part of a summer on a farm in Indiana. The *National Geographic* and *Saturday Evening Post* and the Sears and Roebuck catalog were big sources of information about the outside world. Somehow — I don't know how — I got the idea that if I were a successful artist I could live anywhere I wanted to. Then, in high school, I got a scholarship to go to art school in Boston. The Depression had begun, and but for that scholarship I think I would never have been able to set foot out of the state of Ohio.

Q: Was *Lentil,* with its affectionate portrait of small-town America, your farewell to Hamilton?

A: No, I didn't think of it as that. I didn't think of *Lentil* as being about an exact place. I used bits and pieces of my hometown. The monuments and other buildings are composites, slightly caricatured. The 1930s was the time of American Scene art, when artists were becoming eager to depict typically American subjects instead of just European or classical ones. *Lentil* was connected to that. As a boy I had suspenders and dressed rather like my story's hero, though my mother would never permit barefootedness.

Q: Were there flimflam men in Hamilton, like the ones you wrote about in *Homer Price*?

A: There used to be a Saturday market around the courthouse in the town square, where farmers would sell their produce. Along with the farmers these other people would show up selling things like snake oil — it must have been lubricating oil or something that they doctored up. And corn removers — all sold by con men. I used to listen to those people by the hour with their medicine shows.

Q: What got you started making children's books?

A: Well, one of my boyhood friends was a nephew of the editor May Massee. When I was growing up with him I heard about his aunt, so that was one of my introductions to the field. Once I became interested in children's books, Miss Massee was the first person I went to see.

When I came East from Hamilton, I had only the germ of an idea for *Lentil.* It started out as just a lot of pictures of a boy playing the harmonica. I didn't have any idea whether I was going to have words with my pictures or not. I thought the drawings might lead to a series of lithographic prints, not necessarily to a children's book at all. But once there got to be some words, the words grew, and then the pictures grew. For a time, it just seemed to go on forever, with no beginning or end. But when I met May Massee, it fell into place.

Q: Did the art school you attended in Boston offer a course in children's-book illustration?

A: They had a course in illustration, but not children's-book illustration, and I don't think that anyone had a special course for that then. In those days, you illustrated whatever came along. The *Saturday Evening Post* was the top. If you could get an illustration job from the *Post,* you had arrived! Artists were also very happy to get a job from *Fortune* magazine. In those days if you were in Provincetown over the summer and somebody sold a drawing or print, everybody in town knew about it, and all your friends would gather round and you'd have to treat them. If you sold a painting, it was almost "May I touch you?"!

Q: You set your next book, *Make Way for Ducklings,* in Boston, where you yourself had gone to live.

A: *Ducklings* was a spin-off, too. I had gotten a job as an artist's assistant painting murals of Boston subjects — the State House, the Charles River, Louisburg Square. So these were all subjects I had been thinking about in terms of spatial relationships and scale, and it seemed just natural right after that to put those subjects down on the page.

Q: Wasn't *Make Way for Ducklings* also based on a true story that had been reported in the Boston papers?

A: Yes, and one time I saw those ducklings myself, on the curb, having come across the street to the Boston Public Garden, though not with the police and everyone looking on as in my story.

Q: I've always thought that the story started off in a curious way, with a family of wild animals moving to a big city in search of a safe place to live. . . .

A: In those days ducks might have had a better chance in Boston. At one time my late wife and I had a house on a pond in Bedford, New York, where we saw swans disappear, taken by the turtles.

Q: How did work on *Make Way for Ducklings* proceed?

A: By then I'd moved from Boston to a studio apartment in New York City, and though I returned to Boston to make sketches, it was cold weather and rainy and very unpleasant and I soon realized I couldn't study ducks there. Then an ornithologist mentioned that I could buy live ducks at a certain Greenwich Village market. So I did, brought them home, and kept them in the tub, though not continuously. Once in a while I had to make use of that tub myself! The ducklings were not hard to manage when they were young but their appetites and size increased very rapidly.

Q: You made an unusual choice in having the whole book, text and illustrations, printed in brown ink.

A: It had to be as interesting as I could make it because I didn't have enough of a reputation then for them to take a chance on printing a big book like that in full color. I made the original lithographic drawings in black and white. The ink used in the printing gave them the sepia color. Black and white just seemed such a cold thing for a children's book — and for those ducks. Later when I got to *Blueberries for Sal* (1948) I wondered if I could get away with that blue ink, and I didn't make up my mind till the last minute.

It was a time of experimentation, and artists had to be a lot more involved in the graphic process in those days. The publisher would never have been able to afford to put out a book like *Make Way for Ducklings* for two bucks if I hadn't been very involved. They saved on the platemaking.

I stretched all my know-how to the limit in just making the lithographic plates. I debated for a while whether to do the illustrations in woodcuts or wood engravings rather than lithographs, but when I found out that they would probably take what I had done and print them by lithographic process, it seemed a silly thing for me not to do the lithographs myself. So *Ducklings,* like *Lentil* before it, was done as lithographic drawings on the zinc, though they made transfers from those to put on the printing plates. I never used stones for lithography, as the d'Aulaires did, because that's such a storage job.

Q: *Make Way for Ducklings* is such a good title. Did you think of it right away?

A: No, I didn't think of it at all, as a matter of fact. I think I called it something like *Boston Is Lovely in the Spring.* It was Miss Massee's secretary who thought up a title for it.

Q: Your career was really taking off just then. You had recently won two major art awards unrelated to your work as a children's-book illustrator, the Prix de Rome for your watercolors, and a Tiffany Foundation Prize.

A: Yes, and one day the publicity person from Viking called up and said, *Life* magazine wants to come down to your studio. *Life* was everything in those days. The photographer arrived and took pictures of the ducks, me drawing them, and me playing harmonica with the ducks quacking all over me. Those were wild times. The *Life* article was due to be published when the entire issue was suddenly scrapped — *boom* — like that because Hitler had just invaded Poland.

Q: The sense of warmth, which you spoke about a moment ago, carries over to your detailed depiction of Boston.

A: I was meticulous about pursuing accuracy, though it's not a matter of measurements: it was the *feel* of Boston, a place I enjoyed, that I wanted. No one is going to go strolling or flying over and check the number of chimneys that I put on or the number of bricks. But the detail of a wrought iron fence, for instance, that a child would put his hand on or walk right by or rub a stick on the way children do — that's accurate.

Q: The drawings also have amazing energy.

A: Children like to pore over pictures. And in those days, as I said, I thought of myself as a mural painter. I wanted to cover walls. I found it confining to scale down my pictures and ideas to put them inside the pages of a book. So I tried every trick I could to get as much into those pictures as possible. I paced the illustrations, and gave them a variety of viewpoints — aerial views and others — to create a sense of space and movement and a feeling of something going on.

Q: Like the boy racing by on his bicycle like a bat out of hell.

A: Yes.

Q: Were you surprised by the success of *Make Way for Ducklings*?

A: Yes, I was. I was surprised by the Caldecott Medal because I had never heard of it. Of course, that award had only been around for a few years then.

Q: Do you still like the book now?

A: Sometimes I wake up at night from a dream of being in a warehouse full of books! Fork lifts and trucks full of thousands of copies of the book, *and all of them printed with exactly the same mistakes.* You have an eye that's slightly out of place and that offends you when you see it. It gets to be like a drippy faucet. Now I have to force that out.

With *Ducklings,* I feel a great responsibility of having unleashed something. I get letters from all over the world and a lot of pictures of ducks from children. People also send me postcards and photographs they've taken of ducklings crossing a road with their mother, and cars stopping for them. This is something that happens all over the world. It doesn't know any national or continental boundaries.

Q: Do you think that's why *Make Way for Ducklings* has lasted?

A: People see a lot of different things in that book. It never occurred to me that it would be taken as exemplary of family life. But there must be some sort of reassurance in a story about a father mallard making a promise to return, and then keeping that promise. I couldn't begin to explain it.

Then there are other people who have used *Ducklings* to train children to stop and look in both directions before they cross the street — just traffic know-how. It has, of course, also been an introductory book to Boston for many people.

All my books have somehow gone off and found their own level. There have been libraries that installed reading corners — or "reading nooks," which got to be a big thing at one time — and they would acquire an old boat, for instance, like Bert Dow's, and upholster it and paint it. Or they would have a bathtub with claw feet like Lentil's. To make it comfortable it must have had a soft cozy lining—perhaps even a mattress and some pillows.

I never expected those books to be so popular. Nor did the publisher! And no one could tell that children's books were going to be as widely accepted as they have become.

Q: *Blueberries for Sal,* your first book set in Maine, has an almost musical form. It's a two-part invention in which the bears' and humans' berry-picking adventures become entwined.

A: I'd never thought of it like that, but it is a sort of counterpoint, isn't it? One day I had taken my wife and daughter blueberrying and had taken along my sketchbook and was just lazing there, almost dozing away in the sun when I heard this *kerplink, kerplank, kerplunk* of the berries striking the bottom of Sal's pail. I guess that that was what set the whole thing off—not music, but a *kerplink!* inviting you to sing along.

Q: Did bears come along, as happens in the story?

A: No, the bears were imagined, though meeting up with bears in Maine while blueberrying used to be a pretty common occurrence.

It's odd. A lot of my books are of a locale. The locale of *Lentil* is Ohio—but I did that book in New York City. I think I made the first draft of *Ducklings,* which is about Boston, in Connecticut, and I finished it in New York City. And here was *Blueberries for Sal,* this story of Maine, and when I finally got around to starting the drawings for it, we were staying in suburban New York. I researched blueberry plants at the New York Botanical Garden and went to the Central Park Zoo to sketch the bears.

Q: You said before that when you first saw Maine, you liked what you saw. What in particular about Maine appealed to you?

A: Maine is just a beautiful spot. It gives you an opportunity to get the cobwebs of a place like New York out of your hair and time to observe.

Q: Your books are filled with similar reminders of the rewards of close observation — Sal's discovery of a "magic" feather in *One Morning in Maine,* the children's sighting of a hummingbird in *Time of Wonder.*

A: I think there is a lot of satisfaction in allowing your eye to go roving over the surface of a thing, or an illustration in a book, knowing and imagining and realizing what connects what, and why.

Q: In your second Caldecott Medal acceptance speech, given in 1958 — the year after Sputnik and a time of a great clamoring for better science education — you spoke out on behalf of the need for better art education. Why?

A: People — adults as well as children — so often just don't realize what they're looking at. There's no thought behind it. They'll say to themselves, "Well, that's a bookshelf," or "That's an elephant," and see nothing other than just the fact. There's no sense of relationship — of the relationship of a house to its environment, a man to his environment, of the scale of things. Our understanding of cause and effect is disappearing because people are doing so much looking without evaluating. Television adds to this, with all the tricks they can do. Seeing is really a decision-making process, a matter of evaluating what is around you. And children cannot develop that ability so well as they can by learning to draw.

Q: The Ducklings sculpture in the Boston Public Garden is just the right size for small children to climb on.

A: It was very difficult to decide how large they should be. They're tremendous compared to actual ducklings. I saw the bronze figures for the first time in the sculptor's studio, and when they're indoors they *look* tremendous. It was a shock to me. So I said, "Well, we'll have to take them out."

So we put them on a dolly and got them out in the snow and off under some trees, and took a look — and they were just great. Now I have lots of photographs of people and their children with the sculpture in the Garden. I never thought it would happen, but in a very short time those ducklings have found a life of their own.

HELEN OXENBURY

Born 1938, Ipswich, England

Helen Oxenbury first made a name for herself as a scenic designer. After becoming a mother with two small children to look after, however, she found that theater work was too difficult to sustain, and began casting about for alternatives. Her husband, John Burningham, had already launched a successful career as a children's-book author and artist. Following his example, Oxenbury, after a stint as a greeting-card designer, turned to the picture book as an art form she, too, might pursue at home. She published her first children's book, *Number of Things*, in 1967, and was the recipient just two years later of her first Kate Greenaway Medal, England's equivalent of the Caldecott Medal, for *The Quangle Wangle's Hat* (1969) and *The Dragon of an Ordinary Family* (1969).

With the arrival of the couple's third child, Oxenbury became interested in the possibilities for books made with babies and toddlers especially in mind. The board books that followed during the 1980s were among the first to reach the newly emerging market of college-educated parents eager to introduce their children to books from the earliest ages. Oxenbury's board books have rarely been matched either for the overall quality of their design or for the refreshing touches of comic realism with which she salted the works: babies spilling their juice and splattering their food, parents grimacing and panicking. A master watercolorist and draftsman, Oxenbury has also shown herself to be a canny psychologist capable of capturing the complex mix of emotions with which children and their parents respond to one another over the course of a day.

We taped this interview on November 6, 1989, at the offices of Margaret K. McElderry Books, New York, where Oxenbury was visiting in connection with the recent publication of *We're Going on a Bear Hunt* (1989) — a book that was greeted with general acclaim and has since established itself as a read-aloud classic.

~~~~~~

LEONARD S. MARCUS: What do babies see when they look at books?

HELEN OXENBURY: They recognize faces and other babies, and all the little things they have around them — the dish that they eat out of and their high chair. It would be silly to do a board book with atmosphere and landscapes for a very, very tiny child who has no experience of that. All babies know is what happens in their home with their mom and dad. As an artist, one has to recognize what it is that children recognize.

Q: What else goes into the making of books for the very young?

A: You have to consider that a board book is looked at with the parent. For the child, that's the best part — the parent saying: "Do you see the this?" And: "Where is the that?" So you must have a little bit of something in the book that the mother or father will recognize and laugh about, so that they don't think, *Oh, God, I just can't take that book and look at it again!*

Q: You've given the baby on the cover of *Working* (1981) a faceful of food.

A: Exactly. That's something we all know about, isn't it? Relationships between the child and other members of the family, or friends, can also be brought into the pictures of a board book. By the end of *Dressing* (1981), the baby is dressed and ready to go, and it's implied that a parent is on the scene lending a hand, even though I haven't actually shown that in the pictures.

Q: In many board books — but not in yours — babies are always smiling.

A: When babies are eating or on the pot, they don't smile, because they're concentrating on something else. In making books, what I try to show is how things really are.

Q: Are there other ways in which experience as a parent has helped shape your work?

A: When our first two children were babies, we didn't think that they would even want to look at books. But Emily, our third one, suffered as a child from eczema. To stop her scratching we used to walk up and down with her until we almost fell over, and we used to show her magazines. We were absolutely amazed when she began to point things out at a very young age, before she was one, certainly. And you know how one has catalogs of children's clothes, things like that? She used to look and laugh at and enjoy them. So for this little girl who had eczema that we had to cope with, I went especially to the store to look for board books with very simple drawings of things — and there really wasn't much at all available. That's when I began to make my own.

Q: In your most recent board book series (*Clap Hands,* etc.) (1987), you have drawn four babies, each of a different racial group. Do very young children identify with the characters in their books on that level?

A: I think it probably doesn't matter a damn to them. They only start noticing when they pick up ideas about race and ethnicity from their parents. But there weren't any board books that had a multiracial feel to them, so I thought, *Why shouldn't there be?* Because that's how the world is. I tried to do it very unself-consciously.

Q: Your Out-and-About books are for children who have just outgrown board books. What do the books of that series have in common?

A: They're concerned with those quite traumatic little events in a child's life, such as the first day of school — or a birthday party.

Q: In *The Birthday Party* (1983), one little girl guest doesn't want to surrender her present to the birthday boy, who, in turn, is much more interested in his gifts than his guests.

A: Again, we've all been through those experiences. And the parent looking on is thinking: *Better say thank you,* and the child doesn't, of course. Children just want to know what's coming next. Adults, you see, put children in very trying situations and expect them to perform and behave. Adults love to go for a trip in the car, look at the countryside, and go and have tea. But for a child, to be strapped in the back of the car is the most boring thing in the world. So you can't blame the child in *The Car Trip* (1983) when all he thinks about is teasing the dog and . . . I forget what else happens . . .

Q: He throws up.

A: Oh, yes! He's had too much to eat because eating is all he can do, sitting in the back of the car.

   Eating Out (1983) is about the fact that young children loathe going to restaurants. They'd much rather be at home. But I'm not so much saying in that book that the poor parents shouldn't go out to eat. Why shouldn't they? The point is that they're not the only ones who have a child who can't bear it. I think that when children misbehave, parents think that they're the only ones who've got a child who does this sort of thing. Of course, everybody's child does.

Q: By the same token, children often believe that the things they're afraid of, or can't stand, or aren't good at, are unique to themselves. Your books also show them that that isn't so.

A: That's right. At the same time, though, I'm quite suspicious of books that set out to teach things. A picture book, after all, is primarily a stepping-stone to reading. That is what one hopes will happen in the end. What a book must do is to make a child want to read it, to make him think: "Oh, gosh, now what's going to happen?"— and turn the page.

Q: As a child, did you have books that affected you that strongly?

A: I was a baby during World War II, when very few books were available. I had a large book of Shirley Temple photographs, which I absolutely loved, though I can see now it was pretty dreadful.

Q: It's surprising sometimes, isn't it, what books kids actually like?

A: Oh, yes. My brother and I also had some of the classics, Kenneth Grahame's *The Wind in the Willows*, Beatrix Potter's *The Tale of Peter Rabbit*.

Q: *Peter Rabbit*, like your own work, is for the younger ages. Why do you think it has become a classic?

A: It's a *very* good adventure story. Things happen and all the emotions become involved. It starts off with a safe sort of family situation. The mother goes off shopping and tells the children to be good. But there's the one little rebel, Peter, who does the very thing he's been told not to do; he goes into Mr. MacGregor's garden. I'm sure children identify with Peter. So a slight sort of tension builds because you know he shouldn't be there, and because something's looming. Then he's seen and there's the great chase, and you feel *very* sorry for poor old Peter Rabbit as he gets caught up in the netting. Then comes the relief at the end when he escapes. It's not a morality tale, just good earthy naughtiness.

Q: Were you interested in visual things as a child?

A: I can't remember a time when I didn't draw and paint. My father, who was an architect, did quite a few little pictures for my brother and me. There was one lovely painting of a community of elves living in the roots of a tree which overhung a river. I shall never forget that.

Q: Have childhood memories played a part in your own books?

A: The muddy estuary in *We're Going on a Bear Hunt* is very much based on a place where I played as a child. My illustrations for that book also express, I think, the freedom I felt to go out into the country on my own or with a crowd of other children — which children don't have now. You don't dare let children go around on their own, especially in London.

Q: It's curious, then, that you included a parent in the scenes where the children have gone off hunting for bear. Is it a sign of our times — of children needing to be protected — that you did so?

A: I don't know. Hmmm. The stories I loved as a child were actually the ones where there weren't any adults around—adventure stories with children who just coped on their own.

What I like about *Bear Hunt* is that the text allows the illustrations to do as much work as the words themselves. For instance, in the line, "We're going on a bear hunt," the "we" is never described. We're never told who "we" are, so it is entirely up to the illustrator to create the characters. The scenes with the snowstorm and the mud are also never described, so again it was up to me to decide how they looked. Then the bear: We're not told what sort of bear it is, whether fierce or friendly. The text has a wonderful way of gathering speed, so I had to find a way of not letting the illustrations slow it down. That's why it becomes like a strip cartoon toward the end as the family rush back home with the bear at their heels. At the very end, I made the bear look a bit lonely, as though he would have liked to have played with those kids, who instead have run away from him. You know: "Wait for me! Come out and play!"

Q: These days, publishers—and many parents—seem to think that the more color there is in a picture book, the better. Why do you often choose to alternate black-and-white illustrations with color ones?

A: I had to slightly fight for that for the *Bear Hunt* book. I can remember books with black-and-white illustrations that I loved as a child. Suddenly, when you *knew* you were coming to a color picture, there would be the excitement of turning the page, and finally there it was. It's the contrast that's so dramatic, I suppose.

Q: In your books you often show parents in unguarded moments: a father tired with his feet up on the sofa, a mother half-dressed in a department store dressing room. Why is that?

A: It's almost the opposite to a television commercial, where everything is perfect and the mother produces white clothes out of the washing machine. I find that awful because it's not true, and because it makes people dissatisfied and feel inadequate.

In *We're Going on a Bear Hunt,* when the bear is finally found, it's the dad who runs like hell to get away, ahead of the children, which of course is meant to be comical. I think it's very important to show the child that parents are only human. To show that they have weaknesses is perhaps not a bad thing.

Q: In your drawings you'll sometimes include a discarded bottle or an old tire floating in the river or lying in a lot. Why do you think such details might interest children?

A: I can remember having more fun as a child throwing stones at a tin can on the beach than from playing with any expensive toy. Our own children don't seem to want all the toys that are available. Some parents have a desperate feeling that they're not good parents if they don't buy all those expensive toys.

Q: Why is that?

A: There's a desire to fill every moment of the child's life — with lessons, toys, after-school activities. As a result, many children have lost the ability to be quiet and entertain themselves with fantasy games of their own devising. At least there's a tendency for this to happen.

Q: The Tom and Pippo books are about just such fantasy games, aren't they?

A: That's right. Little Tom doesn't have great expensive toys. He just has his friend Pippo.

Q: Are those books based on personal experience?

A: Tom, I suppose, is my son when he was a little lad. Pippo was his dog, a real dog, not a doll. The two of them were pretty inseparable and the dog used to get blamed for an awful lot of things. Of course, *we* knew what was going on.

Q: The stories are told in the first person, in Tom's voice. So when a parent is reading aloud to a child, the parent . . .

A: . . . *becomes* the "I." That's right.

Q: That gives the parent a chance to see things from the child's point of view.

A: It was because of the warmth of the "I" that I eventually came round to writing stories that way.

I used to visit schools a lot, and sometimes a class of little children would have written their own Tom and Pippo story.

Q: Were their stories very different from your own?

A: They were usually very, very similar, to the point where you knew they'd probably had a jolly good look. . . .

Q: Well, Tom is quite a mimic himself: Tom's father reads, so Tom wants to read, and so on.

A: Yes, and then Tom becomes the father to the monkey.

Q: That type of role reversal must be one of the most basic kinds of children's play.

A: It's a testing, isn't it? A testing things out.

Q: In your books it also becomes comical.

A: One of the most important things is to laugh with your children and to let them see you think they're being funny when they're trying to be. It gives children enormous pleasure to think they've made you laugh. They feel they've reached one of the nicest parts in you. Tom makes a dreadful mess and says: "It was him. It was the monkey." As a picture-book artist, I don't think one can be too much on the side of the child.

~ HELEN OXENBURY POSTSCRIPT, DECEMBER 21, 2009

LEONARD S. MARCUS: Since we last spoke in 1989, you won a second Kate Greenaway Medal for your edition of *Alice's Adventures in Wonderland* (1999). Why did you decide to illustrate Lewis Carroll?

HELEN OXENBURY: I was sort of eased into it. A television company got in touch with me and said that they were going to do a series of Alice episodes. They planned to start with the original Carroll episodes and then go on and write others, and they wanted a more up-to-date Alice. They said, "Could you just go away and draw some Alices for us to see and also a few of the other characters?" So that was what I did. They liked my drawings very much indeed, and it was all going ahead when suddenly the whole department just fell apart. Nothing happened with the film. But I had done so much research and so much thinking about Alice that I went to my publisher with the idea for a book, and that's when I did it.

Q: Did you try somehow to put the very famous John Tenniel illustrations out of your mind?

A: I did try at first — and then I realized it was impossible because like so many other people I had been brought up as a child with those images, which I liked very much — though they are a bit stiff and frightening. Then I thought, either you just go ahead or you allow yourself to be inhibited, and then you find you can't do what you want. I had the chance to use color and to do many, many more illustrations than Tenniel had drawn.

Q: And you made Alice a girl with whom a young reader might easily identify.

A: Children don't quite understand all those pinafores and things now. So I just put her in a simple little dress.

Q: Did illustrating Lewis Carroll whet your appetite for re-illustrating more classics?

A: Not so far. I do so love *The Wind in the Willows,* but that again has been done so many times — including by my husband! Well, that *would* be interesting. I've just finished a book called *There's Going to Be a Baby* (2010), and it's the first one I have done with John. It's about the anxiety of a child that a new child in the family is going to take up the mother's attention. I did the pictures and John did the text. No terrible rows or anything! In fact I think it's worked out rather well.

JERRY PINKNEY

Born 1939, Philadelphia, Pennsylvania

Old-fashioned storytelling played a central role in Jerry Pinkney's World War II-era Philadelphia childhood. Grown-ups in his all-black working-class neighborhood often gathered — as much for their own entertainment as for the children's — to tell time-honored tales about Brer Rabbit, Brer Fox, and John Henry. As a child, Pinkney was always among the rapt listeners in the room; as an illustrator, he has taken special pride in having had a hand in preserving these and other traditional African American folk stories for new generations.

Pinkney produced his first illustrated children's books during the 1960s while continuing to work in the commercial art arena for which he had trained. Responding to the civil rights movement's call to action, publishers at the time were starting to address their past failure to include black authors and illustrators for children on their lists and to publish books that accurately reflected the multiracial nature of American society. For Pinkney, this historic change in attitude opened rewarding new opportunities that he was quick to seize. In the years that followed, Pinkney illustrated numerous books for young readers by Verna Aardema, Mildred D. Taylor, Patricia C. McKissack, Virginia Hamilton, Eloise Greenfield, and his most frequent collaborator, Julius Lester.

But artists don't want to be pigeonholed. If there was a dilemma for Pinkney in the increased demand for picture books celebrating African-American themes, it lay in his unwillingness to be known as an illustrator who worked *only* in that vein. It was largely for this reason that he chose to illustrate *The Little Match Girl* (1999) and *The Ugly Duckling* (1999), Hans Christian Andersen stories that his mother had read to him as a child. When we recorded this interview in his suburban New York studio on October 27, 1999, Pinkney was in the process of gathering reference material for a new edition of Aesop's fables. Almost exactly ten years later, he would publish *The Lion & the Mouse* (2009), the picture book based on an Aesop tale, for which he won the 2010 Caldecott Medal.

LEONARD S. MARCUS: What is it about watercolor that appeals to you as the medium for so much of your work?

JERRY PINKNEY: My first passion is drawing. I have always loved the energy and spontaneity of drawing. And so it was fine with me that when I began to illustrate books in the 1960s, full-color printing was considered too costly for children's books, and I was limited to doing line art, with perhaps two or three additional colors that had to be pre-separated. I thought of the lines of my drawings for those first books as holding lines for the color. Then in the mid-1980s, full-color became available for use in children's trade books, and combining watercolor with drawing seemed a natural way to keep the sense of energy and spontaneity in the work.

Patchwork Quilt (1985) is the first picture book for which I worked in this way.

Watercolor allows me to bring a certain freshness to a drawing that in reality had to be very carefully thought out and planned. I enjoy the translucent quality, the fact that when the paper shows through, you get a sense of light. That is kind of magical for me. That sense of surface, of the paper playing a role in the look and feel of the picture, is, I think, a good part of what attracts artists to watercolor and why people enjoy looking at watercolor art. It allows the viewer, in a sense, to step into the picture, to finish the picture by seeing into it with their mind's eye.

Q: You often let your pencil lines show through.

A: Every project starts with a strong line drawing. If I want the book to look more painterly, then I keep painting over the line and eventually the line will soften and begin to disappear. Now, if I want the line to play a part in the energy of the book, I'll go back over the line. Sometimes I will leave lines from a drawing that I have worked over in order to let the viewer see something of how the picture developed. That is another way of giving immediacy to the work.

Q: When did you begin to draw?

A: I remember always drawing. At first, I drew anything with wheels. Later, when I was eleven, I got my first job, working at a newspaper stand, and would take a pad and pencil with me and draw the people I saw waiting for the bus or trolley. I would also draw the window displays at the department store that was across from my newsstand. By then I was drawing whatever I saw around me.

Q: Did your parents encourage your interest in art?

A: My mother always praised my drawings, and my father, who painted

D rawing is *re*-drawing: it's a rare day when even the most seasoned artist strikes illustration gold with the first few strokes of his or her paintbrush or pen. Making picture books almost always entails an exploratory phase of trial and error, and no two artists, hunched intently over their drawing tables, will either reckon or respond to the options open to them in precisely the same way. Things may get messy — or they may not. Hours may pass — or years. We see the rabbit pulled from the hat, but what makes the onstage magic really happen? The dummy spreads, sketches, and other preliminaries reproduced on the following pages suggest the extraordinary lengths to which twenty-one illustrators of note have each gone to bring their artwork to the point of looking as though it all came about with the wave of a wand.

Anno's Alphabet: An Adventure in Imagination. Study for front and back cover border. Watercolor. In the finished version, Anno has woven the legend "DR. ANNO's ABC BOOK" into the design in a flowing, tendril-like cursive reminiscent of William Blake's calligraphy.

Anno's Alphabet: An Adventure in Imagination. Study for the letter A. Watercolor. When some of Anno's editors were unable to identify this image as an angel, he replaced it with an illustration of an anvil.

Anno's Alphabet: An Adventure in Imagination. Study labeled "Hag," for the letter *H*. Watercolor. In folklore, a hag is a witch or malevolent fairy. Anno discarded this image in favor of an illustration of a horn.

Quentin Blake's ABC. Two studies for "M is for Mud." Pen and ink. The image on the right is closer to the finished art, with the figures in each version growing progressively muddier and more animated.

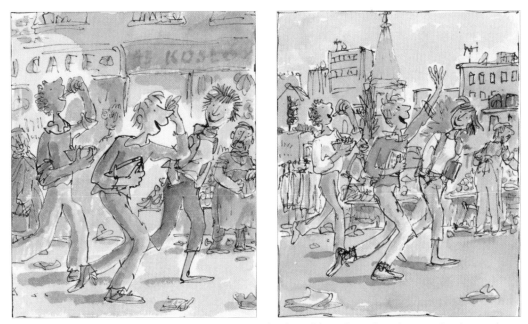

Michael Rosen's Sad Book by Michael Rosen. Two studies for "Eddie walking along the street, laughing and laughing and laughing." Pen and ink and watercolor. In the finished illustration, we see Eddie closer up than in either of these attempts, and with a more simplified backdrop that keeps the focus on him and his friends.

Above: *The Night Has Ears: African Proverbs.* Detailed sketch for the Grebo saying, "Take the drowning child from the water before scolding it." Graphite.

Above right: *Ashley Bryan's African Tales, Uh-huh.* In the finished version of this illustration for "Jackal's Favorite Game," both characters' eyes have grown in size and intensity. Black ink and Chinese white.

Right: *Ashley Bryan's African Tales, Uh-huh.* For the published version of this drawing for "The Foolish Boy," the father's pose has subtly changed to stress how hard his work is. Black ink and Chinese white.

Above left: *Turtle Knows Your Name.* Study for the scene in which the villagers dance around UPSILIMANA TUMPALERADO. Watercolor. For the finished version, Bryan rearranges the dancers to give the scene a more animated feel.

Above right: *Turtle Knows Your Name.* That's UPSILIMANA TUMPALERADO, the boy with a very long name, on the right. Watercolor. In the finished version, he holds a toy hoop and stands out more distinctly against the impressionistic backdrop.

Turtle Knows Your Name. Turtle and the young hero share a delicious dinner of fungi and fish. Watercolor. Bryan's admiration for the French colorists Matisse and Bonnard is clearly evident.

It's a Secret! Study for the scene in which Marie Elaine asks Malcolm, her cat, "Why are you all dressed?" Pencil and ink. In the finish, Burningham's characters appear front and center, and nearly everything else has been stripped away.

Left: *It's a Secret!* Studies of Malcolm the cat in raffish attire and Marie Elaine in her party dress with wings. Pencil and ink.

Above: *It's a Secret!* In the final version of this scene, the supporting characters are rendered in near-silhouette while the faces of Malcolm and friends are clearly delineated. Powder paint on red background.

It's a Secret! Study for "'She's coming.' . . . The Queen of the Cats." Gouache, ink, and pencil. Burningham simplified this scene, postponing the climactic moment until the rooftop feast scene, when all eyes are on the bewhiskered and amiable Queen.

The Very Lonely Firefly.
Dummy cover drawing. Graphite
and crayon on paper. Carle's first
sketches are typically very loose.

The Very Lonely Firefly. The hero takes shape.
Acrylic and collaged tissue paper on scanner
board. Much remains to be decided, including
the color of the firefly's head.

The Very Lonely Firefly. The book's finished front-cover art. Acrylic and collaged tissue paper
on scanner board. Carle leaves white space up top for his name and the title.

Above: *Waiting for Wings*. An early dummy with different-size pages. Marker and photocopies on tracing paper. As the plan for the book evolves, page sizes become more varied.

Above: *Waiting for Wings*. At top, a meticulously drawn dummy spread, with collaged elements. Marker on layered tracing paper. Shown below, a later version of the same spread, in which both the text and placement of the butterfly have changed. Marker and xerography.

Left: *Leaf Man*. For this book, Ehlert has ventured outdoors for some of her art supplies. Marker on colored paper, xerography, and gouache.

Leaf Man. Here, as in the finished book, the intricate die-cut edges along the top of each page combine to create the illusion of a three-dimensional landscape. Marker on tracing paper, colored paper, and xerography.

Old Bear. Lush color studies featuring elements associated with each of the four seasons. Watercolor.

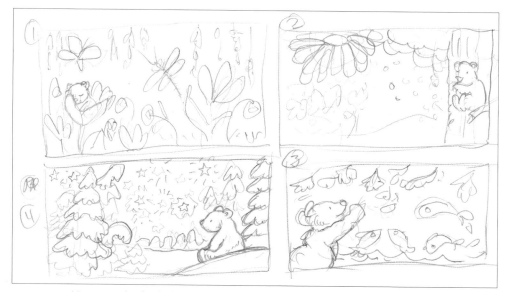

Old Bear. Studies for the hibernating bear's dreams of the four seasons, each of which is given a double-page spread in the finished book. Pencil.

Old Bear. Detailed study for Old Bear's dream of spring. Pencil. The major elements are all in place but much redrawing lies ahead.

Old Bear. A later study for the dream of spring. Pencil. The petals of the flower in which the bear cub sleeps have been redrawn with greater authority, as has the tree near the center of the composition. Time again to think about color.

Old Bear. Detailed study for Old Bear's dream of winter. Pencil. In the finished art, Henkes gives the star-filled sky a more decorative, mystical interpretation.

Henry's First-Moon Birthday by Lenore Look. The first in a sequence of thumbnail sketches for the scene that begins, "This is the chicken pot boiling over." Pencil. In this straight-forward layout, a close-up view (left) introduces a fascinating artifact from GninGnin's daily life, and the more distant view (right) shows it in use.

Henry's First-Moon Birthday. Here the pot itself almost looks alive, like a face with handles for ears and a domed hat-lid tilted at a rakish angle. It's fun know-ing, without having to be shown, whose hands those are. Pencil.

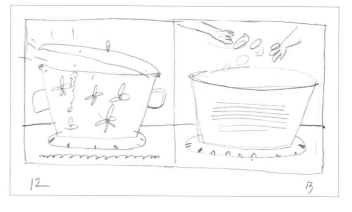

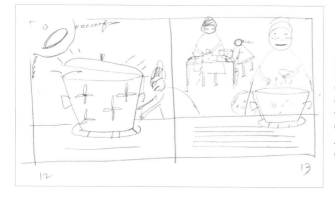

Henry's First-Moon Birthday. In the end, Heo takes this scene as an opportunity to create a complex double-page spread with multiple views across time of GninGnin and her granddaughter Jenny, both swept up in a whirl of activity. Pencil.

Colors Everywhere. Dummy spread. Photography. After shooting and selecting the photographs for a book, Hoban typically taped the images in place in a dummy like this one, and presented the project to her editor in near-finished form.

One Little Kitten. Contact sheet with images marked for possible use. Photography.

George and Martha Round and Round. Study for cover. Crayon, pencil, and ink. Marshall had
yet to find the perfect title for the seventh and last installment in the George and Martha collection.

Undated sketchbook. Ink and watercolor or gouache. Marshall did much of his preliminary thinking in notebooks like this one. The drawing on the left illustrates the Mother Goose rhyme, "Rain, rain, go away" in vintage droll Marshall fashion. The remarkable painting on the right is of Sarah Caldwell conducting the Boston Symphony Orchestra.

Sketchbook, January 1988. Ink and watercolor or gouache. Marshall's notebooks are a crazy quilt of scribbled to-do lists and sketches—some quite elaborately rendered—for works in progress. The George and Martha drawing at top right relates to "Story Number Three: The Artist," in *George and Martha Round and Round.* In a note to himself about the bottom drawing, Marshall questions whether George or Martha is the hippo more likely to sing.

Make Way for Ducklings. Double-page dummy for the spread that begins, "One day the ducklings hatched out." Charcoal on groundwood paper. The dramatic and comic impact of McCloskey's drawings of ducklings in motion owe a lot to his months of sketching live specimens in his Greenwich Village studio.

Make Way for Ducklings. Dummy spread for the lines beginning, "They looked in Louisburg Square." Charcoal on groundwood paper. As an art student during the 1930s, McCloskey lived in this historic Boston neighborhood.

Make Way for Ducklings. Dummy spread for the famous scene, based on a real event, in which a policeman stops traffic in order to provide safe passage for a family of ducks crossing a busy Boston street. Charcoal on groundwood paper.

Above: *We're Going on a Bear Hunt* by Michael Rosen. Study for "Oh-oh! Mud!" Pencil. In the finish, the dad's comically glum expression reveals his second thoughts.

Top right: *We're Going on a Bear Hunt.* Cover and title-page study. Ink. The final drawing reads from left to right, propelling us into the story.

Middle right: *We're Going on a Bear Hunt.* Study for "Oh-oh! A forest!" Charcoal. In the finish, the family and forest are both closer to us.

Bottom right: *We're Going on a Bear Hunt.* Study for "Oh-oh! A river!" Charcoal. The finish feels more expansive.

We're Going on a Bear Hunt. Study for "Splash splosh!" Pastel. In the final version, water nearly engulfs the page, rendering the scene a lot splashier and sploshier.

John Henry by Julius Lester. Early thumbnail sketch for the scene in which John Henry (standing) challenges Ferret-Headed Freddy, the "meanest man in the state" (on horseback), to a race. Marker.

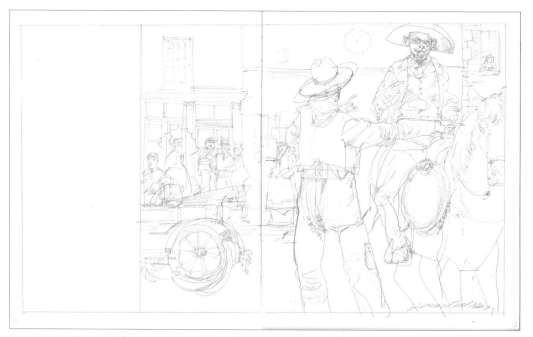

Above and facing page: *John Henry*. Three more detailed studies for the same scene. Graphite pencil. In the finished art, Pinkney dispenses with the vintage automobile, giving a larger role to the admiring young onlooker as John Henry prepares to show Freddy a thing or two about strength, speed, and determination.

A Primer About the Flag by Marvin Bell. Study for the title page. Ink and colored pencil. Always fascinated with chance effects, Raschka here tries ink smudges. In the finished art, he replaces this bold effect with subtler fog-like watercolor washes.

Above and left: *A Primer About the Flag.* Raschka established the look of his characters early in the game but not so the flags, which become larger and more flamboyant in the finished art. Ink and colored pencil.

A Primer About the Flag. A study for a possible endpaper design. Ink and colored pencil.

Five for a Little One. An early "fun" look for the bunny, but one perhaps with more foot- and ear-power than personality. Woodblock ink prints and watercolor.

Five for a Little One.
This color study for the bunny
followed. Watercolor.

ART IS UNFINISHED

C

Five for a Little One. Drawing in a free-flowing, gestural style reminiscent of Chinese and Japanese brush painting, Raschka here considers dispensing with color altogether. Potato prints and ink.

I Saw Esau: The Schoolchild's Pocket Book, edited by Iona and Peter Opie. Final drawing. Pencil, pen and ink, and watercolor. Sendak created the vibrant art for this collection of traditional children's rhymes on the first go-round, in a great burst of bravura improvisation. Here, a breastfeeding baby ends up completely devouring his mother—a provocative image that sits well beside equally challenging depictions of Hansel and Gretel caught in the clutches of a ravenous witch and of the very self-possessed Mickey, who at one point will declare: "I'm in the milk and the milk's in me." © 1992 by Maurice Sendak.

Left: *In the Night Kitchen . . .* Preliminary drawing. Pencil on tracing paper. One of many sketches of Mickey, the doughty young hero whom Sendak modeled in part on comics artist Winsor McCay's Little Nemo. © 1970 by Maurice Sendak.

Below: *The Juniper Tree and Other Tales from Grimm,* selected by Lore Segal and Maurice Sendak, translated by Lore Segal with four tales translated by Randall Jarrell, illustrated by Maurice Sendak. In the finished drawing, the witch's features are more grotesquely exaggerated and Gretel reaches out to push her away as imprisoned Hansel and a powerful guard dog take in the dramatic scene and storm clouds gather along the horizon. Graphite pencil. © 1972 by Maurice Sendak.

"Madlenka's Block" (prototype for *Madlenka*). Study of Madlenka in a Mary Poppins–like fantasy moment. Marker and colored pencil.

"Madlenka's Block" (prototype for *Madlenka*). A delightfully casual sketch of the New York City block (modeled on the one where the artist and his family once lived) that young Madlenka explores on her walks. Marker and colored pencil. It's raining but Madlenka is well prepared!

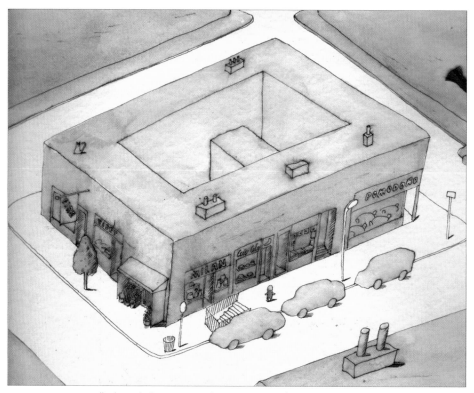

"Madlenka's Block" (prototype for *Madlenka*). The artist tries a more solid, geometric approach. Ink and watercolor.

"Madlenka in Paris" (part of projected "Madlenka's Block" series). Study for one of a set of books envisioned by the artist about his young heroine's travels around the world. Watercolor.

"M & M in Italy" (part of projected "Madlenka's Block" series). Study for a scene set in Venice for a projected book about Madlenka and her younger brother Matéj's adventures in Italy. Pastel on colored paper.

Sylvester and the Magic Pebble. Steig began by making a rough dummy in black and white and continued to rework his compositions as he experimented with color. In the final version of the window scene, for example, a family portrait hangs on the back wall, heightening the emotional impact of Sylvester's disappearance. Top: graphite and ink. Bottom: watercolor, ink, and graphite.

Sylvester and the Magic Pebble. In the final version for this spread, intense yellows and greens play an even bigger role in radiating the joyful mood. Top: graphite and ink. Bottom: watercolor, ink, and graphite.

Love Waves. Wells blocks out the scene—a depiction of a working mom serving her customers—in firm, clear outline. Black line rubber stamp.

Love Waves. In this study, Wells considers adding, in a kind of thought balloon, a note of reassurance: a cozy image of the mother and her child reunited at day's end. Black line rubber stamp, soft pastels, and pastel pencil on French sennelier pastel sandpaper.

Love Waves. Opting to keep the scene focused entirely on the moment, Wells now begins to experiment in earnest with color. Black line rubber stamp, soft pastels, and pastel pencil on French sennelier pastel sandpaper.

Love Waves. For the finished art, she chooses a brighter, more soothing palette. Black line rubber stamp, soft pastels, and pastel pencil on French sennelier pastel sandpaper.

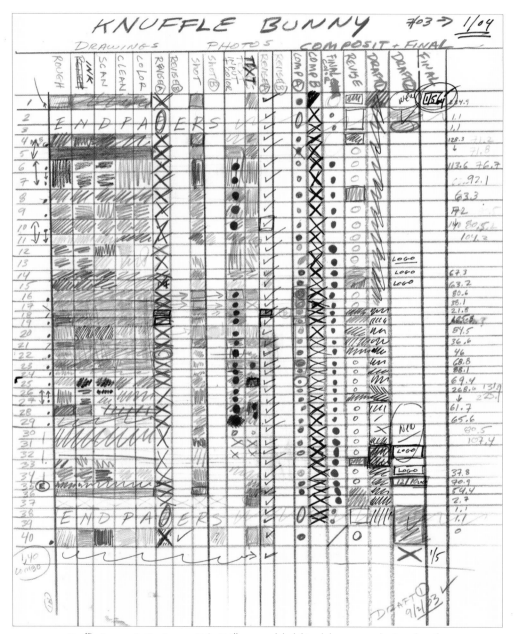

Knuffle Bunny: A Cautionary Tale. Willems modeled this elaborate production chart for recording his progress on the ones he used for animation projects. Pencil and ink.

Knuffle Bunny: A Cautionary Tale. Dummy spread for the scene in which Trixie, having left her toy bunny behind at the Laundromat, first realizes something is wrong. Pencil with printed frames. The composition as roughly sketched out here is essentially the same as the finish.

Knuffle Bunny: A Cautionary Tale. Willems made this first photo "test" before preparing the dummy. Pencil, digital color, and digital photo collage. Getting photographic backdrops to work proved to be a lot harder than he had imagined it would be.

Above: *"More, More, More," Said the Baby*. Rough sketch for Little Pumpkin and his grandmother running. Colored pencil.

Above: *"More, More, More," Said the Baby*. Lessons Williams learned about color theory from the painter Joseph Albers, who was her college instructor, lie behind the daring color choices seen in this study for the "Little Pumpkin" section. Gouache, watercolor, and collaged tracing parchment.

Left: *"More, More, More," Said the Baby*. Williams practices her signature and block lettering skills as she tries out a variety of color combinations. Gouache, watercolor, and marker.

Above: *"More, More, More," Said the Baby.*
A haunting study of Little Pumpkin. Pencil.
A Williams kid is never just cute.

Right: *"More, More, More," Said the Baby.*
Study for Little Pumpkin. Pencil.

"More, More, More," Said the Baby. Color study for the same scene as
above right. Gouache and tracing parchment. For the finishes, Williams
painted a colorful, bordered background for each illustration first. She
then painted the characters separately on tracing parchment, repainting
them as needed until she was satisfied. Finally, she cut out the finished
characters and pasted them in place.

Noah's Ark by Heinz Janisch. Three detailed studies of animal pairs for the Ark. Pencil and colored pencil. Except for minor adjustments in a few of the poses, Zwerger kept closely to these compositions, which are meant to evoke the formal elegance of "plates" (often engravings) in an old-fashioned illustrated zoology book.

houses and was a jack-of-all-trades, used to hang wallpaper in our bedroom so that I could draw directly on the wall while lying in bed! Although my father did not encourage me as directly as did my mother, there was a certain encouragement implied in his making sure that if I wanted to doodle I would have something to doodle on. From a very early age I would go off with him to help with his work, and whenever we went into Newton's paint store to buy house paint there would always be the moment when I walked past the aisle with art supplies. Somehow just in seeing the brushes and pads there was also a kind of encouragement.

Q: Was your father also a woodworker? You show wood-grain patterns in so many of your illustrations. It seems to be a subject for which you have a special feeling.

A: Yes, he was. Woodworking was one of the things my father did quite a bit of, especially toward the end of his life. He was very proud of how he could refinish furniture. He knew about wood grain and mastered a variety of techniques. Now I find that I can endlessly draw the patterns of wood grains and never find it boring.

Q: Were books important to you as a child?

A: I'm dyslexic, so as a child I struggled with reading. I avoided anything with words. Unlike many artists of my generation, I did not even read comic books, and I did not draw from comic books, either. My interest in books came much later in life, through the vehicle of drawing and my appreciation of storytelling in art.

My mother was a big reader, and my sister recalls that she often read us fairy tales, including the stories of Hans Christian Andersen. She also read the Bible and the essays of Ralph Waldo Emerson, and I can recall that as a teenager, despite the fact that I had such trouble reading even simple books, I took up Emerson myself. I had to struggle with him, but I had become so fascinated with his sense of nature and universal balance. Looking back, it seems paradoxical that I would have shied away from comic books but not from Emerson.

I remember *Little Black Sambo* as the only book from my childhood in which I saw a depiction of a child of color. I liked the book for that reason as well as for the fantasy of the story. Our family owned a copy, and my parents, who were very proud people, must have thought it good because they would not have had a book in the house that had to be explained away or that in any way undercut their strong sense of self.

Q: Do you have childhood memories of World War II?

A: I remember the large-formatted photojournalistic magazines, *Life* and *Look*. We had a wardrobe in the upstairs hall at home and it was in that wardrobe that my mother and father kept copies of the magazines, because they did not want us children to see photographs of the war. But often when I was home alone I would go to the wardrobe, take out the magazines, and lie mesmerized on the second-floor landing, looking at them. I remember the powerful impact that those large photographic images had on me and I remember the horror portrayed in some of them, especially those of the concentration camps taken at the end of the war. My parents never talked about the war with me, so the pictures spoke volumes.

Q: Tell me about meeting John J. Liney. You dedicated *The Hired Hand* (1997), which is the story of a younger person's apprenticeship to a master, to him.

A: John Liney, who drew a well-known comic strip called *Henry,* lived in Philadelphia. Having noticed me drawing at my newsstand one day, he introduced himself to me and invited me to visit his studio. Meeting John Liney was a milestone — in ways I did not fully realize right away. By the time we met, I had somehow already gotten the idea that drawing was a noble activity, and I remember thinking then that I had nobler things to do as an artist than to draw cartoons. Yet it made an incredible impression on me just to see that he sat down every day at a drawing board, surrounded by all sorts of wonderful art materials, and made his living by drawing, and was happy doing it. I visited his studio several times. He was an older man, and although for that reason I did not think of him as a friend, we really were friends.

Q: Philadelphia has a long history as a center of the visual arts. Charles Wilson Peale, Thomas Eakins, Howard Pyle, Jessie Willcox Smith, Maxfield Parrish, John Sloan, and others lived there. Did you become aware of that history during the time you were growing up in the city?

A: I did not become aware of that until much later. About ten years ago I became very interested in the Ashcan School painters and was surprised to learn that half of those guys came from Philadelphia. I never entered an art museum or gallery until I was in college.

Q: What about Philadelphia's historic role during the American Revolution and in the early years of the republic? Were you taught to feel proud of the city's heritage while growing up?

A: Germantown, where we lived, was quite a distance from the center of the city. We would have had to travel to get there. And I'm not sure whether other parts of Philadelphia at that time were not segregated, or at least that the impression was given that they were segregated. Certainly there were places that we as black children did not go. So, no, when I was growing up we did not participate in that sense of the grandeur of Philadelphia's history. When I go to Philadelphia now, I do so because of the city's history and rich cultural life. It sometimes feels like a makeup course for all the things I missed out on as a child.

Q: Did you experience other forms of racial discrimination while growing up?

A: It was more something that I was aware of rather than something I experienced myself. But my senior year in high school, an instructor who had always been very fair in his grading made it clear that he did not think it best for the black students to continue on to college to study art, because there would be no future for us. In his own mind he may have thought he was doing us a favor.

Q: But you ignored his advice.

A: Yes, I did. At the Philadelphia College of Art, I majored in graphic design — the practical side of art — in part because my father was skeptical about the possibility of making a living as a fine artist. I was probably unsure about this myself. I thought that if I had a degree in design, I would always be able to find some entry-level job after graduation. The illustration department was located on the floor above ours, and the interesting thing was that they and we were two completely different cultures — different in the way we dressed, the way spoke — everything. When no one was up there, however, I would go up to see what was hanging on the walls. I remember being very impressed. The illustration students worked in the tradition of Howard Pyle and N. C. Wyeth, but things were changing. Milton Glaser, Seymour Chwast, and the other members of Push Pin Studio in New York were looking at design and illustration as interrelated, and their ideas were affecting the way everyone viewed their work. So, as an experiment, the illustration department and the design department at my school decided to get together and exchange projects. Each department came up with a project for the other department to do. That assignment gave me a chance to think more about illustration, which I was already mildly interested in.

Q: As an art student, did you also bump up against abstract expressionism as a force to be reckoned with?

A: Oh, yes! In high school my training had all been practical: how to render products, how to use an airbrush, how to do calligraphy. When I got to college one of my painting instructors said to me, "I'm going to break you yet!" I was doing realistic paintings because that is what I had been taught. But to painters of that time, abstract expressionism was *it*. So it all just hit me — *boom!* I began to paint in that manner myself and continued to do so for years. I think that if I were to go back to painting I would paint abstractions again. In fact, if you look at my illustration work in an abstract way, just look at the backgrounds, the foliage and tree trunks, and move away from the figures, you'll see that interest in abstraction expressing itself.

Q: When did you leave Philadelphia?

A: I married, started a family, and left art school after two and a half years. We moved up to Boston, where I went to work for the Rustcraft greeting card company. Boston had a strong design community and a strong painting community. I felt a need at that time to be around other African-American artists, and from that standpoint as well Boston was a good place to be. I became somewhat active in the civil rights movement — involved with voter registration and various fundraising projects and community group meetings — and found those experiences energizing.

Boston, of course, was also a publishing center, and when I later went to work for a design firm called Barker-Black, I was assigned to illustrate a book project that they had under contract. During the 1960s publishers were interested in publishing African-American material and were eager to hire black illustrators. So the opportunities were there, and I found that as a book illustrator I could combine my design training in problem-solving with my passion for drawing. It was amazing. Everything fell into place.

Q: Were you looking at picture books with your children at home? Did the books you became acquainted with have an impact on the direction of your own work?

A: I'm sure I noticed how hard it was to find a book with black children as characters. That must have had an impact on me. We looked for such books for our children. And I can remember when Ezra Jack Keats's *The Snowy Day* was published in 1962. I understood the impact of *The Snowy Day* but I didn't see it at the time as an example of a kind of book that I could imagine myself doing. I began by illustrating African folktales and then went on to illustrate folktales from other cultures. I did not yet see myself as an artist who might one day illustrate a contemporary story such as *The Patchwork Quilt.* In any case, I still thought of editorial illustration, rather than book illustration, as my idea of a noble calling and as the thing I most wanted to do.

I continued to do books because of the satisfaction I took in creating a well-made object that I could hold in hand. Later, my awareness of the need for books on African-American subjects, interpreted positively, became a second reason. I began to feel that through such books I could make a contribution to society.

The Boston and New York art communities were two separate communities. I began to feel that I wanted to be in New York, that I would find a wider range of opportunities there. And so in 1970 my family and I moved to New York.

Q: Were you still doing advertising and editorial illustration?

A: Yes, that work provided me with most of my income.

Q: Tell me about the Seagram's black history calendars you designed in the 1970s.

A: When large corporations began to see that minorities represented a potential market, they began setting up departments to figure out how to target that market. I think they genuinely also wanted to make a constructive contribution of some kind. Seagram's decided to commission a series of black history calendars. I did four calendars, including one called "The Black West," for which my wife, Gloria, wrote the legends. I loved doing those calendars. I started collecting history books around that time, and it was also then that I became acquainted with the New York Public Library's Schomburg Center for Research in Black Culture.

Q: When did book illustration finally become the main focus of your work?

A: It was not until around the time that I illustrated *Mirandy and Brother Wind* (1988) that I reorganized my work life. After accepting a teaching position at the University of Delaware, I told my agent for commercial work that I wanted to take some time off to concentrate more on illustrating books.

Mirandy marks the point in my career where I was beginning to do more intensive research and to associate research with a sense of discovery. I no longer felt I was just illustrating a book. I was *in* the book and beginning to create storytelling through pictures. I was learning about a part of my culture that I did not know about and using that learning experience as fuel for the art.

Q: So you came to enjoy research.

A: I love research. The Schomburg used to be my main source of material but by now I have put together my own extensive files on the Underground Railroad, the slave trade, plantation life, and the like. If I run into some detail for which I lack specific information, as I did while working on *Minty* (1996), for example, I just call a friend who is the curator of costumes and furniture at the National Park Service. He is able to supply me with whatever I need.

Q: Why did you dedicate *John Henry* (1994) to your father?

A: I did so because in some ways my father was a heroic man to me. He was a very independent man. At an early age he decided to work for himself. I think he really thought he was the strongest person in the world! We would always have a conversation about whether he should have an aluminum ladder instead of the monstrous wooden one that he liked to use, and always he would refuse to change. For him it was "the heavier, the better."

I grew up with the story of John Henry and know that I must have been impressed by the image of a black man beating a steam drill. And so when my agent and I were talking one day about new projects, John Henry came to mind. The public-domain retellings I found were not very good. They were stereotypical — and vicious, in a way. And so my editor at Dial, Phyllis Fogelman, and I asked Julius Lester, whose three volumes of Uncle Remus retellings I had already illustrated, if he would write the text.

Julius and I had not actually met or been in direct contact with each other during the time I was illustrating the Uncle Remus collections. But when we proposed the John Henry project to him, he called me, wanting to know what was my interest in John Henry. He said he had not thought much about the story and wasn't particularly interested in it. I told him about my childhood memories of having heard the story at home. As we continued to talk, he began to relate John Henry to Dr. Martin Luther King Jr. That association, he said, would be his inspiration.

Like *Mirandy*, *John Henry* was a turning point for me in that I was able to create illustrations that parallel the text without mimicking it and to add my own pictorial story lines. One reason that I love working with Julius is that he inspires visual images other than the ones he's actually describing. In the opening scene, Julius writes about the animals all coming out of the forest to see the young baby. This gave me the idea to have the animals follow John Henry all throughout the book. In the spread where a boulder is being dynamited, for instance, I show John Henry holding back two burros, even though the animals aren't mentioned in the text. But I knew that burros would have been needed to carry materials to the work site and that they would have bolted at the sound of the dynamite blast. So this became another way to show John Henry's incredible strength.

The art is much more developed in *John Henry* than in earlier books. There are a great many characters in the pictures, and they're always active in some way. Instead of having the drawing lines show through, I brought more depth to the watercolor, with the result that edges define forms rather than lines. It takes a lot longer to paint that way.

Q: I wondered about that look of solidity. Was it because John Henry is a mythic figure that you wanted to make him appear more securely anchored in the real world?

A: Well, that's part of it. That's the intuitive part of my working process. I'll have a certain vision for the way a story should look. You'll notice that John Henry always breaks the planes of the book. I wanted him to be too big for the book to contain. That was part of my vision, too.

Q: Tell me about your interest in drawing animals, which you have done across a wide spectrum, from naturalistic to personified.

A: Before doing the first book of Uncle Remus tales, I had been illustrating a story retold by Verna Aardema called *Rabbit Makes a Monkey of Lion* (1989), for which I did not want to render the animals either naturalistically or in a fully anthropomorphic style. When I came to do the Uncle Remus tales, I first tried to do the illustrations in the same manner as *Rabbit,* but saw they weren't working. I finally resolved the problem by posing for the animals myself. I had Polaroids taken of me acting out the different animal parts.

I have a great interest in and sense of wonder at animal life. Sometimes I show the qualities I see in the animals themselves. But Arthur Rackham, with his fantastic approach to the natural world, has also been an inspiration to me.

Q: When did you first meet Julius Lester?

A: I met Julius at a conference where we were talking about the Uncle Remus tales. By then, however, I felt I already knew him through his novels and autobiography. There is a connection between us. We're the same age.

He grew up in the South and I grew up in the North, and I have been able to learn a lot from Julius about how someone who is black and from the South might respond to a particular situation. He has helped me to understand some aspects of segregation and prejudice that I saw mainly in historical terms but had not been able to relate to personally. For instance, I thought of Uncle Remus as a symbol of stability, as one of the older wise people of the community, whereas Julius saw him as a less positive symbol — sort of Uncle Tom-ish, telling tales for the white boys' amusement. I wanted to show Uncle Remus as a figure of strength. Julius did not want me to depict him at all.

Q: Would you agree that African-American children's books have now entered the mainstream?

A: Yes, I would. The books are no longer just sold in stores in a special "African-American" section, and I think that large numbers of books are being purchased by non-African-American parents for their children. I would love to see us get to the point where we no longer need to have a "multicultural" section in stores and libraries. It would be a great leap if artists such as myself could be talked about more not only in relation to our subject but simply in terms of our work as artists and storytellers.

Julius and I talk a lot about what we would like to see in children's books with an African-American subject, how we might possibly be able to enlarge on what is available. We find a lot of historical books being published, and lots of remembrances, but we don't often find fantasy. We also look for areas we don't know much about. I was aware of Julius's interest in the West, and so I sent him a copy of the Seagram's black history calendar. He remembered the story from his collection *Long Journeys Home: Stories from Black History* called "The Man Who Was a Horse" and decided to rewrite it as a picture book, *Black Cowboy, Wild Horses* (1998). One of the things we talked about then was myth, the fact that myths take a long time to create, but that you have to start somewhere. So we took the true story of the life of Bob Lemmons and tried to make him into a mythical character, which is basically the way Americans think of the West anyway. So each project that we've done starts with a shared vision. That's what cements the collaboration and makes it very balanced. Because we're both energized by the subject itself, we're better able to listen to each other.

In the case of *Black Cowboy, Wild Horses,* Julius had wanted the book to be very quiet and to simply deal with the man and his horse and nature and the wild mustangs. Whereas for me as a visual storyteller, even though I loved the story as he wrote it, I didn't find enough to work with visually to make the book exciting. So Julius and I spent a day together discussing the possibilities of bringing more action or more tension to the book. He listened to my ideas, we brainstormed, and Julius gave me what I needed.

Q: Why did you want to re-illustrate *Little Black Sambo* as *Sam and the Tigers* (1996)?

A: First of all, because it is a book I remembered from childhood. While doing some research at the Charles L. Blockson Afro-American Collection at Temple University, my wife, Gloria, spotted a shelf with other illustrated versions of *Little Black Sambo* and with other books written by Helen Bannerman. I began to think that if there had been more than one version, there could be another version, too. It seemed to me that during the 1950s and '60s, Little Black Sambo became somewhat frozen as a symbol of insensitivity toward children of color. People still referred to it as that, and that it would always be that way unless it was changed.

Q: How did you come to do *Journeys of Elijah* (1999)?

A: One of the things I have been trying to do of late is to speak of and celebrate not only my own culture but other cultures as well. That is the direction in which I want my work to go. Recognizing other peoples' differences in terms of culture or race is one of the ways that we can come to terms with and celebrate the world. So here was a manuscript that dealt with the worldwide migration of the Jews, and with the message of the prophet

Elijah, and that was also a collection of eight folktales from seven countries and several historical periods. I saw illustrating this book as an opportunity to express my interest in different cultures and to learn more about other peoples and cultures in the process. That is the part of my work that I find especially rewarding, because it's what you don't know that can become an open door to understanding.

JERRY PINKNEY POSTSCRIPT, JUNE 20, 2011

LEONARD S. MARCUS: Your work is currently the subject of a major retrospective at the Norman Rockwell Museum [in Stockbridge, Massachusetts]. What went into the making of the show? What role did you play?

JERRY PINKNEY: I have had many exhibitions, but this one is the largest one by far. A year and a half or so before it opened at the Rockwell in November 2010, two curators from the museum came to my studio with an overall plan and with a wish list of specific pieces they wanted to include. But they also wanted my input. In some instances, they asked for a suggestion for an image to fill in what they saw as a gap in the plan. In other instances, they wanted my thoughts on the best possible image for making a particular point. The process was collaborative to some extent.

Q: Did looking back at so much of your work prompt you to see any of it in a new light?

A: Yes, it did. I was surprised to see that certain projects that I had not thought of as being related to one another were related after all. For instance, in my first books, such as *The Adventures of Spider* (1964), I wore more of a designer's hat and was not so much interested in narrative. Even so, in my pictures for those very early works, the natural world always plays the role of a kind of supporting character.

Q: Did working on the show make you more aware of how you have grown as an artist?

A: I noticed that stylistically my work changed out of a need for greater clarity in the depiction, for example, of my characters' facial expressions. I was finding my way toward understanding different ethnic facial types and toward a style that allowed me more descriptive detail and greater historical authenticity.

Q: Were there certain pieces that you felt *had* to be in the show?

A: I felt it was important to include examples of the early work — illustrations from the 1960s and 1970s that people coming to the show would not necessarily recognize. The early work was needed in order to set the tone for everything that followed. Oftentimes, a project that I would do for a client such as *National Geographic* or the National Parks Service taught me the research skills or gave me the historical background that I later needed for books like *Minty* and *Black Cowboy, Wild Horses*.

Q: Does art that is created for the printed page change when it's framed and hung on a museum wall?

A: Some of my illustrator friends were always waiting for the time when their work would finally make it into the galleries and museums. I never thought about my work in that way. I was mainly interested in honing my craft and in expressing certain ideas that mattered to me. It was really about the commitment I had made to my work. Having my work exhibited has simply reinforced for me the sense that what I have done — the ideas I have communicated, the style and technique I have brought to it — is in fact a kind of art. I suppose it's a validation. But it hasn't changed the way I do anything.

CHRIS RASCHKA

Born 1959, Huntingdon, Pennsylvania

C hris Raschka reports: "Usually a number of events will be going on around me to start me on a book. I will have read a poem or seen a picture. . . . I will be brooding about something going on in my life, and then I will remember something that happened to me as a child. Some of this will just come to me; some of it I will actively pursue. . . . So then I will have this thing I want to get down."

Raschka is one of the most consistently original picture-book artists of his generation, a restless shape-shifter who has worked hard to make what he does look improvised, and who time and again has risked falling flat on his face to create vibrant, raw, kinetic graphics that appear poised to whirl or lift off the page.

An accomplished violinist, Raschka has made favorite jazz musicians the subject of two of his books and has taken the rhythm and flow of music as an ideal to strive for in all his attempts at grafting pictures to words. At the award ceremony in New Orleans in which he received the 2006 Caldecott Medal for *The Hello, Goodbye Window* (2005), Raschka's collaborator, author Norton Juster, took the stage to entertain the assembled crowd with a jaunty tune on his harmonica. In a more contemplative mood, Raschka himself spoke that evening about the difficulty of feeling both happy and useful as an artist. Raschka had once considered becoming a doctor — a surefire path to being useful to others — but abandoned the plan in favor of painting because the latter gave him so much satisfaction. Had it been a good choice? The awarding of the medal, Rashka now said, made him feel that his books must also be useful in their own way. "And for that," he told the audience of librarians and publishers, "I am very, very thankful."

From the first time I saw a review copy of *Charlie Parker Played Be Bop* (1992), I have looked forward to every new book by this artist. We were introduced early on in his career by the editor who discovered him, Richard Jackson, and our paths have crossed from time to time ever since. This interview, however, was our first long conversation. We recorded it in Raschka's small, cluttered studio on Manhattan's Upper West Side, on July 24, 2009.

∿ ∿ ∿ ∿ ∿ ∿ ∿ ∿ ∿ ∿ ∿ ∿ ∿ ∿ ∿ ∿ ∿

LEONARD S. MARCUS: Tell me about your experience at the Chicago Art Institute.

CHRIS RASCHKA: This was definitely a formative moment for me. I was studying watercolor painting in college. I was on a spring break. It was my last year of school, and I went to the Art Institute of Chicago, which was the art museum I had grown up with. And because I knew that the museum had many works by Sargent and Homer, who were both masters of watercolor, I asked a guard where I could see their work. He looked at me and said, "Go down here." I came to the entrance to the Department of Prints and Drawings, went in hesitantly, and was approached by an elderly gentleman who asked me why I had come. He began to quiz me, asking which American watercolorists in particular I was interested in seeing. I said, "Sargent, Homer," and he said, "And who else?" "Maurice Prendergast," I said. That was good enough for him, so he brought me into a neighboring room where several minutes later a clerk came out with an enormous dolly with enormous wooden portfolios each containing about twenty matted paintings. The first watercolor he lifted out was a Sargent, covered with tissue paper. It was big and gorgeous and amazing, and I just sat and looked at it and then at the others in the portfolio. But it was all so overwhelming that I didn't stay all that long. I couldn't stand the responsibility. I've always loved those paintings.

Q: What appeals to you about watercolor?

A: I would say its immediacy and, in a sense, its fragility. When you apply paint to the paper, it either works or it doesn't, whereas with opaque mediums like oil or acrylic you can just paint over what you've done. You can keep going. But with watercolor, traces of what you have done will always be there. You can kind of go back in and rub out. Lately I've been doing more of that, which creates its own nice effect. In general, though, watercolor is very direct, and you very much see the evidence of every brushstroke. And you count on each layer glowing through those painted over it. You never know quite what you've got until it's done. That is the glory and the drama of watercolor. That's why I like it.

Q: Does painting that way make you feel decisive?

A: Decisive and nervous. I worry about the cost of the paper, too! In fact, I've just been working in watercolor on a book called *Little Black Crow* (2010). I did the whole book, all along having a lot of trouble getting the right feeling. Then I brought it in to my art director, Ann Bobco, who said it was "Wonderful, wonderful." And the next day I had second thoughts and decided to redo everything. Now I'm almost done with the second version, which I think is better.

I like Chinese brush painting, too. I don't want to go completely in that direction, in an imitative sense. But I enjoy using elements of traditional brush painting, as I did, for instance, in *Five for a Little One* (2006).

I often go to the Met and paint there. And I like to study the examples of brush painting on display in the museum's Asian galleries. Chinese calligraphy embodies what I love in painting. In it, you can see the movement of the brush. The history of the movement of the brush is present. You can tell if the character was painted slowly or fast. You see so strongly the character of the painter — even in a single word. The painters took that same impulse of calligraphy and put it into their paintings. I like the rough painters, the ones whose work initially looks almost primitive because it was created so rapidly and with such intense emotion. The whole thing might seem to be tipping over slightly because it's done so quickly and not fussed over. Those are the ones I really love.

Q: Did you know early on that you were going to be an artist?

A: I went to St. Olaf College, a small liberal arts college, and my degree was in biology, which was what I always knew I would study. As a child, I had always loved animals. I had always been a drawer, too, and had taken art classes, but I never considered that art would be part of my working life. I had intended to go on to graduate school but took a number of detours, the first of which was a year spent working with handicapped kids in a children's home in West Germany. My original plan was to take a break from school and go to India to work on a crocodile farm, but I landed up in Germany instead. Working with those children was a moving experience, and when I got home someone suggested that I apply to medical school. I put that idea aside for a couple of years and went with my wife as Peace Corps volunteers to the Caribbean, where we both started painting like mad. That is when I first realized that I might make some sort of career in art.

When I finally reported to Ann Arbor for medical school, it hit me that once I walked through those doors, art and painting would stop for me. I spent a sleepless night trying to decide what to do, and ultimately I phoned the school — I was already in town — to say that I had changed my mind and would not be enrolling. It was awful!

Q: Were you afraid of ending up like Arlene the sardine — confined to a can?

A: I never thought of that, but the analogy works! Actually that book grew out of my time working with the children in the Caribbean and was the first book I ever did. All of our food at the home came as donations, and my story of Arlene grew out of my contemplating the path the sardines we ate one day had taken to get to us.

Q: Did you have many books as a child?

A: My mother is Viennese and my father is from Detroit. I didn't have a lot of the classics, but I did have some German picture books, including one called *The Happy Stone Age Children*. I did not own but loved the Madeline books. And I remember vividly the first time I saw *Where the Wild Things Are*. A copy of it was lying on the kitchen table at my best friend's house. I remember clearly — I was already nine or ten — being made to feel that this was somehow a mysterious, shocking book. I had never seen anything like it. I was fascinated by the cross-hatching — the etching quality — that felt alluringly like something from the adult world.

We had *Struwwelpeter*. I was moderately appalled but recognized it as an artifact of days gone by. I had a book with Wilhelm Busch's "Max and Moritz" stories, which are fairly disturbing, too. But the pen line is gorgeous.

I was never a big comics fan, but I certainly loved *Peanuts* and studied and drew Charlie Brown. When I was ten, I had a funny little yellow cloth briefcase that I took to school each day. I carefully drew Charlie Brown on one side and Snoopy on the other. I was the class artist, sort of. At home, my mother would call on me whenever a birthday card was needed for a family member. I would get cranky and complain about not having been given enough time. I was already feeling the pressure of deadlines! She would assure me that it didn't have to be special. But of course it did.

I would say something provocative to my mother like, "I think I'll jump over that wall." She would respond with a vivid German expression, *"Unterstehe Dich!"* ("Stand under yourself"), meaning, "Don't you dare!" My father was a historian and very much interested in words. My mother is an archivist and librarian and, though not a native speaker, probably knows English grammar better than any of us. She was quick to correct anyone who made a mistake. So I certainly grew up with a very focused attention to language. My mother spoke German at home and we would answer in English. My father ran a refugee camp in Austria after the war. My mother was a volunteer there and that's where they met.

Q: How did you go from being a watercolor painter to being a picture-book artist?

A: The afternoon of the Friday that was to be my first day of medical school, I cracked open the paper and applied for the first decent-sounding part-time job I could find. It turned out to be a job as the personal assistant to a private attorney. I was his driver, and I found the exculpatory evidence in a murder case he was handling. I would see the *Michigan Bar Journal* and one day decided to ask about doing illustrations for the magazine. I was hired with the stipulation that I would draw each illustration in a different style, in order to give the impression that the magazine had not just one illustrator, but several. This, in a funny way, was great training for me. The editor was a very grumpy old newspaperman who hated it if I ever made one of the lawyers I illustrated look comic. But I illustrated tort reform, water regulation — all sorts of things that were a challenge to illustrate. I learned a lot. I was afraid of heading into fine art and instead did some editorial illustrations for the *Ann Arbor News*. And then someone suggested I try children's books. It was then that I stumbled on a picture book illustrated by Vladimir Radunsky called *The Pup Grew Up.* I liked it so much that I thought, *This is what I want to do.* I read on the back flap that the artist and his wife lived in New York. That's when I decided that I had to live in New York, too. Once we got to the city, I would work on children's-book ideas in the morning and various illustration assignments in the afternoon. I did *Charlie Parker Played Be Bop* and *Yo! Yes?* (1993) during that time. I had joined an illustration group that met once a month, and one of the friends in the group suggested that I send *Charlie Parker,* which was in quite finished form, to Dick Jackson. "He likes weird books," she explained. So I mailed it to him in California, where he was then living, and he wrote back and asked to meet me. Later he told me that he hadn't known quite what to make of *Charlie Parker* and he had wanted to see what was behind it. The positioning of some of the text changed. Otherwise, the book I showed Dick was in finished form. My main worry had to do with the degree of abstraction. I was drawing a real person. But I wanted to express bebop and jazz and experimentation with a very immediate and fluid line. So I would draw very quickly and not erase and just work with whatever line came out, which gave the drawings a pretty rough and immediate look. I was afraid that people would find that disrespectful. But I was trying to embody the spirit of bebop in every aspect of the book. I would look at photographs but put them away before I started drawing. Because Charlie Parker had many health issues, sometimes he would be thin and sometimes not, so it was hard to know what image to choose. The one thing that didn't change from photo to photo was his beautiful eyes. And I know that as a musician he always stood quite still, and I wanted to capture that feeling of stillness. I tried to capture that stillness. I wanted it to be quite unfussed-with.

Q: You have made a number of picture books about music and musicians. Are you a synesthete?

A: Only by decision. When I do the music books, I try to translate the purity of one art form into the other. I impose my own set of rules. There is so much lyricism and rhythm in the brushstrokes of the Chinese brush painters. It's a way of embodying time in the painting. Many of the Chinese scrolls were painted in an afternoon. It's as if they hold that time, just as a piece of music holds the time it takes to perform it. I've been interested in the artists who were interested in these connections, such as Paul Klee and Kandinsky.

Q: The style of your Thelonious Monk book suggests the influence of Klee. You worked out a system for choosing the colors for the illustrations.

A: The color wheel starts with red, yellow, blue, and divides into twelve tones in all. The Western musical scale consists of twelve tones. So I decided to link the two scales by randomly assigning the color red to the tonic, or base note, of the musical key in which *Mysterioso,* a piece by Monk that I've always loved, is set. Starting with red as the keynote, I figured out that the piece began with blue-green. That is how I chose the background colors for each of the later illustrations, too. I split each double-page spread into eight or sixteen even-ish spaces to mimic the time-beating of music, and was about to bring the art in to my publisher when I realized that because I had divided each image so evenly, I had not left room at the center for the gutter — the small central vertical strip of each page that would disappear into the binding. So I had to cut each painting in half and insert 1⅝ inches of additional art in the middle. If you look closely at the book, you can see what I added. That's what happens when you get too caught up in your own system!

Q: With *Yo! Yes?,* you seem to have set out to make the most minimalist picture book imaginable.

A: My father used to do little back-and-forth wordplays with me in which the game was to communicate with just one word at a time. In *Yo! Yes?* I brought that game into a picture book. The text is really a script for two children to act out.

In the early 1990s, when I was working on that book, the word *yo* was first making itself felt. You almost never saw it in print. It felt like a word that was being born and was about to be launched into the world.

Q: Have you studied picture books of the past, apart from the ones you knew as a child?

A: A literature professor I met in Ann Arbor told me to read Barbara Bader's *American Picturebooks* and to join the Society of Children's Book Writers and Illustrators. With Bader's book as my guide, I then began to look at the many picture books she wrote about. I tend to love the picture books of the 1940s and 1950s, including Little Golden Books such as *The Seven Little Postmen,* which tells a fantastic journey from beginning to end and yet somehow makes you feel very close to what's happening at every point along the way. I also began to read other kinds of children's books that I had not known as a child — E. Nesbit's fantasies, for instance, and *The Phantom Tollbooth.* Jules Feiffer is another illustrator I admire greatly. His work is so gestural. You can sort of feel his hand going as you look at those drawings. One of the hard things to achieve with gesture is to figure out how it fits on the background. That's why his drawings are often without a background. When you have a gestural line, as soon as you paint up to that line you wreck a lot of the beauty of the line, because it's a different energy, in a sense. To get to the line, you have to paint very carefully. It's just no good. But if you gesturally do a background, then you also wreck the line. Even if you do a gestural line on top of a gestural background, it often doesn't work. The purest gestural drawing is calligraphy, which is a beautiful series of movements of the brush. Charles Schulz's line drawings are so beautiful, but when it's colored in, it often loses its strength. The color suffocates these beautiful lines. The genius of his artwork is his fantastic abstraction, the placement of a nose and eyes done absolutely right.

Q: Who are some of the other illustrators whose work you admire?

A: Ludwig Bemelmans and Roger Duvoisin and William Pène du Bois —

even though he's such a careful artist. I like *his* carefulness. And John Burningham and Quentin Blake.

Q: Where were you in your career when your son was born?

A: My first book had appeared in 1992 and several more were in the pipeline when I became a parent in 1995. The first books to be influenced by the experience of being a father were the Thingy Things books. Those were very much for him. Since then, he has had more and more influence. The Thingy Things books were very much taken from his daily life as a three-year-old getting up in the morning, not wanting to wear long pants or short pants; the reverse psychology that parents try on their children and the silly jokes they share; hide-and-seek; that kind of thing. My wife was teaching six- to nine-year-olds in a public Montessori school in Yonkers, and I would often have contact with those kids too, and would sort of point my thoughts toward them as I was trying to create something.

When I first came to New York with the thought of possibly getting involved in children's books, I thought that as a way of educating myself I should have some regular contact with children. So I volunteered in the education department at the American Museum of Natural History, and would go every Monday, and would be stationed in one of the galleries and approach a class that was there on a field trip to offer my services. Finding the right level on which to engage children of different ages was the great challenge. You quickly learn that with the very little children, you ask, "Is an elephant little or big?"—and you go from there. Once I was stationed in Ocean Hall and was standing under the giant model of a blue whale, which is suspended from the ceiling. I had just pointed out the belly button of the whale to a group of fourth-grade Catholic school girls, when one of the girls asked: "How can you tell a male whale from a female whale?" I replied, "A male whale has a penis and a female whale has a vagina." Suddenly, all these little heads tilted upward as the jaws of the chaperoning parents and teachers dropped. I thought: *I'm going to be run out of the museum.* Somehow it had been the only thing I could think to say.

Q: What did you think of Norton Juster's manuscript for *The Hello, Goodbye Window* (2005)?

A: I was thrilled to create something new with Norton Juster. The text was not the kind of thing I had illustrated before. It was very much a real story. I liked the tone of the child's voice and I wanted to find that same tone artistically. At the time I was getting started, I happened to see a show at the Met of the work of Philip Guston — huge, abstract expressionist paintings with thickly applied paint. They reminded me of the kids' art I was looking at just then. I thought, *This girl is supposed to be about six. I would like to embody some of the qualities of the kids' drawings and Guston's paintings in the illustrations.* The first drawings were very crayon-y and I also hand-lettered the text in many colors, as I imagined a child might. That turned out to be too much. Then I started scribbling in oil pastel, doing it in layers and then scratching it back with a folding bone. I would draw in lighter to darker hues and then scratch back so that the lighter hues would show through, so that I could draw a little bit in reverse. In the end I added a heavy pencil line to bring it all together. I was experimenting to see if that would work to get to this feeling I wanted of looseness that kind of dissipates into abstraction in places but with a character always still there. I loved the Madeline books for the "roughness" of the drawing. Norton's response was so gratifying. He sensed what I was trying to do. Another painter I love is Pierre Bonnard. His admonition was "You must make a painting that has no holes in it." I put too much color in the early drawings. It was airless, too heavy, and overdone. You couldn't feel the lightness of the scribble. When I pulled back and made it sometimes a little ambiguous about what was what — what was "chair" and what was "rug"— it made it easier to absorb visually and more pleasing. That's something that still often eludes me.

Q: What does?

A: Keeping things pretty immediate and transparent, and not too careful. Just getting it right.

Maurice Sendak

Born 1928, Brooklyn, New York; Died 2012, Danbury, Connecticut

Maurice Sendak, the children's-book world's preeminent artist, began his career in the early 1950s, at a time when the young children depicted in American picture books were typically angelic-looking, carefree, and blond. These idealized images were a far cry from the scrappy, unbeautiful immigrant youngsters Sendak had grown up with in tenement Brooklyn — and had been sketching since childhood. The "Sendak kids," who first made their appearance in print in *A Hole Is to Dig* (1952) and *A Very Special House* (1953), had fun all right, but they also got angry, lonely, and bored. Insisting that young children wanted — even needed — to see the full range of their own emotional experiences reflected in books, Sendak did more than anyone to free the picture book from its sentimental moorings in the Victorian past.

By the time Sendak won the 1964 Caldecott Medal for *Where the Wild Things Are* (1963), he had already garnered five Caldecott Honors and was the illustrator of more than fifty books, of which he was also the author of seven. The maverick attitude for which he liked to be known sometimes stirred up controversy, but few critics disputed the sheer power of his illustrations. As his work was singled out for exhibition at museums around the world and adapted for the stage, film, and television, Sendak came to play a pivotal role in raising the professional status and popular appreciation of children's books and their illustration generally.

A largely self-taught artist, Sendak was nurtured for much of his career by the legendary Harper editor Ursula Nordstrom. In more recent years, he has sought out the mentor's role for himself as the co-founder and director of the Night Kitchen Children's Theater; as an active collaborator in the worlds of opera, dance, and film; and as the presiding presence at an informal annual workshop called the Sendak Fellowship.

When we recorded the first of these two interviews at the artist's Connecticut home on July 7, 1988, Sendak was absorbed in overseeing the printing of *Dear Milli* (1988). We taped the second interview by telephone on June 14, 1993, in advance of the publication that year of *We Are All in the Dumps with Jack and Guy*. Five years passed before we were next in touch, when I was completing work on my book *Dear Genius: The Letters of Ursula Nordstrom,* and he painted the extraordinary portrait of Nordstrom that appears on the cover.

➤ INTERVIEW 1—JULY 8, 1988

LEONARD S. MARCUS: When you were ill as a child—as you often were—your father told you that if you looked out the window and didn't blink, you might see an angel. In many of your children's books, the characters stare out at the reader. Are they looking for angels?

MAURICE SENDAK: I remember that incident clearly, as if it were yesterday. It hurts not to blink, and I didn't blink until my eyes watered, but I did see an angel. And when I saw him or her or it go by, I screamed and my father came rushing in. And, of course, in *Where the Wild Things Are,* Max doesn't blink once.

Q: You have said that it is your ability to recall the "emotional quality of particular moments of childhood" that distinguishes you as a children's-book illustrator. Yet at various times in the past you have also dismissed your children's work as secondary, and said that you wished there was no real notion of children's books per se. Do you still feel that way?

A: No. I think part of the reason I felt that way was due to resentment; the establishment critics looked contemptuously, or at the very least patronizingly, on the art in children's books. Now that I have spent nearly ten years in the theater and have gotten to be sixty years old, that resentment has dissipated. I like being a children's illustrator; I'd *rather* be one. Children are the best living audience in the world because they are so thoroughly honest. "Dear Mr. Sendak, I love your book. Marry me. Yours truly." "Dear Mr. Sendak, I hate your book. Die soon. Cordially." How could you not love those responses?

Q: Do you get many letters from children about your books?

A: Predominantly I get form letters. "Our teacher said we should write to our favorite author. We like your book *Where the Wild Things Are* very much. Where does Max go? When does he come back? Will you send us a free copy of the book, a photograph of yourself, a vial of your blood, your left ear. . . ." Sadly, very few letters come directly from children.

Q: *Where the Wild Things Are* remains the book you are best known for, notwithstanding the theater work and the many other books you've done over the years. How do you feel about that?

A: Well, that isn't entirely true, but it is to a large degree. It is not my favorite book, but it is a book I'm extremely fond of, and very proud of. It's fine if that's the one I'm going to be known by.

Originally, *Wild Things* came out in spirals of scandal. People said it was too frightening, too ugly, that it wasn't a children's book, and so on. Bruno Bettelheim denounced it on the grounds that it would keep children up, was frightening. He also didn't like that Max was denied food. He did come around to agreeing with me years later. But his initial reactions did me a disservice. It was a very peculiar book for children back in the 1960s.

Q: And yet a committee of librarians got together when the book was still quite new, and awarded your book the Caldecott Medal.

A: I think that is probably the most astonishing fact of my entire life. I was thirty-four. I had already been in the business since I was eighteen, and had been a runner-up for the award five times previous to that. The Caldecott Medal helped sell the book, but it also helped give me the power to continue to do the kind of books I wanted to do. It didn't make me feel that I could do even more outrageous books, because I didn't think my books were outrageous. The fact that other people did has always been a puzzle to me.

Q: Over the course of the book, the pictures change in size, and eventually the pictures displace the words altogether. Is that meant to reflect Max's development in the story?

A: Well, it's based on a theory of picture-book making that I suppose I evolved myself, since I never took a course in bookmaking. It's a theory based on the work of artists I love, primarily Randolph Caldecott, Jean de Brunhoff (creator of the Babar books), and William Nicholson. That device is a way of dramatically picturing what's going on; as Max's rage engorges him, those pictures fill the page. When his anger turns to a kind of wild jungle pleasure, the words are pushed off the page altogether. And then he deflates like any normal child; he's getting hungry, he's getting tired, and he wants to go back home.

Q: In your new book, Wilhelm Grimm's tale *Dear Mili* (1988), two of the last pages are all text. As Mili and her mother are reunited, it's the pictures that have been pushed off the page.

A: It's the same reasoning in reverse: there is no time for pictures there; the music of Grimm's prose takes over. It would be an irritant to see what is being said at that point, so I let people read it and enjoy the music and the imagery; they don't need me to draw it for them. The illustrator must have more respect for language than he has for picture making; he must assume the backseat.

Q: How did the Wild Things dolls come about, and how did you feel about turning your characters into toys?

A: I'd always wanted the toys because I'm a toy maker, or was, with my brother, Jack. I helped design the Wild Things dolls, basing their proportions on the early Mickey Mouse doll, which I adored.

Q: The majority of your children's-book characters have been boys — boys whose names begin with *M* and who bear a striking resemblance to you as a child. From what you have observed, do girls identify as much with Max as boys do?

A: As many or more girls identify with Max. For one thing, he is wearing a unisex suit; you can't tell his gender. And any female child can look as maniacal as Max does. In the little plays that are put on by children all over the country, Max often is played by a little girl. In the opera, his role is sung by a soprano.

Q: The backgrounds in the illustrations of *Wild Things* look like stage flats. They are not as fully rendered as the figures, who stand out contrastingly in relief, as do actors onstage.

A: I didn't think of that at the time, but it makes sense, if only because once the book was published, a ballet company in Boston choreographed *Wild Things* and an endless parade of musical people came along wanting to do something with it. The opera that eventually grew from it is wonderful and makes me happy.

Q: Is *Outside Over There* (1981) still your favorite book, as you said it was at the time of its publication?

A: *Higglety Pigglety Pop!* (1967) is my favorite in sentiment, because it is a tribute to my dog, Jennie, whom I loved so much, and because it is the only sad story I've ever written that turned out to be funny. But overall, *Outside Over There* is my favorite. I think it is the most beautifully structured book I've written. I never imagined that seven years later I would still be doing a version of *Outside Over There,* but *Dear Mili* is an extension of that same subject — what can happen to vulnerable children. The two books belong together emotionally; *Dear Mili* is the grace note. It's the solution, the salvation.

Q: The mother in *Outside Over There* looks really out of it as she sits there in the arbor, waiting for her husband to return home from sea, and leaves it to her older daughter to take care of the baby. Do you think of the book as a fable for our times — as the story, with tragic overtones, of a withdrawn or irresponsible parent?

A: No, I don't. The whole fantasy unfolds very quickly. It doesn't take twenty-four hours. You have a mother who for one moment thinks of something else: every mother does. And in that one moment something happens that she doesn't notice. I dare say it happens every single day. It's like Max and his mother. Now, if Max's mother had been in a slightly better mood on that particular day, she wouldn't have screamed "Wild thing" and he wouldn't have said "I'll eat you up." She might have said what he really wanted her to say, which was, "Darling, you're hilarious, come and give Momma a hug," and he never would have gone on his journey, and there would have been no book. My books are all about that quirky minute when things just don't work out. Mothers were kids once, and they grow up to be just regular people. They cannot always be watching the child.

Q: In *Outside Over There*, the sunflowers are watching out.

A: Well, nature is watching out, and Ida is watching. She wishes to hell she didn't have a sister, and she wishes to hell that she wasn't dumped with this responsibility while Mother's sitting there gaga, and at that minute, she wishes this kid was dead and that she could be free. But the minute she wishes her dead, she un-wishes it. That's what the book is about — this minute of distraction. And that's why I call those three books — *Wild Things, In the Night Kitchen* (1971), and *Outside Over There* — a trilogy. They're all about one minute's worth of distraction. One noise in the kitchen has Mickey doing a weird thing. One temper tantrum, one wrong word causes all of the Wild Things to happen; one minute's dreamy distraction allows the kidnapping in *Outside Over There* to occur. I only have one subject. The one question I am obsessed with is, how do children survive?

Q: When did you first think of the three books as a trilogy?

A: When I did *Wild Things* I knew that it was such a good idea that I would have to play variations on it. Even then, I was thinking about it in musical terms. I wasn't going to make *Max II*; it had to be a different book about a wholly different world. And when *Night Kitchen* was done, it was full of exciting reverberations. Then it was on to the third variation. I somehow knew that the third book would have to be about a girl.

Q: You have said that the baby in *Outside Over There* is Mili in your new book. I want to ask you about your personal mythology, how you come to make those connections.

A: Well, it's all bits of things of my own particular life. Memories of things, social and political things that occurred in the world that frightened me as a child, things that I have to play with, re-create, or exorcise. The baby is immensely important because as the youngest, *I* was the baby. I was always the baby, even when I got to be a middle-aged man. I grew up in the era of famous kidnapped babies, which played a part in *Outside Over There*. It was a re-creation of the Lindbergh kidnapping, which was so traumatic to me as a child. People say you mustn't frighten children, but you can't, because they already *are* frightened, they already know all these things. All you can do is console them.

Q: Was this missing from your childhood experience?

A: Nobody consoled me when Charles Lindbergh, Jr., was found dead in the woods. It wasn't that my parents were cruel and therefore denied me consolation. It was that they wished I didn't know, and so they pretended to themselves that I didn't. For my part, I was too ashamed to ask, like the Henry James little girls who don't ask questions because they know it would be inappropriate. Well, I was a normal kid: I knew what was inappropriate — and I knew how to keep my mouth shut, even when I was dying to know.

So, like any normal kid, I made up my own answers. I thought, if a famous baby could die, a blond and beautiful baby, what could happen to an ugly, short, black-haired baby like me? *Outside Over There* was my fantasy in which the baby got saved. I changed history in that book. I did what I couldn't do: I brought him back alive. And I grew up to do a book that made it acceptable for me. Just as children take in everything and then, finally, because no one around them has the sense to explain the situation, they explain it to themselves. This is what my books are all about: explaining difficult life situations to myself.

Q: *Dear Mili* is a Christian miracle tale. Was this story difficult for you, being Jewish, to illustrate?

A: I saw it as a contemporary story of mothers forever gratuitously losing children because of the stupidity of men who go off soldiering. We read about it every day, in Vietnam, South Africa, you name it. In every country in the world, crying mothers and crying babies. It is the subject of human life. And for me, as a Jew, it was also very much the subject of the Holocaust: mothers and fathers separated from their children forever.

My father's entire family was destroyed in the Holocaust. I grew up in a house that was in a constant state of mourning. My bar mitzvah was one of the most tragic days in my father's life, which infuriated me; I didn't have the brains to understand what he was going through. That very morning a telegram arrived saying that members of his family had been confirmed dead. I remember my father falling down, and me being in my little suit all ready to go, and the rage that was stirred in me by these dead Jews who constantly infiltrated our lives and made us miserable. But we got there, and they sang, "For He's a Jolly Good Fellow," and my brother and my mother held my father up on either side, and he got through it all. So it was very important for me to distill into this little story, however gently and subtly, my own Holocaust experience, to pay homage to those dead Jews. Their graves are in the book. Some of them are living in paradise with Mili and her guardian-angel friend.

Q: Do you think some readers may find it strange to come upon these references in an overtly Christian story?

A: I found it very appropriate to take this simple and very moving story and pay homage not just to Christian children but also to Jewish children, and black children, and Palestinian children, all of whom have died miserably and for no other reason than the stupidity of mankind.

Q: In the illustrations of many of your books, you turn the gaze of the characters directly toward the reader. But in *Dear Mili,* the figures typically look away while the landscapes go wild all around them.

A: The people in *Dear Mili* are symbolic. The mama of the story isn't Mrs. Jones down the street. The dramatic action did not so much lie in them. Then, where *did* it lie? I turned to the idea of a living forest. At the beginning it's Arcadia. It's heaven for a minute. Then it's William Blake mad. Then it's early German Romantic glorioso. Then it's the sensuousness of English landscape painting. Then it's Van Gogh going demented in paradise. This of course is an exaggerated, hyperbolic way of describing what I did. But I kept the book moving through nature.

Q: At the beginning, when the war is mentioned, you have made the distant cannon fire look something like exploding sunflowers.

A: I didn't think of that.

Q: It calls to mind . . .

A: *Outside Over There* . . . and Vincent van Gogh. It took steps to get to a religious story, a spiritual story. Van Gogh is one of the artists I trusted most to help me. He was a religious man and had wanted to be a priest when he was young. He had read the Bible and decided to go down into the coal mines and live with the poor. But the church fathers said, "Are you out of your mind? You're giving us a bad name!"— and kicked him out. And so he found another means to preach. He painted.

Q: You seem to describe Van Gogh in much the same terms as you described children earlier, as people who find their own answers to questions.

A: Absolutely! I believe in sunflowers and in all the brazen, blazing pictures Van Gogh painted and utterly trust his ecstatic vision.

Q: Mark Twain once said that it's important never to let your schooling get in the way of your education. We've been talking just now about some of the artists from whose work you have learned. When you were young, however, you apparently did not enjoy going to school.

A: But I have many honorary degrees! I wish to heaven my father was alive to see them because I was the only child he could afford to send to college, and I was the only one of the three who refused to go. That was the irony of his life. If only he could see that he could have saved all that money by his son's just going off for a weekend and coming home with another degree. That would have made him so happy!

Q: There's something very weighted and deliberate about the way you have drawn Mili; her feet are very big.

A: I like to draw feet; one of the Wild Things has enormous feet. I have no interest, apparently, in proportion. But it does have another meaning when I draw children: these characters have a rootedness, they're planted.

I suppose what I love about Mili is that she's very much like the children in my other books. In spite of everything that's going on in her life, Mili proceeds with the kind of heroism that is natural to a normal child. She trusts her mother; when her mother says go, she goes, even though she doesn't comprehend why. And in a sense she comes back as an emissary, as an angel to take her mother to heaven with her. But she has the same kind of trudging, hard-working quality that I love in children. They're trudging children; they go and do what they must do.

LEONARD S. MARCUS: Your new book has the intensity of a fever dream. It must have grown out of some compelling inner need. What was that need?

MAURICE SENDAK: Partly, it was an old artistic conundrum. I actually began *Dumps* (1993) in 1964, right after *Hector Protector* (1965). I was so entranced with nursery rhymes then that I wanted to do another book right afterward that from my point of view would be more accomplished than the first one. The two rhymes in *Hector* aren't joined in any way except by the slim fact that both are about rather repellent little boys. I wanted something more complicated than that for the second book.

I had done a lot of research in the nursery rhymes, found "Dumps" and "Jack," and did a dummy for the new book. I didn't like the dummy, and so I put it away. But I kept it, because I knew that a rhyme called "We Are All in the Dumps" was made for me!

That was part of the urgency, as it continued to cook in my little Night Kitchen brain for all these thirty-odd years. Then one night, when I was in Los Angeles to work on an opera, I was driving down a very posh street on the way back to my hotel and saw a kid sleeping in a box. His naked feet were sticking out of the box. The juxtaposition of the posh street and the kid just seemed crazy, and it made me think of the two nursery rhymes that I had come across so many years earlier. A little later, I did some research and found that Rio de Janeiro is circled by shantytowns with just children living in them, and that those children have created their own little society, which is what happens in my book. Anyway, the idea started to come to life, and it just hooked into the old rhymes, which now suddenly had a whole new meaning.

With *Dumps* there was also the excitement for me of doing a book that was not quite about me. Suddenly, I felt free to do such a book in which my self was not the central subject.

Q: Does that freedom come with age?

A: I think it comes with age. It also confirms what I said many years ago but that only now makes sense to me: that *Outside Over There* would be my last picture book. What I meant, really, was that it was the last picture book that was to be an excavation of my soul, the last archaeological Sendakian dig! I think I only *knew* it was the last when, later, I was doing the illustrations for *I Saw Esau* (1992), and found myself thinking, *My God, I'm happy doing this book. That must mean I'm free.*

Q: You could be describing an end to therapy.

A: In a sense, yes — a very rich sense. Critics have said that the book was a throwback, an attempt to recapture my earlier styles of illustration. I wasn't conscious of anything of the kind. I just knew that the verses were jubilant and that I was working on a book without the familiar anxieties and inhibitions that had been part of my entire creative life — a very functional part to be sure — until then. It was like shedding a snakeskin, and *Dumps* is definitely the child of *Esau*.

Q: The illustrations in *Dumps* could be camera close-ups of the tableaux you drew for *I Saw Esau.*

A: Precisely. With more than a decade's career on the operatic stage behind me, there is also a theatricality about the book that I'm very proud of.

Q: Both rhymes are cryptic. Was Iona Opie able to give you any special insight into their meaning?

A: She said nothing was known about them. I made some minor changes. The original of one line reads: "The babies are bit." I changed that to: "The baby is bit." So I asked Iona, "Is this kosher?" She laughed and said, "That's what they're for!" That is *exactly* what they are for: to transform and change and use over and over again.

Q: The headlines that appear on the cover and elsewhere throughout the illustrations are very contemporary.

A: The device of the newspaper headlines developed as I composed the book. It came, as often happens, as the solution to practical problems. For instance, when the moon cries, you have a choice. Do the kids have umbrellas to keep themselves from getting soaked? Well, if they don't have houses, they don't have umbrellas. So what do they use? Newspapers, old newspapers. So the newspapers became their clothing and they became their "houses without walls." I then thought, *The newspapers must say something, but what?* Once you are putting in headlines, why not headlines that have a satiric edge, even a painful edge?

Q: Some are very painful. You've talked often in the past about having been terrified as a child by news of the Lindbergh kidnapping case. Do you think that news about homelessness and AIDS are having the same kind of impact on children now?

A: Of course. It seems to me that there are so many more ferocious horrors — stories of children getting shot on the way to school, the story of a four-year-old leaving his sibling to die at a fire, and hospitals jammed with AIDS babies. They make me and my Lindbergh fantasy seem small stuff.

Q: Hasn't most of children's literature been based on the premise that kids can somehow be protected from the harsher realities?

A: Yes, but that runs counter to what I firmly believe, which is that children *do* know what's going on. I mean, when the Lindbergh baby was kidnapped, I knew at age four that something had happened to this child that could happen to me. I think that all small children know things we wish they didn't. But wishing is not going to make that go away. Of course, you don't want to tell kids about things that are beyond their comprehension or that are unlikely to happen. The idea that children today know that they can be shot on the way to school petrifies my brain, because I don't know what they do with that knowledge.

Q: So there's no way kids can escape from an awareness of that kind of violence and suffering?

A: There's just no protecting them. We're confronted with a terrible dilemma, which is having to tell children things that we know are hard for them to hear, yet that they have to know to protect their lives. It's like not wanting to put the word *condom* into a sex education pamphlet. Kids have sex so much earlier now, but people don't want to use the word *condom*. I mean, if you want to kill kids, why don't you take them out in the street and shoot them? Why not *help* them, instead? When do we give up this nonsense about words that are not permissible and knowledge that is not permissible, if in fact they save lives? It's a phony morality.

Q: In its depiction of homelessness and references to AIDS, your book makes an angry appeal for an end to the moral complacency of our society. Shouldn't that kind of plea be addressed to adults, not children?

A: Absolutely — in fact, this book is also being marketed to adults. I didn't fight for that, but it was a blessing that it turned out that way. I've been struggling with the constraints of being a children's-book illustrator/writer for years.

The discomfort has nothing to do with my passion for children, but with grown-ups there's always the subtle implication that your work is not very important. That's always plagued us in this business. The book *does* take up some serious issues with adults, such as where the hell are they in an emergency?

Q: But what about the child reader?

A: What the book really says is, "You kids are heroes. You'll make out." Children will persevere if they can. They'll find a family. That's all they need, that's all they want — to be loved and cared for and fed. That's what I hope children will see in it.

What sort of message do children get out of "Hansel and Gretel," one of the most dire tales ever written? That story is like a punch in the face. Do they get any joy out of hearing that the stepmother loathes them and wishes them dead? That the father is a wimp? It's only their own courage and resilience that keep Hansel and Gretel alive. Now, *Dumps* is no more frightening than that famous story.

Q: But "Hansel and Gretel," like other fairy tales, takes place in a vague, once-upon-a-time fantasy realm, while your story has the immediacy of the morning's headlines. Doesn't that make your story scarier?

A: It may to you, and to other grown-ups, but not to the kids hearing it. All that once-upon-a-time stuff is cosmetic embroidery, a device. Who has time for devices these days? Adults don't and children don't. I think the world is in a dire situation, and I'm surely not alone in feeling that is so. So why hold it off at a distance? It doesn't make sense to do that anymore.

Q: The word *AIDS* recurs, like a mantra, in the newspapers of your illustrations.

A: My life has been totally changed by the loss of my friends, so many I can't count. How do we not talk about it? It's like trying to keep your mouth shut about something that is devouring you. But the big question will be, is this appropriate for children?

Q: What is your answer?

A: There will be people who will object to AIDS as a subtext of this tale. I couldn't care less. If people condemn me, fine. If they are tired of the subject and angry at this book, fine. If they want to put their heads in the sand, fine. Don't tell me children don't know about AIDS. That's ridiculous!

Q: Do you feel that by creating this book you have become a political activist?

A: Yes, but I don't want *Dumps* to be seen as a political tract. It's still me, it's still a picture book to be read and, I hope, enjoyed. It still has all my idiosyncratic fantasies, and to me it is no different from the subject of any other book I've ever done: It is about the heroism of children. Kids see that. You know, things get simplified so fast. This book is not suddenly stripping away everything I've ever done and making me a political commentator. No way.

Q: But for you, dealing with a subject like AIDS *is* something new.

A: When you lose good friends who are much younger than you, then you begin to see the world as upside down. Students I adored, whose work was magnificent, who were far more gifted than I was at their age, are dead and gone. Older people whose work I admired are gone. It takes my breath away. It's become part of my life, part of my nervous system, part of my terrible grief. If that makes me political, so be it. There is grief in this book, but there is also joy. I know there is because I felt joy doing it.

Q: You are old enough now to be a grandparent. Often grandparents have a different, more relaxed relationship with children than do parents. Has there been a comparable change in your relationship to your audience, or in the way you make books for children?

A: That is a curious and interesting thought. It must be true to some extent, because when you are young you are caught up in the intensity of recovery, of truth-telling, of making sure you got it right.

Q: Recovery from what?

A: From your own childhood. So, yes, I would say the grandfather metaphor is suitable.

Q: Notwithstanding the book's intensity, there's a very relaxed feeling to the drawing style of *Dumps*.

A: You see I'm no longer concerned with drawing. I'm counting on many decades of experience to come through for me; style and technique have become second nature. My heroes, too, have become a part of me in my old age: Dickens, Blake, everybody I've ripped off and stolen from! Instead of paying homage to them as a trembling student, as I did in my earlier works, I feel as if I've swallowed them whole.

One of the few graces of getting old — and God knows there are few graces — is that if you've worked hard and kept your nose to the grindstone, something happens: the body gets old but the creative mechanism is refreshed, smoothed and oiled and honed. That is the grace. That is the splendid grace. And I think that is what's happening to me. I'm afraid of getting old, I'm afraid of my body failing me. And yet there's this other side, this young side. *Mamma mia!* How many people can claim such a thing?

∽ MAURICE SENDAK POSTSCRIPT, MAY 12, 2011

LEONARD S. MARCUS: It looks as though you had fun making your new book, *Bumble-Ardy*. Even the title suggests that.

MAURICE SENDAK: Actually I didn't. It was a very difficult time. I was working on it when my partner and friend was dying of cancer. We set up a room in the house to be like a hospital room. Eugene died and then I had coronary bypass surgery. I was doing the book to stay sane while all this was going on.

Q: It's a book about someone — a pig-child — who insists on having a birthday party even if he has to give it to himself.

A: Well, one of the beauties of being an artist is that you can create a whole new world, with circumstances that are better in your invented world than they are in the real world.

I had been reading a fabulous book about Verdi [*The Man Verdi* by Frank Walker], whom I adore. Verdi was in his late seventies and had written what he said would be his last opera, *Aida,* when from out of nowhere a young poet called Arrigo Boito came into his life. Boito had composed a wonderful opera about Mephistopheles and was going to write another opera about Nero, and he gave himself up to Verdi in collaboration. A whole new world of Italian music was springing up, and Verdi was seen as old. Boito got Verdi all excited about the possibility of doing another opera, another kind of opera. In fact, Verdi composed his two best operas, *Otello* and *Falstaff,* in his eighties. And so I thought that if I were going into old age I would want to do what Verdi did, which is to write extraordinary things, and to really find myself. I'll be eighty-three shortly, and I want to be renewed. We all want to be renewed, don't we? *Bumble-Ardy* was a step toward renewal.

Q: How do you see the hero of the story?

A: Bumble-Ardy is a very wicked little child, as far as I'm concerned. He's not to be trusted. He's never given permission to have a party, but he has one anyway. Sweet Adeline doesn't want anybody to come to the house, to drink her special drinks. Adeline is a simple, ordinary woman — wonderful and healthy and strong — and she loves him in spite of everything. Does he love her? "You bet!" he says, as if that were an appropriate answer. But can any child love who has been so mishandled by his original parents? Thank God that Bumble-Ardy's parents are dead, so we don't have to wonder what they did to him. We only know that they were famous, and famous people have unhappy children for the most part. They don't have the time to take care of them. So he's a troubled pig-boy. He's a kid you've got to watch.

Q: Maybe Sweet Adeline expects too much of him. I thought he gave the perfect answer when she becomes upset with him and, desperate to calm her down, he says, "I promise! I swear! I won't ever turn ten!"

A: Yes, I like that. For me that's the best line in the book. He thinks that's really a promise.

Q: How were your birthdays celebrated? With parties and presents?

A: No parties. Gifts. I remember one birthday standing at the banister and people coming up and my wanting to see the present before I would let them in the house! Was it worth letting them in the house? That's very Bumble-Ardy. I was not a happy child, and it wasn't enough not to be happy. I had to make everybody else unhappy, too. I was very successful at making everybody miserable — except my brother, whom I adored. I felt he saved my life.

Q: It seems that you were looking back at some of your earlier books in this one. "Some swill pig" sounds a lot like "some swell pup." And one of the party guests — although you have made him a pig — bears a striking resemblance to the Oliver Hardy bakers of *In the Night Kitchen*.

A: You could say that. Oliver Hardy would be a good person for this book — a swell guy with a nice fat face. That same pig appeared in another project I worked on just a few years ago, a staging of *Peter and the Wolf*, which I translated into Yiddish and sang on a stage in New York City. Thank God very few people knew I was doing it! But the kids in the audience loved it — even though it was all in Yiddish. Instead of a wolf it was a pig: "ein Schwein." That is the pig that you say looks like Oliver Hardy. I liked him so much in my *Peter and the Wolf* that I wanted him for this book, too.

Q: Having grown up in a kosher home, do you associate pigs with the forbidden, with guilty pleasures?

A: In a way. We didn't have pig in our house, though God knows most of the people who came there were pigs. My bar mitzvah was a declaration of freedom.

Q: You mean you went out and had a ham-and-cheese sandwich?

A: I might as well have.

Q: The colors in *Bumble-Ardy* are among the warmest and brightest in all your books.

A: It was not a conscious choice, but yes, there is a palette that is different from that of my other books. It's Verdi-esque. Verdi was such an enormous help to me [as I worked on the book]. I had lost my sister recently, too, which meant that my whole family was gone. There were five Sendaks and there were five Wild Things, and now there's only one Sendak and he's about to bite the dust too! Life, as I said before, was very difficult at that time, and so it was natural that there would be a change in the look of things. Also, I was impressed with my own strength in doing this under the circumstances under which I was living.

Q: There is a house without walls in *We Are All in the Dumps with Jack and Guy,* and Bumble-Ardy lives in one, too. Do you see the two books as somehow linked?

A: I never thought of *Bumble-Ardy* in that way. But I still have the same deep feeling for children who are in dire trouble. I see Bumble-Ardy as a lonely, unhappy kid who is doing the very best he can to be in the world, to have a party. I was ungainly. I was heavy. I probably looked like a little pig. I don't know. You can start making up any kind of story if you want to, as you well know.

Q: The party scenes in *Bumble-Ardy* look like something out of a Coney Island sideshow.

A: That big face on the midway at Coney Island. I loved that! We lived only two [subway] stations away from Coney Island and we used to go to the boardwalk and beach there very, very frequently — my mother, father, sister, brother, and I. For my father the one calamity was that my brother and sister and I never learned to swim. My father, who was very macho, was a strong swimmer and was terribly disappointed to have children who didn't swim. Once when my mother was sitting in a beach chair — I can still see the big umbrella — she called to my father, "Throw them in! Throw them in! They'll swim!" So he did. Then he looked down and there were the three Sendak children lying perfectly still, not fighting for life! So he had to schlep us up out of the water and dump us on the sand. He was deeply resentful and disappointed that he had three dopey kids who just lay there. They weren't fighting to live. Somehow that got into this book.

Q: You have given Bumble-Ardy a costume party and a cowboy outfit for a gift. Did you like to play dress-up?

A: No, that wasn't one of my things. All I liked to do when I was a kid was draw. My childhood was like my adult life: drawing pictures with my brother, putting the comics up on the glass window and tracing the characters onto tracing paper or drawing paper and then coloring them. That and making things was all we ever did. My brother and I built the entire World's Fair of 1939 in miniature out of wax. The floor of our room was covered with little waxen buildings. Nobody else could come in.

Q: Maybe that was your real goal.

A: Oh, it was fantastic. My brother, who was four years older than me, was the gifted one, much more talented than I. Most of the work was his. I was his assistant.

My sister at that point had her own room. She was nine years older and had innumerable boyfriends. I had a yo-yo collection that was beyond belief, and the reason I had it was mostly that I would stand in the doorway of the living room watching her and her boyfriend. Finally she caught on about how to get this kid out of the way. Give him a yo-yo!

Then one day my sister abandoned me at the 1939 World's Fair, and that incident is the essence of *In the Night Kitchen*. The book is a reenactment of standing in front of the place where bread was baked by little men in white caps — Oliver Hardy–type men — as they waved to you, and the smell of bread and cake pouring out of the building. I was standing there with hundreds of other people waving back at the little midgets dressed like bakers when I turned around and my sister was gone! The next thing I know I'm screaming and crying and policemen take me to a big place with tons of kids who have all been abandoned like me. At least I was old enough to give them a name and an address.

Q: How could she have done that?

A: She was with a date. She had had to take me but she didn't think twice about leaving me. I was allowed to call my mother from the police station, and my mother was crying, and my sister was already home, and I said, "She did it to me, she did it to me!" Then I got into the police car and I was being driven home and I said, "Please put on the siren when you get to the corner of West Sixth Street." And the police were so eager to calm me down that they did turn the siren on, and when they stopped in front of the building, everybody was looking out the window, calling, "Moishe, Moishe, poor little Moishe!" And then I went upstairs and the first thing I did was point to my sister and say, "She did it on purpose!" Later I heard my father clobbering her. It was a great day! If they had asked me, I would have become a policeman then and there. Then everyone could have been spared my *meshuggeneh* books.

My sister being so much older than me, for years I hardly knew her. But when the war came and her beautiful husband was killed in action and my parents said, "Get married again! You're a good-looking woman," I thought, *How can they do this? How can they be so hard on her?* And that's when she and I became really close. We remained good friends and I loved her very much. My brother was *in* my life. My sister was there to take care of me.

Q: Where did the name Bumble-Ardy come from?

A: I needed a name that rhymed with party. It was as poetic as that! So many things are so mundane in how they get created. It's all in the way you fashion them to look interesting and make people get excited and want to talk about them.

Q: Is Sweet Adeline based on a real person?

A: The only reason my father came to this country [from Poland] was that he was in love with this girl. His father was a rabbi and was outraged that his son should make a spectacle of himself. The girl was a scandal and everyone in their small Polish village paid to put her on a ship and get her out of sight. So she went to America, and my father then drove his siblings and parents crazy because he wanted money to go on the next ship. He said he couldn't live without her. My grandparents refused to help. They cursed and disowned him, and said the prayer for the dead. But his sisters and brothers collected the money he needed, and so he followed this girl to New York. But when he got there just three weeks later, he found that she had already married somebody else, and that she had a delicatessen on West 87th Street and Broadway! So he went to see her and he said, "What's the matter with you! You got married to this Shlomo here?" And she said,

"Philip, Philip, don't worry! Nothing's changed!" Later she and my mother became very good friends, and I always wondered if my mother knew the whole story. I adored her. Unlike my mother, she was a very giving, very emotional woman. Plus — free hot dogs! Come on, I loved her!

Q: What was her name?

A: Ida. My Ida. Sweet Adeline is like Ida, whose arms were always open. "You love me? You still love me?" I can see myself rushing into her arms and feeling how big and warm her breasts were and how delicious she smelled of hot dogs and knishes and everything.

I knew two Idas then and both were special, wonderful women from the old country. Mrs. Perlis, to whom I dedicated *The Nutshell Library,* was another Ida. My mother was a very unhappy-by-herself kind of woman, and the only person who could bring her out of her unhappiness was Ida Perlis. Once she and I were alone in the street. I said, "What is that line of lights? Are all those cars?" And she said, "That is a boulevard." Even now I get a chill when I say the word *boulevard.* It has always seemed magical to me.

Q: Might there also be a little bit of Ursula Nordstrom [Sendak's long-time editor at Harper] in Sweet Adeline, who steps in almost as a mother to give Bumble-Ardy the things he needs: not everything he needs, but nonetheless an awful lot of what really matters to him?

A: Could be. She gives him the basics: love and consideration. And she forgives him at the end. I would have to say that that was not in my mind. But I'm grateful that it was in your mind, because it makes a kind of sense. Even to the big body, the clumsy affection. It was clumsy but it was real affection. How could I have lived without Ursula? It's amazing that that happened. God, I had great people in my life. It looks like a happy book. That's the funniest thing about it. But this was survival. I was working very hard to survive.

PETER SÍS

Born 1949, Brno, Czechoslovakia

Asked about the first pictures that captivated him, Peter Sís recalls: "When I was a little boy, I saw Albrecht Dürer's engraving of a rhinoceros, . . . [probably] in a museum in Prague. . . . This picture was pure magic. Mysterious and beautiful. It was everything I found, and still find, inspiring about art. . . . In that [Communist controlled] society, where everyone was carefully guarding against showing any true feelings, that rhino became a perfect symbol of the tender soul and heart, protected from the outside world by its thick skin."

Sís had the benefit of artist parents who fed his love of drawing and protected him from some of the harsher aspects of life under Cold War–era Communist rule. He studied art in Prague and emerged a skilled animator and illustrator with a well-developed talent for expressing his ideas

216

in powerful, dreamlike images ranging in mood from haunting to droll. After coming to the United States for a visit and deciding to remain there, he found work as an illustrator for the *New York Times* and other newspapers and magazines. He was eager to tackle more personal — and more ambitious — projects as well, and, following a pivotal encounter with Maurice Sendak, he embraced the picture book as his principal art form. In the many picture books he has created since that time, Sís has shown a gift not only for distilling complex bodies of thought and information — the life of Charles Darwin, the history of the Cold War — but also for depicting the most ordinary corners of the everyday world through the kaleidoscopic lens of a young child's imagination.

Sís is a tall but sprightly, gregarious man, and a regular at conferences and conventions. We were bound to meet, and we had many enjoyable conversations in hotel lobbies and crowded reception rooms. When we sat down together for this interview, it was in Sís's lower Manhattan studio in a building not far from the city block depicted in the Madlenka books. The old-fashioned, largely residential neighborhood on the edge of Little Italy had only recently attracted the attention of high-end developers, and the sound of jackhammers could be heard from the street below as we talked on July 23, 2009.

〜〜〜〜〜〜〜〜〜〜〜〜〜〜〜〜〜

LEONARD S. MARCUS: I read that when you were growing up, your parents not only encouraged you to draw and paint but even gave you assignments and deadlines.

PETER SÍS: My father did that. I didn't appreciate it that much at the time. He would say, "I want to see by Saturday how you would deal with . . ." and we would agree on some subject. He was very pushy and loud! I didn't do this with my own children, and now I sort of regret *that*.

It was also a great advantage for me that my father traveled a lot and was open to books and art from all over the world. He would tell me that the world was a big place. Czechoslovakia at the time was a closed society. People were xenophobic and didn't see the big picture.

Both my parents were artists. Other parents didn't approve of their children wanting to be an artist. You know, "You'd better get a serious job, become a dentist or lawyer." But my parents were very encouraging. I remember my father saying, "One day when you will be in New York . . ." At the time it sounded like an impossibility. He loved jazz and had wanted to move to New York himself but had not been able to find a way.

When I was ten or twelve, my father brought home the first books by Saul Steinberg. I grew up with them. I admired the fact that Steinberg seemed to enjoy himself so much as an artist. That was the feeling I got from looking at his drawings. And it was through Steinberg's art that I also felt I had some connection to New York, though I couldn't imagine ever getting there.

Q: Was it clear early on that you had the talent to be an artist?

A: Supposedly.

Q: What about school?

A: For much of my early life, I did not get much encouragement from school, where art, like everything else, was taught from rigid rules. Let's say we would be drawing a stuffed duck and I would want to make something funny out of it. That sort of thing wasn't appreciated at school. My father was always there to defend me. A few times he went to school and argued with the teacher. In high school, I was in a special art school. But even there I had conflicts. I was a teenager then, of course. The teachers didn't appreciate rock 'n' roll. When one of them asked who among us planned to be professional artists, I raised my hand, and the response was, "You! You can't even draw properly!" I was seventeen, and they put me down to the point that I was devastated. I got home and I remember my father went to school right away, and after a few hours of major arguments — he was a film director and a big personality — they agreed to leave me alone. He created that space for me. If I hadn't had a father like that . . . it was really quite awful.

It's so easy now to say it was all political. But the school was also following the nineteenth-century tradition of classical art education. You learned to draw from plaster models of hands and heads, and if you changed the formula, the teachers were not tolerant. From there I went to the Academy of Applied Arts and had a wonderful teacher, who was very understanding. He built me up. It's amazing how much the right teacher can change you as an artist, as a person. That's why it's very difficult for me to teach. I don't want to have to critique a student. I would rather not have to say I don't like their work, because I know how damaging that can sometimes be, how I almost didn't survive that. I think it's much more important to be an inspiration.

Q: Was traditional art encouraged by the regime in order, indirectly, to discourage original thought in general?

A: It's so hard to explain in America. Things in Czechoslovakia were gradually changing during the 1960s. It didn't happen overnight. For example, Merce Cunningham visited Czechoslovakia during those years, along with Robert Rauschenberg. It was unbelievably exciting for us. We thought that everyone in America was dancing! My father was opportunistic in that he took advantage of the regime to make his films and write his books, and at the same time he was also open, in an underground sort of way, to what was happening in the arts in other parts of the world. There was a great hunger for information from the West. Somehow we knew about songs and TV shows, and sometimes we didn't stop to think too much about what was good artistically and what wasn't. We felt that everything that lay beyond the Iron Curtain was magical. It took me some time to realize that that wasn't so.

Q: Your father made documentaries?

A: Yes, and he was sent by the government to Tibet for an assignment that changed his life as well as our whole family's lives. Eventually he made feature films, including some comedies. He came just before the Czech New Wave, led by Milos Forman. They all knew him.

Q: What kind of art did your mother make?

A: She drew very well and made ornaments you might wear on your lapel. But the expectation was that after a woman had children she would no longer work, and my mother followed that pattern. She would always draw with my sister and me when we were stuck in a waiting room or some other situation. She would decorate our clothes hangers, make them look like monkeys. She was always doing things like that.

Q: Tell me about Tibet.

A: My father was there for nineteen months, though as a child I had thought he was gone for many, many years. He was twenty-eight when he was drafted into the Czech army, and the tradition was that if you were a filmmaker, you made films — if you were lucky. His film unit was sent to Communist China to teach them how to make films. It was all very exotic to him; he knew very little about where he was going. They had crates and crates of equipment, and it was freezing, and they were shooting a film about building a road to Tibet, which they were told was ruled by a diabolical leader. Somehow he got ahead of the construction crew and reached Tibet first, where he met the Dalai Lama, who was then eighteen or nineteen years old. My father realized that the Dalai Lama was not anything like what he had been told to expect. This caused a fundamental change inside him. In a way, it opened his eyes about the Communist regime. Then my father came down with a terrible illness, and then he returned home. We loved hearing his stories, which he gradually perfected. As teenagers, my sister and I finally got sick of them! My father wrote a very popular cookbook, *The Counting of the*

Noodles in the Spring Soup, which also included some of the stories he had brought back from Tibet.

When I first began illustrating here, the editors I met gave me other people's stories to illustrate. They didn't trust my own stories. But then my father, who was by then retired, visited me here, and said, "I know how you will become successful in America." He suggested that I, too, write a cookbook with Chinese recipes and stories from Tibet and call it a "secret diary of my father." I made sketches for the whole book, and I showed it to editors. But no one could quite decide what kind of book it was. Of course the book I did years later about Tibet is a version of that original idea.

Photographs of Tibet for me had become all mixed up with my father's fantastic stories, and with the mandalas and other religious art. When I met the Dalai Lama myself, it was hard to realize he was a real person and not something out of a dream.

Q: How did you get into making picture books?

A: It's so strange. Both my father and that wonderful professor I spoke about earlier taught me that "anything goes" in art, but I started as a filmmaker because making animated films was, in a sense, a comparatively safe thing to do under the regime, and not only because my father was a well-known filmmaker. The action in animation would move along, and it would be harder for a censor to pinpoint the intended meaning or context of a given image or moment. And when I would be asked — as all artists were asked — just where in the animation I was going to have an image that showed my loyalty to the regime, I could always say it was coming in one of the next frames, and that I simply hadn't gotten around to drawing it yet. In contrast, if I had put my art down as individual images on paper, or as illustrations for a book, it would have been easier for someone to get hold of it and judge it — possibly condemn me for what I had done. It was like staying one step ahead of the sheriff. It was all about disguising one's true thoughts and beliefs. Thinking that way was exhausting, but it was the art of survival. During that time, it never occurred to me to illustrate books.

I came to the United States to make a Czech government–sponsored film, and then I decided to stay and was without means in Los Angeles. A museum director I met there sent samples of my work to Maurice Sendak. I knew nothing about what a portfolio should be like, and nothing about publishing. When Maurice called me, one of his first questions was, "What are you doing in Los Angeles? It's the worst place in America." It helped that I was in Los Angeles while I was still deciding whether or not to go back to Czechoslovakia. It was a very hard decision. But the palm trees and crazy California irrationality made the contrast much clearer than it would have seemed had I already been in New York. When I came to Los Angeles, I was invited to all sorts of parties. I met Loretta Young, King Vidor. I knew it wasn't true, but I wanted to believe that all of America was just like a Raymond Chandler novel. But then people in L.A. started telling me my art was too kooky. I tried teaching in an art school but didn't know how to teach and lost most of my students. I was decorating eggs for $100. That's when Maurice Sendak called and said, "So you want to be in children's books." That wasn't really my plan, but I knew I was lucky he called and decided to go along. He said, "I will be in Los Angeles," and offered to meet me. I knew nothing, almost, about children's-book art. I knew about Maurice Sendak and I knew Tomi Ungerer's work from *Graphis*, the Swiss design magazine. In Europe, the only American art for children that was talked about was Disney. And there I was in Los Angeles, where the art all seemed that way, even in the galleries, where I saw paintings of sunsets and whales. Maurice and I met and he sent me to the American Library Association convention, which is what he was in town for, with a little note of introduction. He told me which editors to go see. I got lucky again, because while I was waiting on the convention floor to introduce myself to Greenwillow's publisher, Susan Hirschman, I somehow got into a conversation with her art director, Ava Weiss, who had grown up in Czechoslovakia. She said, "I will look at your portfolio." She did and said she was definitely interested in my work. I naively thought that after I illustrated my first book, *Bean Boy* (1984) by George Shannon, that I was set, that Greenwillow would simply take care of me from then on. I had no idea how things worked in America. When I moved to New York, I went to see the people at Greenwillow and said, "Here I am." And they said, "So, here you are." I arrived in New York with a very long story about a rhinoceros and showed it to lots of editors. Everyone disliked it. Some editors just said, "This is stupid!" and I was done in one second. Others were very kind and spent hours telling me why it was no good. To pay the rent, I did a great many illustrations for the *New York Times*. Until then, it hadn't occurred to me to be an editorial illustrator either. The *Times* loved my work right away. I thought, *This is great.* I came up with the idea to draw with dots. Nobody else was drawing that way, and I wanted my work to be different. It was a very time-consuming way to draw, but soon everybody wanted it — just as I had hoped. So all of a sudden I was working day and night, living in this little apartment in the Village. I was getting into *Newsweek, Time, Esquire,* the *Atlantic Monthly* and was sometimes paid very well. It's surprising that I stayed with the books, which didn't pay nearly as well. I think it was because of my editors, with whom I enjoyed working and because it was satisfying work that had a chance of lasting. My second book was Sid Fleischman's *The Whipping Boy* (1986), which was fortunate for me because it won the Newbery Medal. Then Frances Foster helped me shape the story that became *Rainbow Rhino* (1987), which was the first book I wrote myself. I had also begun to realize that editorial illustrators have their moment and are then replaced by someone new. There seemed to be more of a future in making books.

It evolved that I began to bring my simpler, more cheerful stories to Greenwillow and my more complex ones to Frances and Knopf. I enjoyed the excitement of New York, but it was also a lonely place for me at first. One day I was walking on Eighth Avenue and suddenly there was this woman who was waving at me, and I thought, *Finally I've met someone!* Then I realized she was hailing a cab. I clipped a similar story that appeared in the *New York Times* about a busload of tourists who had all started waving back to another woman — or maybe it was the same one! — who had also been waving not at them, but to hail a cab. So, from those two stories came *Waving* (1988). I had the joke and Susan saw right away that it could be a counting book. The pictures I did for that book and two others from the same time were related to my film work. You could place the pictures side by side and they would flow from one to the next as in a storyboard.

Q: Is being simple hard for you?

A: I think I tend to overdo things in my illustrations. I admire Tomi Ungerer's work so much because it seems to be so simple. Of course, that doesn't mean it is simple for him. In London I had as a tutor Quentin Blake. His work looks simple but he would go through many attempts to get the exact effect he wanted. It was a great challenge for me to do a book like *Fire Truck* (1998). What helped was that my son was the right age for a book like that — just as my daughter was the right age when I did *Madlenka* (2000). I did those books for them. I still have a dream of doing a very simple book, but now the children are teenagers, so it's not the same. I think all my books look best in the first sketches I do for them, even before I make the dummy. Sometimes I joke and say that because they pay me money, I feel I have to do that much more work. It's as if I'm afraid that people might say, "It's too simple." It takes a lot of daring to be simple, and I always have the intention to do things simply.

The story of *Komodo!* (1993) was very different at first. Susan reshuffled the pictures and moved bits and pieces of the story. She did it so quickly. She had the idea to use the same picture twice, once as reality and the other time as a dream. I was stunned when she suggested that.

Q: Did the Czech government try, during the years you were growing up under Communism, to suppress stories about the legendary — but the nonetheless historical — figure Jan Welzl, the hero of your book *A Small Tall Tale from the Far, Far North* (1993)? Welzl was such a free spirit.

A: Because Welzl was such a great folk hero, he was too big for them to contain, so they didn't even try. His story is amazing and of course no one had even heard of him here, so I had to tell a very compressed version of his adventures. I think it's one of my best books in terms of art but that I couldn't do him enough justice. He was *such* a romantic hero. He showed me, and I think my father and many other Czechs, that it was possible to venture out into the wider world. The really sad thing is that, although he was a great hero and adventurer, when he returned to Czechoslovakia he was treated as something of a clown. People would invite him to a bar and he would tell them his seemingly far-fetched stories about the gold rush and eating bear paws and watching the sunset with the Eskimos—and they would make fun of him even though all of it was absolutely true. My father adored him. He must have identified with him to some extent.

There was this big movement in Central Europe called "Tramping," which started when Buffalo Bill visited Europe with his traveling show. I think my grandfather saw him. People became fascinated with the Wild West, and even now, every Sunday, they dress up in what they consider Wild West outfits and take the train out of the city, and build a fire and camp and sing cowboy songs. They sleep in the open and drink beer. They did it under the Nazis. They did it under the Communists, even though it wasn't encouraged. It's a very romantic movement. This was their Shangrila. I think Welzl was part of it and that in a way my father and his Tibet stories were part of it.

Q: How did you come to terms with the story of Charles Darwin in all its complexity?

A: My editor Frances Foster always says in her quiet way, "Another ambitious project!" I had boxes and boxes of material. Darwin fascinated me, not only because he was a great thinker but also because he understood the society he was dealing with. He knew that not everyone would accept his ideas and he knew how to hold his cards close to his vest. One of the challenges of making a book about his life was that his voyage on the *Beagle* was relatively brief and that his life was a very long one, and that he spent much of his life thinking. It was hard to find a way to *show* that in the flow of a book. That's why in one of the illustrations I put him in a greenhouse, surrounded by growing things.

Q: You put maps in your illustrations, and mazes and fantasy structures, and mysterious floating symbols. It's like a private pictorial language. Where does all that come from?

A: I look at a lot of things. Maybe my tendency to take on ambitious projects comes from a wish to prove something to my father, even though he's not here not anymore. But also I enjoy it. And I think it comes from the things we hide in our mind, and the way we can see things in terms of different layers. I enjoy it when someone looking at one of my books discovers something he or she hadn't seen before, or even something that I hadn't intended to be there, but is. It's like a book within a book.

The Wall (2007) took a long time because it was a difficult story and I still wasn't able to tell it fully. I might hear a Beatles song that I love and think, *This is so simple! How did my books get so complex?* Not only do kids here not know about the history of the Cold War, but even children today in the Czech Republic and Poland and Hungary don't know because their parents don't want to talk about it.

Q: One of the last images in the book — the one showing an aerial view of the land on either side of the wall, with areas on one side marked with names like "Happiness" and "Liberty," and on the other side with "Terror" and "Lies"— reminds me of Saul Steinberg's drawing of America, which from his New Yorker's point of view was about 95 percent Manhattan.

A: I had a chance to meet him once. Our work was being exhibited together at a bookshop gallery in New York. I thought, *I will finally meet my hero!* But he must have been in a very bad mood that day, as I could tell by what I heard him say to the person just in front of me. So I never spoke to him.

Q: Steinberg, who was also from Eastern Europe, loved to make drawings that were like imaginary "official documents" of one kind or another. It was as if he was forging — in both senses of the word — a new identity for himself.

A: I think so. One of his books was called *The Passport*. I was also fascinated by his imaginary maps. During Communist times, I would sometimes forge a train ticket or a letter if, for instance, I wanted to visit Norway and didn't have the right documents. It was another way of getting around the system. The other day I sent an e-mail to someone and put at the end of the message, "Sent from my BlackBerry," even though I don't have a BlackBerry. I fooled my friend — so it worked!

I met a woman in Florida once who didn't know who I was and asked about the work I do. I told her I made children's books. She asked what kind. That's always hard to explain, so I said, "Special books." She replied, "Like Peter Sís?" That felt good!

The first time I returned to Prague it was amazing. It was still under Communist rule. I had become a U.S. citizen in May of 1989, and I immediately went to Prague — seven years after I'd left. I went to see that everyone I had known there was still alive. I was hoping that some policeman would stop me just so that I could say, "I have an American passport." The only thing that happened was at the airport when I was going through the Passport Control, somebody asked me, "Is this your first time here?" I almost think it was a joke, but I'm not sure.

WILLIAM STEIG

Born 1907, Brooklyn, New York; Died 2003, Boston, Massachusetts

with

JEANNE STEIG

Born 1930, Chicago, Illinois

William Steig was one of the *New Yorker* magazine's most celebrated artists when, at a friend's prompting, he first turned his hand to picture-book making. He was nearly sixty years old at the time. His first two children's books, *Roland the Minstrel Pig* and *C D B!* both appeared in 1968. For his third picture book, *Sylvester and the Magic Pebble* (1969), Steig was honored with the Caldecott Medal for 1970.

Although known primarily throughout his long career as a visual artist, Steig was also an inspired writer whose stories for young readers combine the dreamlike strangeness and clarity of fairy tales with the teasing wit of his own visual gags. Powerful emotions shape even the most comically far-fetched situations in which his characters find themselves, as when in *Doctor De Soto* (1982) an earnest mouse-dentist willingly risks his life to treat a surly fox in pain.

Steig was at once a very funny and a very serious man. Chatting over a brown-bag lunch one afternoon, he was quick to investigate the comic potential in the sour pickle placed before him and the sculptural possibilities of a nearby pair of plastic forks. As in his stories about a magic pebble, a magic bone, a lost harmonica, nothing in this artist's world was ever too small or too insignificant to warrant its fair share of his attention.

Steig met his fourth wife, Jeanne, a sculptor and writer, at a party in Brooklyn Heights in the mid-1960s. They lived together for the next forty years. Among the children's books the couple collaborated on are *Consider the Lemming* (1988) and *A Handful of Beans* (1998). On the morning that we met to record this interview in the Steigs' spacious, art-filled Boston apartment, Bill, at 87, looked amazingly spry and trim in a plaid shirt, jeans, and high-top sneakers, and his wife, who knew all her husband's stories, stood ready to jog his memory with an occasional gentle prompt. Our conversation took place on July 14, 1994, just as, less than a block away, final preparations were being made for Boston's outdoor Bastille Day celebration.

WILLIAM STEIG: Interviewers always ask me the same questions, like "How'd you get into this racket?" Stuff like that.

LEONARD S. MARCUS: I promise not to ask you that.

A: You can. . . .

Q: I *would* like to ask you about *Zeke Pippin* (1994). It feels as if you were revisiting some of your earlier books in this more recent one.

A: I do that all the time. Apparently I've written only one book and keep varying it.

Q: For instance, in *Farmer Palmer's Wagon Ride* (1974) there's a pig named Zeke who gets a harmonica from his father as a present.

JEANNE STEIG: I didn't remember that pig's name was Zeke.

A: I didn't either! It certainly wasn't conscious. Ezekiel, by the way, is my favorite name. If I had another son I'd call him Zeke.

Q: You like the way the name sounds?

A: What else is there to like?

Q: There's the biblical association.

A: Oh, that association doesn't mean anything to me.

Q: Did you ever want to be a musician?

A: No, but my son is a great musician, a jazz flutist.

Q: The reason I ask is that music plays a part in so many of your stories.

A: I think that's because of my son, and because I had a brother who played jazz music.

Q: Music sometimes even saves the life of the heroes of your stories; for instance, in *Roland the Minstrel Pig*. If Roland hadn't been playing his lute when the king came along, he would have fried.

JS: *The Amazing Bone* (1976) does a sort of trumpet number when it's trying to save Pearl.

Q: And Farmer Palmer is able to stop the runaway wheel in its tracks by playing on the harmonica he is bringing home for his son. So music takes on the power of magic.

A: And Farmer Palmer is a pig, right? Pigs would be the last animals who'd play harmonicas, because they can't purse their lips the way you're supposed to. It worried me that in the book he doesn't really look like he's playing.

Q: You've said elsewhere that *Pinocchio* is a book that meant a lot to you as a child.

A: I loved it as a kid. Still love it. In fact I read it every few years. I know Sendak finds fault with it. He likes Disney's *Pinocchio* better, which seems insane to me. There's something about the moralizing of the original *Pinocchio* that bothers him. He's right about that — but it's still a good story!

Q: At various points in the story, both Pinocchio and Gepetto stand falsely accused of various misdeeds, and in the end Pinocchio has to find his way back to his father in order to make amends. That element of the story resembles, does it not, the plot of *The Real Thief* (1973), which is also about the burden of living with false accusations?

A: In that connection, I remember that anytime a teacher of mine said, "Who stole so-and-so's fountain pen?" I always felt guilty.

Q: You mean even if you hadn't actually done it?

A: Never did anything, no. But somehow I always felt they were gonna accuse me.

JS: Bill had three brothers, and it was always important to all four of them to establish "who did it."

A: Who was responsible for some misdeed.

Q: So you were afraid of being accused?

A: I just felt guilty, like "I almost did it," or, "I could have done it." I don't know.

JS: You feel guilty if you see a cop!

A: I feel guilty if I'm driving and I see a cop.

JS: When you're driving you usually are!

Q: Another possible connection between *Pinocchio* and your stories is that Pinocchio starts out as a piece of scrap wood.

A: You mean, the harmonica's garbage, too?

JS: You have a whole book about a garbage collector, *Tiffky Doofky* (1978). And you married a garbage collector. I collect junk. [*To LSM*] And make sculpture out of it. I'm a sculptor.

A: When we walk down the streets of New York, I've got to keep her away from garbage cans.

Q: Does the idea of "found objects" appeal to you aesthetically?

A: No.

JS: What about that storage battery you found when you were a child?

A: Oh, right. When I was two years old, we moved from Brooklyn to the Bronx, and I found in the garbage can outside our house — kids could hang out in the street in those days without getting killed — I found a storage battery, one of those things shaped like a tall glass, and it was beautiful, everything was clean, sharp. And I said, "Look at the beautiful things people throw away."

Q: Is that your earliest childhood memory?

A: No. I can remember my first automobile ride. This was before I was two. Somebody let me sit next to him in his automobile. This new miracle. That was in Brooklyn.

Q: Were you thrilled by the ride?

A: I remember being impressed that this thing was moving without horses. Most vehicles were horse-drawn when I was young.

I also remember that when I was very young a certain kid came into our house and I wanted him kicked out but my mother told him he could stay. That got me really angry. I remember that as an injustice.

Q: You wanted all the attention for yourself?

A: No. Something this kid did displeased me, and I told him, "Get out!" But she said, "You can't do that." So I felt she had betrayed me by letting him stay.

Q: Going back to found objects, Sylvester finds something — not junk, but an ordinary pebble — that turns out to have magical properties.

A: I guess it might be related to my searching in garbage cans. But Sylvester didn't find the pebble in a garbage can, did he?

Q: My idea was just that the pebble is such an ordinary thing that most people wouldn't have thought it worth keeping.

A: Are you trying to say something about my psychology?

Q: Not in so many words. [*Laughter.*]

JS: Good luck to you!

Q: I'm just trying to see what your stories have in common with each other.

A: You mean what motivates me? You know I've said in interviews that I do it for money. Why do you write stories? That's the way I make my living. One doesn't always analyze why one does something. I began writing kids' stories because Bob Kraus said he was going to be a publisher. He said, "Will you write a story for me?" I said, "Sure." And it's what enabled me to give up drawing for advertising, which I always felt unclean about, because I didn't think that was a proper function for art, to sell things, except to sell itself.

Q: Did you find that you enjoyed writing?

A: I'd often thought of writing when I was young, you know, like every other guy. In fact, I occasionally wrote a few pages, and thought it sounded pretty good. I never thought of selling my writing except when I was young. I thought it might be a nice way to make a living. I'm probably one of the few guys who enjoys what he does. Somebody told me it must be less than one percent of the population who enjoys what they do.

Q: I wouldn't be surprised.

A: I wouldn't be surprised either. And even *I'm* not satisfied because I do some things just because they're practical, like write another story. But once I get into it I enjoy it.

Q: Did you draw much as a child?

A: Not really. We were encouraged by my old man to copy things. He thought that was a good way to learn to draw, by copying things.

Q: Do you think that's true?

A: I don't know if it's true or untrue. The best way to start somebody drawing is to give him or her a pencil and paper.

Q: Your father was an amateur artist himself?

A: Yeah. There's something on one of these walls that he did. He encouraged me to draw, but mostly he encouraged me to make some money, because he felt he had supported me for long enough. This was when I was fifteen and was starting college. I worked for him in the summertime. He was a house painter and he used to pay me in malteds. At the end of the day he'd buy me a malted. He figured I owed him these days of work because he'd worked for me up until then. Anyway, he supported me for something like twenty years, and then I supported him for twenty-five years in greater style than he supported me. But he was a nice guy. I make him sound like he was some kind of a bad egg.

Q: Did your mother also paint?

A: Yes. She was very good. That's hers over there [*pointing toward the living room*]. See the cow? To the right of the cow there's a [painting of] a vase with daisies in it. Everything in this house was done by a friend or a relative.

Q: If your father wanted you to make money, he made an unusual choice when he urged you to become an artist.

A: Here's something I say very often. My father was a socialist, and he couldn't afford to send us to school to become professionals. He said, "If you work for someone, you're being exploited. If you're the boss, you're the exploiter." He said both of those are undesirable positions to be in. So he encouraged the arts.

Q: Were there a lot of like-minded people living in your neighborhood?

A: He had a lot of European friends and they were all socialists.

Q: You did go to art school. . . .

A: Yes. First, I got into City College when I was still fifteen. I spent most of my time there in the swimming pool and in fact was on the swimming team. My father didn't think my life at the school was preparing me for the future. Then somehow I got into art school, something called the National Academy of Design Art School. My father was pushing me. Then briefly I was in the Yale School of Fine Arts, but I was disappointed in the school. So in the middle of the night one night, I packed my bag and sneaked out of the house of the friend I was staying with in New Haven and came home.

Q: Were you interested in the experimental art movements of the time, for example, in surrealism?

A: No. In those days there were very few people who were influenced by modern art. Stuart Davis was influenced by the Armory Show in 1913. But, no, I didn't appreciate modern art when I was in my late teens or twenties. I didn't appreciate Van Gogh or Cézanne either, though my kid brother did.

Q: Was there a point at which that changed for you?

A: Of course. Otherwise, I would have remained a dodo.

Q: You did those books of symbolic drawings during the 1930s and '40s.

A: You're going to ask me, *How come?*

Q: Certainly not!

A: All that stuff embarrasses me.

Q: In the foreword to one of those books, *About People* (1939), there's a reference to various theories of automatic drawing. Is that an idea or technique that has been especially important to you?

A: That's the way I start drawing sometimes. I draw without knowing what I want to do. Sometimes interesting things happen.

Q: Do you think of it as a kind of daydreaming?

A: I don't think of it that way, no. It's something that happens after I've been drawing for a while and it only happens when I'm alone. There are a lot of *New Yorker* artists who work right in the office. You can stop by, chew the fat with them, and they just keep working on their drawings. I can't understand that. In fact, even here in my own house, I can't draw if somebody's visiting Jeanne three rooms away. And I noticed living in the country that I always did my very best work when I was snowed in.

Q: Are you often surprised by what you draw?

A: Not over-surprised, but things happen that you don't expect. But you're not interested in my drawing.

Q: Sure I am.

A: If I change my paper and my pen, a whole lot of things happen, because sometimes . . . I've found a rough paper will steer you in a different direction, make you think along different lines — the fact that your hand is doing this [rather than that] brings something else out. When I'm illustrating my kids' books as compared to when I'm just drawing, I feel very constrained because I like to draw on impulse, not because "now he's standing under a tree. . . ."

Q: You spoke before about a childhood experience that left you feeling betrayed by your mother. Similar feelings would seem to be in the background of *Zeke Pippin*.

A: All kids feel misunderstood. Did you feel misunderstood as a kid? Of course kids are misunderstood. How can you understand a kid unless you are one?

Q: So you weren't drawing on a particular memory when you wrote that story?

A: No, never consciously. What would suggest that?

Q: Just that, as in other stories of yours, the emotion is so strongly felt that it doesn't seem it could have been contrived.

A: That's a compliment!

Q: I think so.

A: You mean the writing sounds like it was felt? I'm not aware that the story is related to any experience. I'd have to look at the book again.

Q: *Spinky Sulks* (1988) is another story about a kid who feels burned by his family's treatment of him.

A: I don't think that's from my experience. I mean not directly. I couldn't sulk when I was a kid. My father would give me a kick in the ass if I sulked too much.

Q: The story could be wish fulfillment, then. [*Laughter.*]

Your drawings of Spinky, Irene, and Leonard remind me a little of Crockett Johnson's drawings of kids.

A: I wasn't a big admirer of his.

Q: Your child characters, though, like his, look very solid. Do you think of children as being durable, able to take care of themselves?

A: No, I don't. I think kids are very fragile, actually, sensitive, easily hurt. Don't you? I guess they have both qualities — sensitivity and strength.

Q: Irene goes out into the storm and is battered by the elements, but somehow manages to get through it all.

A: Yeah, but I don't think that's related to my experiences. I mean everybody's been out in the snow and . . . as an adult I had trouble once in a snowstorm getting home because I was on foot and the snow was falling very fast. . . .

Q: Were you ever caught in a really treacherous storm? There really are so many of them in your books.

A: I *love* storms. I just love them.

Q: Do you seek them out?

A: Not now, but I remember when I started living in the country, I used to love to run out in a big thunderstorm to get wet, start screaming with the thunder, stuff like that. Storms are dramatic. Everybody likes that. There's also something nice about being sheltered indoors when it's stormy outside, and looking out, and feeling you're secure, and that you'd rather be in than out.

Q: As a city child, did you already have a strong feeling for nature?

A: I think it's automatic that kids love nature. I can remember in the Bronx the first time I saw a tomato growing in a lot — a junk lot. Somebody apparently had dropped a tomato there; obviously it was in the garbage. And here was this tomato hanging out on the plant. It was like a revelation to me. When I was a kid there was a lot of natural world around. There were parks; we saw trees.

When I lived on Brook Avenue in the Bronx, the New York Central Railroad ran past our house. We were on Brook, then there was the railroad, and then there was Park Avenue. And choo-choo trains would come right past our window, with big smoke and all that. And then there were bridges going from Brook Avenue to Park Avenue, across this depression where the trains ran. And when the train came by, there'd be a lot of smoke and steam. So that when the kids saw one coming, they'd get up on these bridges to get enveloped in this smoke and steam. It was part of our fun. "Hey, the train's coming!"

Q: I would like to ask you about your work for the *New Yorker*. Did the artists who worked for the magazine get to know each other?

A: Yeah, sure. I started during the Depression. The *New Yorker* paid forty dollars a drawing in those days. The next payer was something like fifteen dollars. There were two magazines called *Life* and *Judge* that also printed humorous drawings. So you'd always go to the *New Yorker* first, then you'd go to *Life* and *Judge*. And the last place you'd send a drawing to was the five-dollar market. During the Depression there were a lot of little magazines that printed cartoons — humor — which they thought the people needed because of the Depression.

Now, here's a story I tell everybody about the *New Yorker*. I submitted my first cover and they said, "We like the idea but not your rendition." You know, "We don't think it's good enough. Can we buy the idea from you?" So I said, "Let me think it over." I came home and told my mother, and she said, "Don't do that! Don't sell them the idea. They'll always expect you to sell 'em the idea." So when I came back the next day I said, "My mother told me not to sell you the idea." So they said, "OK, we'll take the cover as it is." That was my first cover. I'd been working for them awhile by then. Anyway, that's one of my stories.

Q: Were the drawings in your early books first published in the *New Yorker*?

A: No, no. There was a book called *The Lonely Ones* (1942). The *New Yorker* turned that down, and Ross regretted it afterward because it proved to be very popular.

Q: You must have gotten to know E. B. White.

A: E. B. White invited me to a gathering at his house when I first worked for the *New Yorker*. I sat around; I was too scared to say a word, and he never asked me again. I guess he felt I wasn't comfortable. I was a shy, shy kid.

Q: Maybe he was shy, too.

A: Not from my perspective. He wasn't shy at that gathering.

Q: Did you become interested in his children's books at some point?

A: Not especially, no. I saw them, sure. I always admired them.

Q: You and he write about the beauty of the universe in much the same terms.

A: That's a natural thing to do. The universe *is* beautiful.

Q: Have you read William Blake? I feel there is a lot of Blake's "The Tyger" in your children's books.

A: Oh, yeah? He's one of my favorite writers.

Q: For instance, in *Amos & Boris* (1971), it's just when Amos the mouse is floating along, admiring the beauty of everything, that he rolls off the deck of his boat and is sent scrambling for his life into the water.

A: And you relate that to Blake? That's amazing. I *love* Blake. I used to . . . every time I saw a book with Blake things I would buy it. I don't understand a lot of what he writes, but I know it's wonderful. He's one of my heroes. *Was.* Because I don't think about him now.

Q: Were you interested in his visual art, his illustrations?

A: No, I couldn't get into that. I don't think of myself as that good an artist. My work has become good, in an unusual way. And I know I have influenced a lot of people. A lot of people who draw children, for instance, say they learned how to draw kids from me, from looking at my stuff. I was able to draw certain expressions that hadn't been done before.

Q: When you did the drawing in *The Lonely Ones* that bears the caption "People are no damn good," did you mean it to refer only to adults or to children also?

A: Only adults, of course. It's interesting about that book. I got a letter from a chaplain who said that the book had had a very soothing effect on guys who had been through the Battle of Iowa Jima. I used to cherish that letter. Soldiers aren't necessarily the most cultivated guys. Usually not. But somehow this book affected them.

Q: Did you know the founder of Summerhill, A. S. Neill?

A: Oh, you know that I was associated with Wilhelm Reich, then, who was Neill's teacher. No, I never met Neill. But of course I met Reich.

Q: You said somewhere that you consider Reich one of the most important people of our time.

A: I think he was *the* most important person of this century.

Q: What was the essence of his greatness?

A: He demonstrated that space is not empty but filled with what he called orgone energy. He discovered for example that a stone, though not alive, is full of energy, which is alive. That when you die, your matter dies, but not your energy. That people's great problem is that their energy is bound up in what he called muscular armature; in other words, that most people are standing on their own balls most of the time.

Q: Did you think of some of your early drawings as depictions of people who were "armored" in the Reichian sense?

A: Yeah, that's true, of *The Lonely Ones,* for example. When I met Reich he had that book on his table. He liked it. Then later I illustrated a book of his. He was a remarkable man. He could look at you and tell you all about yourself. For example, when I was in treatment with him, once I came in and lay down on the couch and then he came in and said, "Oh! I see you're a clown today." There was nothing clownish about me. But all morning before seeing him I had been doodling and drawing clowns. I would have said that was just arbitrary. It could have been devils, could have been something else. But he saw something. Then I realized that when I draw a clown, it's not just an arbitrary choice.

Q: A. S. Neill wrote about the "self-regulating child."

A: That was a phrase of Reich's. I guess he meant that children naturally have a lot to do with their own well-being. That doesn't mean they don't need help. They're still children. But they start out life having sound natural impulses relating to their basic needs.

Q: Reichian therapy, then, was a stripping away of the "armor" to get back to those sound impulses?

A: Yes, it worked best when he was the therapist. Also, the effect isn't necessarily permanent, because the guy goes right back into the same society that screwed him up to start with.

Q: I have a theory you're probably not going to like. It concerns Reich and your book *Shrek!* (1990). Reich apparently thought there were three layers to people. There was the armored outer layer. Then there was a second layer where your wild, aggressive impulses come out. . . .

A: The outer level is the artificial person — what you present to society. In between is the drek. And underneath that is the beautiful human being.

Q: Well, here's my idea: could the "drek" be Shrek? He's an ogre at first, and it's only after he comes to the room where he has to face himself in all the mirrors that he becomes capable of falling in love.

A: I guess there is some of that in there. Sure.

Reich wound up in jail, and died of a heart attack. They burned his books. Did you know that? His work is still available, but no one has latched on to it. But when I first read a book by Reich, I said I always knew that somebody had the answer to what our problems are, and I thought, *This is it*. So I went right to him.

ROSEMARY WELLS

Born 1943, New York, New York

osemary Wells first hit her stride professionally in the early 1970s as the creator of cozily diminutive picture books for preschoolers that gave both young and old something to smile about while also pulling no punches about the emotional bumps and bruises that small children endure. Wells paced *Benjamin and Tulip* (1973), *Noisy Nora* (1973), and other books from this time with the pithy economy of a film short or vaudeville routine. By the late 1970s, she had distilled her approach even further, and with the publication in 1979 of her first set of four board books about Max and Ruby, Wells set the standard for a genre aimed at babies that was itself then in its infancy. In those landmark books, she demonstrated the possibility of creating memorable characters, simple but satisfying stories, strong emotional crosscurrents, and a robust sense of fun—all within the space of a few small pages.

Curiously, although trained as a visual artist, Wells has always felt more at home as a writer. In addition to her many picture books, she has produced a steady stream of fiction for young readers over the years, including *Through the Hidden Door* (1987), *Mary on Horseback* (1998), and *Wingwalker* (2002). Meanwhile, out of concern for preserving a valued place for books in the lives of children born into the digital media age, Wells has re-illustrated and/or recast a small shelf of children's classics, from Mother Goose rhymes to *Lassie Come-Home* (1995), and she has become a tireless advocate for literacy. Wells is an artist on a mission! We recorded this interview over dinner at one of her favorite Italian restaurants in New York City on October 18, 1999.

LEONARD S. MARCUS: What kind of child were you?

ROSEMARY WELLS: Very cheerful. Very focused and directed. Very stubborn. I would do anything I liked with a passion and was completely unwilling to do anything I didn't see any reason to do — math, for instance. So, as you can imagine, I did not do very well in school.

Q: When did you become interested in art?

A: I was drawing, apparently, at the age of two and a half. My mother was my first editor. She had a system. Every Friday evening, for as long as I can remember, she would take all my drawings for the week and pick the good ones that, as she put it, were to "go up." This meant that the drawings she had chosen would be thumbtacked to the mantelpiece and kept on display until the following Friday. My mother would say, "These are wonderful"— and just ignore the rest. That is how I learned what was good.

I was so supported and loved by both my parents. My father was a writer and my mother was a dancer, and I think they both must have said, "Ah, well, this is wonderful. Of course she's an artist, and this is what she'll do." They were very glad that I wasn't a dancer, because my mother hadn't liked parts of that life very much — all the travel and the physical ordeal. But they welcomed the life of an artist. Money was never discussed in my family. The point was to do a thing well and then money would come.

Q: I read that you were an only child. Yet you have written and illustrated so many books about sibling rivalry. Has doing those books been a way for you to imagine a kind of childhood you did not have?

A: No, I wouldn't say so. For one thing, I was only *sort of* an only child in that I had a half brother, Peter, whom I saw on weekends and in the summertime. I cannot really say why I do lots of books about sibling rivalries. Since I've had children, obviously, it's partly because I have two children. But I did *Morris's Disappearing Bag* (1975) long before I had children. It had to do with an outside awareness that I can't explain and not much to do with exploring my own experiences.

Q: I think that *Morris's Disappearing Bag* is quite a strange book. The image of the magic bag has a seemingly mythic dimension.

A: Well, there are three great dreams of childhood. One is to have eyes in the back of your head. One is to fly. And the third dream is to be able to disappear. I remember very clearly as a child seeing on television Jean Cocteau's *Orpheus,* about a man who could walk through walls. I was fascinated with that idea. I could not believe how wonderful it was. He even got out of jail by walking through the cell wall. So I was always interested in oddities of that kind. I think that is because I was brought up by a mother who, although she was born in New York City and was an American, had a Russian soul and learned all sorts of superstitions from her fellow dancers in the Ballets Russes de Monte Carlo. She believed in all sorts of strange things. I was close enough to it all as a child to take this kind of belief completely for granted: even if I did not believe it myself, I accepted that it was part of the world.

Q: Tell me more about your parents.

A: My father, whose name was James Warwick, was a playwright. His drama, *Blind Alley*, was produced on the *Playhouse 90* television series and later made into a rather well-known film called *The Desperate Hours*. My father came close to being blacklisted during the McCarthy era because his best friend was Melvin Douglas, and Melvin's wife, Helen Gahagan Douglas, ran against Richard Nixon for Congress and was smeared horribly during her unsuccessful campaign. My father stood up for Helen and became so closely associated with the Douglases that the McCarthy people started looking at him.

He stopped writing after that episode and never wrote again. He was a wonderful writer.

From the time I was tiny, my parents made me so aware of language and its power, its poetry and music. We had classical music playing in the house all the time. They believed that culture should enlighten people, not pander to them.

The one single experience I can remember from my childhood that is so relevant to what I do and to how I feel about my work is just a very slight memory without words. It's a memory of my mother when I was very, very tiny, probably three, stacking the Victrola with seventy-eight records of *Giselle* or *Coppélia* and . . . I can see her! She has on sailor shorts with three little buttons on each side and a halter. It's summertime. . . . And she put on that music and she simply danced all through the house. She did the whole ballet. From that experience I learned just how it is with art. No one said to her, "Now do this." She simply danced to that music and *became* the dance. It just came to her out of the air. It came from heaven.

Q: Compared to all this, school must have seemed a little boring.

A: For the most part, yes. But I had lots of friends and fun, too.

Q: What kinds of books did you read as a child?

A: I read absolutely everything. Not nearly as many children's books were published in the 1940s and '50s as are published now. But so many of the books of that time were very well written and had a comforting factor to them for children, as if the author was saying, "Hey, I'm really on your side and I understand who you are and no one else does!" I didn't mind reading the same books over and over again. I used to pile up all my favorite books in bed when I wasn't feeling well, and I would read them all morning long if I stayed home from school or if it was a rainy day. Then I'd listen on the radio to my favorite melodrama, *The Romance of Helen Trent* — "Can a girl from a little mining town in the West find happiness as the wife of a wealthy and titled Englishman?" I loved it! Then I would go back to my reading in the afternoon.

I loved the Beatrix Potter series. I loved everything that Robert Lawson wrote and illustrated. His books were magic to me, particularly the longer ones such as *The Great Wheel* and *Mr. Revere and I*. Those books made me love history, which was also my father's great passion. History was one subject I always did well in at school.

Q: Did the art you saw in books become connected in your mind with the art you yourself were making as a child?

A: Oh, yes. Everything I saw in books I copied. But I wasn't just looking at children's books. My grandmother had an enormous house with a huge library in which I saw, for instance, *New Yorker* cartoon books and books by the English political cartoonist David Lowe.

Q: What about comic books, which many parents of that era tried to discourage their children from reading? Did your parents feel differently?

A: My mother hated comic books and forbade them. But I got hold of them anyway. I just learned to keep them away from her.

Q: What prompted you to become an artist who made books and, in particular, a children's-book artist?

A: I didn't have any idea that I was going to become a children's-book artist, not even in art school at the Museum School in Boston, which was a hotbed of abstract expressionism. What happened was that I got married, and then I needed a job. We needed money. My first job was as an assistant buyer in purses and bags for the Lorraine shops in Boston. That lasted about a week. My second job was as a salesgirl at Lauriat's Bookstore. That was close but no cigar. I still didn't know what to do. I knew I could draw, however, and I thought, *There must be a way you can get a life as an artist. How do you do it?* I decided to try the Boston publishing companies, knowing that they published illustration. My portfolio consisted of invented book jackets for all my favorite classics. They were terrible but wild. I brought them around to Allyn and Bacon, where I was hired to substitute for an art department file clerk who had gone away for the summer. I completely ignored the files and threw myself into an American history book with a passion. By the time the summer was over, I was already editing and was given a permanent position as a book designer. I never had to worry again. Over the next six years I parlayed that first work experience into other jobs, learning the business as I went along, and then became an illustrator, and then also writer.

After we moved to New York, where my husband was studying architecture at Columbia, I got a job at Macmillan. Susan Hirschman headed the children's-book department, and one day I gave Susan a little dummy I had done of a Gilbert and Sullivan song. She accepted it on the spot and published it. She said to me, "Sit down, Rosemary. You're a Macmillan author now!" Except perhaps for "Marry me!," those were the most wonderful words I ever heard. I did sit down, and Susan proceeded to show me dozens of books from Harper, where she had worked under Ursula Nordstrom. She spent hours teaching me what was appropriate in a picture book, how children read them, everything she knew.

Q: How else did you go about learning about picture-book making?

A: Watching Sid Caesar's *Your Show of Shows* and Jackie Gleason's *The Honeymooners* on television as a child had already taught me about comedy and timing. All of my books are tiny theater pieces, and you'll find that it was from those shows that I learned to do what I do.

Television then was in its infancy and took its patterns and formats from the stage. Even the movies — musicals, for instance — were conceived in a theatrical way, as if staged. My entire sense of language and of story and plot come from my father and from theater. That is how I think about my books.

Q: During the late 1960s, Susan Hirschman and others were making a specialty of publishing picture books for very young children, and you yourself, from your early books onward, have very often been drawn in that direction. Had the time somehow become right for this new focus?

A: Very possibly, but I have no idea why. By then I had left Macmillan and had begun publishing for Phyllis Fogelman at Dial. Phyllis probably perceived an opening — a hole that needed to be filled — and moved right in to fill it. That is what the most creative people always do. A generation earlier, Margaret Wise Brown, who regarded children as people, had seen the possibility of an authentic literature for very young children. No one had ever attempted that before. Phyllis as well was part of Ursula's "charmed circle" at Harper, and she wanted to continue that tradition. As for myself, I don't think about the children who read my books. That is, I don't think about who my audience is going to be. I relate to children as individual human beings, not as a group or species! As I work, I simply think about the book itself.

Q: When did you first think of yourself as a writer?

A: I knew right away that, even though I was an illustrator, the stories were more important, and I wanted to do them. I was a far more accomplished and polished writer early on than I was an illustrator. It took me a long time before I was even a self-respecting artist, not just a loopy cartoonist. It took me twenty-five years to bring my art to the level of my writing.

We were talking earlier about childhood influences, and here I would like to make what I consider a crucial distinction. None of the actuality of what a writer or an artist is able to do has anything to do with childhood. Childhood affects subject matter. Those stories I choose to write, those subjects I choose to illustrate, have to do with experience, or with likes or dislikes that are conditioned. That's nurture. But talent is nature. Children's literature is practiced extremely well by a given number of people in every generation — maybe twenty in all. Talent is a gift from God. In my case, my writing talent is far greater than my drawing talent, which I have had to prune and school and develop.

Q: *Benjamin & Tulip* (1973), which is one of the first books you both wrote and illustrated, stands out as a far more raw book emotionally than are most books being published for young children today.

A: It's about the way kids are. As a child you know who in your class is capable of pushing you around. Every child does. I don't ever try to put an adult happy face on childhood. This is one of the problems I have with adult political agendas being filtered into children's books — "everybody's happy together or at least everybody should be" themes, with no reality to them. The reason children have responded to *Benjamin & Tulip* is that in Benjamin they see Norman Buck, who used to wait after school for me and my best friend Ginny O'Malley and push us off our bicycles and roll us down the hill. There have always been bullies. This is childhood, and I try to write about it without prettying it up for grown-ups.

Q: The late 1960s and early '70s was a time of small picture books. Besides your own, there were, for example, the very small books by Martha Alexander and Mercer Mayer. Did you enjoy working on that very intimate scale? Why aren't more books like those being published now?

A: I still love little books. They're for little hands, and children love them, too. But now most books are large because publishers want a book to serve as a poster for itself. They want it seen across a big store. They want a book that is a big presence.

Q: You have often said that you based Ruby and Max on your two daughters, Victoria and Beezoo. Why did you draw your characters as rabbits rather than as people?

A: I always used animals. One reason is that animals are easier for me to draw. I have found it hard to draw really appealing children. Real children are very grubby and are not always nice to look at. So while I wouldn't want to idealize children, I also would not necessarily want to show them as they really are, either. And to go back to *Benjamin & Tulip,* that is a story about children pushing each other around. If I showed that happening between real children it wouldn't be publishable, and it wouldn't be funny. But with animals it becomes one step removed from reality, and therefore acceptable.

Q: Tell me about Angus, your first West Highland white terrier. You based some of your early animal characters on him, did you not — even animal characters that are not depicted as dogs?

A: If you look at the bunnies or any of my other animal characters, you'll see that they are all secretly West Highland white terriers, who are among the most expressive of dogs. Westies have ears that give you amazing signals and expressions. Their eyes and their body language are expressive, too.

They're very dominant little dogs. If you get one, it trains you; you don't train it. Yet they are also very warm. They kiss you and they talk to you endlessly!

Q: Given your great affection for the dogs, why did you wait so long to make books that feature a West Highland white terrier, as you have in the McDuff series?

A: If you go back to *Tell Me a Trudy* (1977) by Lore Segal, you'll find the first time I put a Westie in one of my books. But there are reasons why I didn't want to have a Westie character. Dogs don't fit into my world of soft, mystical bunnies. The bunnies live in their own world. Dogs are domesticated. Dogs are going to have a collar and a tag and a master.

Q: Did you envision a board-book format for your first Max and Ruby stories right from the start?

A: No, I didn't know what those stories were. To begin with, I simply thought of them as very short story books, meant to be sixteen pages long, or half the usual length of a picture book. I was thinking possibly of cloth books. It was Phyllis Fogelman at Dial who came up with the format we used. They became the very first board books with real stories and characters.

Q: Why did you decide to re-illustrate the Max and Ruby board books? What considerations were involved in remaking those books?

A: I have also re-illustrated *Noisy Nora* (1973), *Morris's Disappearing Bag,* and *Timothy Goes to School* (1981). The considerations are about the same. You leave all the good parts but change what you could do better now. The pictures have changed because I'm a more sophisticated artist and have learned other techniques. And one thing I didn't want to happen is to have what I consider my life's best work in stories illustrated by a "less than her best" Rosemary Wells. Better to re-illustrate them myself than to have some-body else come along and do so in fifty years' time. These were particularly nice projects — *Morris* and *Timothy*. I re-illustrated them in 1999 with my new-old editor Regina Hayes at Viking. A very young Wells worked on the "original" *Morris* and *Timothy* with a very young Regina Hayes at Dial in the early '70s.

In *Max's Birthday* (1985), I changed the dragon in the original version to a lobster because I had done *Max's Dragon Shirt* (1991) in the meantime and no longer found the dragon in the earlier book very convincing. If you look very carefully at the lobster, you'll see that he comes straight from the Little Nemo comic strip. I think the lobster is much funnier.

Max and Ruby are a lot bigger. The characters fill the page better. They have on their birthday clothing. Their actions are more anatomically believable if not exactly correct for made-up bunnies that are sort of bun-nies and sort of West Highland white terriers. It's graphically more pleasing. The "around and around the lobster went" page is very decorative, which hadn't happened in a Max book before.

My way of working also changed. Back then I would first draw a char-acter in pen line. The line and the expression would be all right, but they did not have very good definition because I had never been taught how to vary the thickness of the line, or about the beauty that comes of using line well. I would fill in the color and the background last. Now I do the opposite. I take the page as a space. I put a little box around most of my drawings, which makes each one its own little world. And so I compose in that space, drawing the character first in pencil, and then I go over it in very light blue pen. Then I color in everything and only at the very last do I do the black line.

Q: Tell me about your working relationship with Susan Jeffers. It goes back many years, does it not?

A: I met Susan Jeffers in 1966 at Macmillan. We were both designers under Ava Weiss. Our collaborations can be explained by the fact that there are things that I can write, and that Susan can draw, that I can't draw. As Phyllis Fogelman, who was my editor at Dial for many years, once said, "Rosemary, *everything* you draw is funny." That is true. But not everything I write is funny and so there have been times when I needed a different illustrator.

Q: In an article called "The Artist at Work: The Writer at Work," which appeared in the March/April 1987 issue of *The Horn Book,* you stated that you were glad to have entered the field at a time when original writing was encouraged and retellings of classic stories were less emphasized. Has there been some change in the children's-book field that has prompted you, in more recent years, to become more interested in retelling classic texts yourself?

A: I still think I was lucky to come into the field when new writing was what publishers most wanted and when young artists and writers were given a lot of time to develop — six or seven books before their books were expected to sell. And I still think that retelling and re-illustrating old stories is not a very important thing to do. I've done *Lassie Come-Home* and *Rachel Field's Hitty* (1999) and don't foresee doing any more.

Children's reading patterns have changed since the time those two books were published. No one was reading *Lassie* or *Hitty* at all anymore. I felt the story of *Lassie* was a wonderful one about the loyalty of a dog and the absolutely terrific effort that an animal will make for love. *Hitty* was a great favorite of Susan Jeffers. I came to it late because I didn't like dolls as a child. Hitty is such a marvelous character, but some parts of the original book are racist and we simply can't have any group of people in today's children's literature portrayed as superior or inferior to another group. The 1920s, '30s, and '40s was a time when nearly all children's books were written by educated, usually well-meaning white people, who were sympathetic to people of color but who sometimes expressed their attitudes patronizingly or in other ways that are simply no longer acceptable. And so to preserve *Hitty* at all, the book had to change. So I gave Hitty a variety of owners that accurately reflected American history, and I think I made them as real as Rachel Field would have done. It was not hard to write in Rachel Field's voice, because my grandmother used to speak in exactly the way that Rachel Field writes. So I just recalled her voice and it was great fun for me to do.

Q: How did *My Very First Mother Goose* (1996) and *Here Comes Mother Goose* (1999), the two nursery-rhyme collections edited by Iona Opie and illustrated by you, come about?

A: Amy Ehrlich, the editor in chief of Candlewick Press, was another old friend from Dial. I had known Amy and worked with her on many of my best books. Amy asked me if I would do an enormous Mother Goose for them. At first I hesitated. I began to think of all the Mother Geese I knew. There would be a picture, the rhyme in maybe fourteen-point type, and the reader would keep turning the pages, on and on, and it just wasn't any fun. I didn't want to do that. But then I got into Mother Goose with Iona herself. Iona loves to say, "This is the Shakespeare of the kindergarten. This is the shortest great poetry of the English language." She also says, "This is the greatest short poetry of the English language." With her help, I realized that Mother Goose rhymes are a gold mine of almost surreal, random poetry, that these are the words of our great-great-great-grandfathers and mothers, who were harness makers and shoemakers and milkmaids and farmers who didn't have radio or any books at all — just the handed-down oral storytelling tradition. This was the poetry of real people who could not read or write but still had the English language at their command.

So I set aside everything else I was doing and took each poem and made a drawing without regard to size or format or the overall length of the book. And when I was done I sent this pile of 165 paintings and sequences of paintings to Walker Books' designer, Amelia Edwards, who put them all together and made a book. She did it once and she did it twice.

Among my favorites are the jump-rope rhymes because they come from the children themselves and they're always the most fun. When children repeat something hundreds and hundreds of times, you know it's going to scan well and there's not going to be an extra syllable. That kind of poetry is so completely rounded and beautiful that the sense of it doesn't matter. The rhythm and rhyme is everything that matters. This is one from the second book:

> *Manchester Guardian,*
> *Evening News,*
> Here comes a cat
> In high-heeled shoes.

It's wonderful because it has no relation to anything except its own logic.

Q: It takes you out of this world.

A: Yes, but at the same time, this is very serious art. It's not "product."

Q: Do you think that children today know Mother Goose rhymes to the same extent that they did when you were growing up?

A: No. Everybody's in front of the TV. Childhood has changed in ways that scare me. When I was a child, kids were expected to organize their own games, and they did. Boys played pickup baseball. They organized their own teams. Maybe everything wasn't fair. But they did it. And girls played a lot of hopscotch and jump rope. We organized the games ourselves. The parents weren't interested. They didn't come around and say anything. And this is what we did because we didn't have television. Children had a world of their own making, and if it wasn't always fair it didn't matter, because that's how it was, and they learned a lot from the experience. Adults didn't listen to their rhymes. Nobody cared. But now children's culture has been completely taken over by television. And so no, children don't know the old rhymes the way they used to. They know commercials instead. And they don't make up their own rhymes the way they used to, either.

One of the scariest aspects of all this is that commercial culture has taken over what I like to call the "popular crowd" or peer group. Everybody has to wear Gap clothes, or whatever the fad is, because television has taken over what's cool. It's not that you didn't have to be cool when I was growing up. Everybody wanted to be cool. But it wasn't quite so in-your-face or so early. Now there is very little childhood left. The more time that is spent in front of a screen, the less childhood. We're ending up with children who are well trained in materialism. And that is the reason I became involved in the "Read to Your Bunny" campaign, which is the first time I have ever been involved in any kind of public advocacy. The campaign — "the most important twenty minutes of the day are the twenty minutes you read to your child" — just came to me because of this. Children who don't have reading-aloud experience with their parents on a regular basis are missing out on one of childhood's most important experiences.

Q: I asked if you would bring along some books other than your own that you might want to talk about. What did you choose to bring?

A: The first, a catalog by Chris Beetles, is a compilation of artwork by the English watercolorist for children's books of the 1920s and '30s Honor Appleton. Not many people have heard of Appleton, but I've learned enormously from her work. Her art is so toy-centered and beautifully drawn. In *Here Comes Mother Goose* I drew upon Cecil Aldin, Appleton, and the French artist Bernard Rabier, who was clearly an inspiration for Dr. Seuss.

The Doors of San Miguel de Allende is a book of photographs of doors found in a certain town in Mexico. I look at these photographs if I need to calm down at the end of the day. As I look at them, I sometimes also find architectural details that I need for my illustrations. But most of all, these pictures put me in a kind of meditative mood.

And here is a book called *Wheels: The Magical World of Automated Toys.* Many of the toys photographed in this book appear as real vehicles in my children's books—the yellow car driven by a cat, for instance, at the beginning of the "As I Was Going to St. Ives" chapter of *Here Comes Mother Goose.*

This is *The Friendly Book* by Welleran Poltarnees, who does marvelous compilations of art from historical children's books, which I love to pore over. And here is *French Trademarks of the Art Deco Era,* which I find just addictive. A book such as this gives me a sense of the world graphically from the time when I was young. And somehow trademarks and graphic symbols manage to become tiny but complete worlds in themselves. They would be enough—just one square inch of black-and-white art—to transport me as a child thousands of miles away. I had to learn the secret of that, and that's what I have been trying to do. Such images, along with fabric designs and biscuit-tin labels and toys and dollhouse furniture and comic strip art from the 1920s and '30s, are now a visual subtext in my work, especially in the Mother Goose books.

Q: You seem to have used the Mother Goose books as a laboratory for experimenting with new techniques—collage, for instance, for the *"Manchester Guardian"* rhyme. And for the one that begins "Early in the morning at eight o'clock," you devised imaginary postage stamps for imaginary countries.

A: Children love mail. I was fascinated with postage stamps when I was little. I also make my own rubber stamps and stamp them all over my artwork now.

Q: Why did the Mother Goose books in particular become the ones that prompted you to try so many new techniques and approaches?

A: Because the rhymes are so wild and there is no narrative line or character I have to follow episodically, scene after scene. With Mother Goose I could, in a sense, relax.

Q: Do you have a favorite among all your books?

A: *Voyage to the Bunny Planet* (1992) is my favorite of all the books I have ever done. That set of three small books and *Mary on Horseback* (1999) are my best writing. By the time I had children, my mother lived next door to us in Westchester County and I was able to see my childhood almost repeated through them. I could see how my mother affected my own children as she became like a second mother to them. She was such a free spirit, so pure in what she liked and disliked. I wanted to give my mother to the children in those three books — Claire and Felix and Robert — to have her give them the same huge comfort that I think she gave to my children.

But the Bunny Queen is really the mother of us all in heaven, coming down and pulling you away from the awful, blistered feet of the real world, and the socks running down into your shoes and the food you don't like to eat and the people who tease you and the fact that you can't do a cartwheel or that you're cold or hungry or not feeling well. The Bunny Queen is there to rescue you. They're really very meditative books. It's about the power of the mind to heal everything and transport the soul.

Q: We seem somehow to have come back to that book of doors, which you said earlier also puts you in a meditative state of mind. What exactly is it about the doors that you find comforting? Do you like to imagine what might be on the other side of the doors?

A: Not really. The doorways are all possibilities, and there are eighty-five of them in the book. It is enough to see them, rather like being six years old and knowing your mother and father are asleep in their bed in the middle of a dark night. If you know they are there, you need not open the door.

MO WILLEMS

Born 1968, Chicago, Illinois

As a child, Mo Willems recalls, "All I was being told was, 'No. No, no, no.'" Now one of the great appeals for him of being a picture-book artist is that he gets to give other children the chance to do what he so often longed to do then: turn the tables on the grown-ups and be good and loud about it. Now Willems says, "I go to a library, and I've got five hundred kids yelling 'No!' to me at the top of their lungs. . . . It's a very super-cool thing."

Willems's early experience as a stand-up comic proved to be good training for getting up in front of a throng of squirming six-year-olds. So were the years he wrote and did animation work for *Sesame Street* and other children's television shows. A comedian soon finds out that he can lose his audience in the blink of an eye. Animators likewise learn to get to the point, and to be ruthless about tossing out even the greatest idea if it doesn't move the story forward. Lessons like these have served Willems well as a maker of picture books, an art form that for him comes with the added appeal that over the span of thirty-two pages he can be his own boss. Now Willems himself is the only person who can yell "No" to him — except of course for those five hundred children. Willems is one of those rare talents who really did "burst on the scene" and whose books really are "something new." We recorded our conversation at the Housing Works Bookstore Café, in lower Manhattan, on the afternoon of December 2, 2009.

❧ ❧ ❧ ❧ ❧ ❧ ❧ ❧ ❧ ❧ ❧ ❧ ❧ ❧

LEONARD S. MARCUS: Tell me about growing up in New Orleans.

MO WILLEMS: Even though I'm the son of Dutch immigrants who moved there when I was four, I consider New Orleans my hometown because of how it shaped me. New Orleans is a great place for storytellers, and I was lucky enough to have spent a slightly dissolute youth in blues bars listening to folks sitting around telling each other outrageous stories. When everyone ran out of stories, they would barrel out of the bars, do something colossally stupid, and come back with new tales to tell. Eventually, I started doing stand-up comedy there along with a young English teacher, a hyper fireman named Blaze, and a host of other eccentrics.

After high school I moved to London to do stand-up. I had friends in London and had already spent a couple of summers taking drama courses there. I was young, hungry, ready to learn, and a big Anglophile, so my brief time there was formative.

Q: Was doing stand-up comedy good preparation for making picture books?

A: Certainly. Not that I was ever very good at it, but the challenge of coming up with new material and learning to read your audience was important. All those late hours in smoky clubs taught me to stay on my toes and never fall in love with a joke. Most importantly, it gave me a sense of what's *not* funny. Once you can instinctively tell what doesn't work, whatever is left probably will.

Q: Were you the class clown in school?

A: Um . . . If school was a circus, I was the guy who cleaned up the elephant crap. Especially in elementary school, I was a deeply unpopular kid who wore weird clothes and had weird foreign parents, including a mother who worked!

Consequently, things like being cast as the lead in the eighth-grade play, *L'il Abner,* became less a victory than an excellent opportunity for my classmates to ridicule me. For one thing, I was so skinny, the costume folks had to sew fake muscles into my shirt. Unfortunately, every time I lifted my arms, the muscles plopped down under my arms, so I looked like somebody's grandmother.

At the first rehearsal, the girl who was cast as Daisy Mae announced that under no circumstances would she touch me before, during, or after the performances. Immediately the teachers replied, "All right. We can work around that." So the big, romantic love song was choreographed in such a way that she and I were singing back to back, with not even our backs touching! I flew to London the day after high-school graduation.

Q: Did you do a lot of drawing as a child?

A: Absolutely. My dream was to be a daily syndicated cartoonist. My free time was spent reading and copying *Peanuts* or drawing my own cartoons. In second and third grade, the class bully wouldn't beat me up in return for my drawing him a cartoon, so I was turning out a new cartoon every day.

Q: Just like Scheherezade!

A: Or like working in cable television. By high school I was doing cartoons both for the school newspaper and a strip for the local real-estate newspaper called "Surrealty." That's when I illustrated my first book—a collection of eccentric New Orleans-isms that had been compiled by two local college professors. Fortunately for posterity, no copies exist. . . .

Q: Despite being unpopular, did you do well in school?

A: Sure, my grades were fine. At my prep school it was cool to be smart, so nobody was making fun of me for that. On the other hand, one of my cartoons was banned because I had used the word *fart* in it. I had to submit an official letter of apology in which I wrote that I hoped the whole stink would blow over soon. . . .

Q: Tell me more about your parents.

A: After I was born, my mother, justifiably, was looking for a way to get out of the house, so both my parents took a pottery class. My father, who had never thrown a pot before, fell in love with it. My mother, who had never gone to school, fell in love with college and eventually went to law school. So, when I was about eight, my mother became a lawyer, and my father quit his day job and became a full-time potter.

In retrospect, much of my philosophy about making books comes directly from what I learned while hanging out in my father's studio as a kid. It's where I developed my deep respect for craftsmanship. His idea was that every piece of pottery should have a utilitarian purpose and that the form of the thing should derive from its use.

That's how I think about my bookmaking. I'd rather be a craftsman than an artist. An artist waits for an audience to understand his or her work. But a craftsman tries to understand the audience. For me, the printed book is the thing, easily obtainable and reusable. That's much cooler than seeing my work on a museum wall.

I think it's different now than it was for artists of Maurice Sendak's generation, who insisted that picture books were filled with Art with a capital *A*. Partly that's because the battle's been won; there are lots of galleries and museums catering to original illustration.

Ultimately, for me, that's gravy. I'm less interested in the original than in the reproductions, because it's the reproductions that are out in the real world doing the real work.

Q: Did you become interested in making picture books while you were in England?

A: No. The first time I thought about it seriously was after I'd been working at *Sesame Street* for a few of years. It was a confluence of slowly realizing that I *enjoyed* the challenge of writing for children more than the "grown-up" stuff I'd been doing and a weird chance phone call.

One day I got a call from L.A. from some people who were making a television series based on a book by Maurice Sendak, *Seven Little Monsters,* and wondered if I might want to be involved in some way. The backstory was that Sendak had pitched some films based on the idea for *Sesame Street* years back, and when CTW [Children's Television Workshop] rejected them, he turned them into books. I remember thinking to myself, "*Sesame Street* rejects some of my ideas every week!" Maybe one of them could become a book. I even tried to do it with CTW, but they told me in no uncertain terms that I would never have a book published, so I should just go back to making little cartoons.

Q: How had you gotten to *Sesame Street*?

A: Luck, mostly. I'd been doing sketch comedy in New York hosting a bi-weekly show called the *Monotony Variety Show,* for which the audience-to-performer ratio was generally about one to one. Somehow, I got a freelance gig in the research department of Children's Television Workshop, where I hawked my show. The people at *Sesame Street* heard about my sketch work and invited me to audition as a writer for the show. Eight months of audition scripts later, I was in.

Q: What did you learn at *Sesame Street* that has carried over into your books?

A: Clarity, brevity, and that funny is funny. *Sesame Street* is where I not only learned how to write for kids, it's where I learned that I *wanted* to write for kids. Before that, I'd set my sights on writing for snarky twenty-somethings like myself. As an animator, *Sesame Street* is where I created my first continuing character, Suzie Kabloozie, and my first abstracted backgrounds that served as emotional templates as opposed to locations, a technique I used in the Pigeon books and *Leonardo the Terrible Monster* (2005).

As writers, we were required each season to attend a weeklong seminar on child development research, which, frankly, could become onerous. But one year we had a fabulous speaker who told us, "I saw a sign in a school that said, 'Everyone is number one.' Well, that's a statistical impossibility. Someone is going to be number eighty-three and somebody is going to be ninety-two." That rocked my world!

Philosophically, a lot clicked for me that day. Kids, like me, are constantly failing at things, but we live in a culture that is terrified of admitting even the slightest mistake. Personally, my legion of personal and professional failures have turned out to be quite helpful for me in the long run. Maybe I should write about failure. Besides, failure is always funny.

Q: As in Leonardo's story.

A: Right. That is the book that took me the longest to write. I probably started it fifteen years before it was published. In the beginning it was about the Big Bad Wolf's cousin, the Little Bad Wolf. Now, Big Bad was a very successful wolf—ate a lot of grannies and so on. But when Little Bad bit somebody's shin, people would smile and say, "That tickled. Isn't he cute?"

Somehow, I could never find the moment of redemptive badness for him, the thing that would make him good at being *really* bad. Then one day, when she was about three, my daughter walked in and said, "ROAR! I'm a terrible monster!" And of course she wasn't. She was adorable.

But, that phrase clicked and suddenly, by turning the wolf into a monster, the "bad" to "terrible," the story came quickly.

Q: As you began making picture books, were you inspired by other artists' books, either books you were looking at then for the first time or those you remembered from childhood?

A: The first Pigeon book was certainly informed by *Where the Wild Things Are*. I became interested in Sendak's manipulation of the audience's response by changing the sizes of images over the course of the story. In my case, I decided to change the background colors instead.

As a child I had many books illustrated by the Dutch artist Fiep Westendorp, who was sort of the Mary Blair of Holland. My way of drawing is strongly influenced by her style, which was very angular, with pastel colors, a scratchy line, and highly stylized elements: her feet, the noses, the hands were abstracted almost to the point of symbolism.

Now, however, I'm really trying to stay away from overt influences, which I worry can become a crutch. The best way to avoid becoming trapped in trends is to ignore them.

Q: When you did the first Pigeon book, did you have it in mind to see just how simple you could make an illustration that worked?

A: Sure. The idea was to make the drawings seem like they were done as quickly as possible, like Japanese calligraphy. It's also important to me that a five-year-old be able to reasonably draw the characters in my stories. The books themselves should be merely a point of entry for their own creations, based on copying my characters.

Q: I read that you wrote a letter once to Charles Schulz.

A: When I was five I wrote to him, asking if I could have his job when he died. One thing I loved about Charlie Brown was that he was the only pop-culture star who wasn't always smiling. I hated Mickey Mouse and his pals always merrily dancing around like they were on lithium.

Charlie Brown was miserable, but funny. I could laugh *and* sympathize with Charlie Brown. I liked that balance, and I still do.

One of the great lessons I learned from Schulz's strip is that no one in the strip has any idea they are in a funny strip; for them their situations are deadly serious. That's something I am careful to carry over in my work: the Pigeon thinks his books are tragedies!

Q: In *Leonardo,* you seem to have gotten very interested in typography.

A: Typography is really just another form of illustration for me. The type I chose for *Leonardo* is great fun because it has little claws *and* gives the story a vaudeville feeling.

The shape and size of my books are also essential to telling the story. For *Leonardo,* I wanted the book to be big enough to be awkward in a child's lap so as to emphasize Leonardo's smallness. My first book was square because a square picture frame is what I was used to from television. After that, I suddenly realized I could have fun playing around with different aspect ratios.

Q: How do you think about the writing in your books — the role it plays in relation to the pictures?

A: For a story's text to work, it needs to be incomprehensible. Otherwise you wouldn't need the pictures. My job is to let the audience figure out what's going on by themselves. So, in *Leonardo* I didn't *say* the monster was small. I created a situation (large book, lots of empty space surrounding a small drawing) where kids feel the smallness on their own.

Q: Is it true that you drew *Naked Mole Rat Gets Dressed* (2009) using one of Charles Schulz's pen nibs?

A: During a recent tour I realized I was going to be near the Schulz museum in Santa Rosa, California, so I contacted Schulz's widow and met her for lunch. I was taken to Sparky's office and shown his unfinished drawings, which was a thrill of a lifetime.

To top it off, I was given one of his pen nibs, which is a kind that isn't made anymore. I thought, *Awesome!* I don't believe in magic or love at first sight, but there was an emotional quality to having it — particularly because it turned out to be so hard to use. That pissed me off! Schulz had a much thicker, more interesting line than I could get with this pen.

Q: Is *Naked Mole Rat* like *Peanuts* in some other way? Do you think of it as a tribute to Schulz?

A: Certainly the designs of the Naked Mole Rats are top heavy, as if they're about to tip over. Initially I did this just to be funny. Later, however, I realized, *Oh, my God, these Mole Rats are Snoopy!*

For every book, I set a personal aesthetic challenge. For this one, the challenge was to draw characters without mouths and still find a way to indicate when they're happy or sad. The emotion comes into the drawings in the placement of the eyes and in the posing. As an animator you learn that if you draw your character in silhouette and you can't tell what he's thinking, it's a bad drawing.

Like with the writing, the less I put of the intended emotion in my drawing, the more the viewer then has to supply for him or herself. That's what James Marshall did so well in the George and Martha books.

Q: Tell me about making *Knuffle Bunny* (2004).

A: The whole Knuffle project started by accident. One day I was sitting in my art director's office with her and my editor, telling a funny story while we waited for some printouts. Immediately, Alessandra Balzer, my editor, said, "That's a book!" I said, "No, no. It's just a funny little story." But she insisted (and Alessandra is very good at insisting), so I went home and thought about it seriously. In the process of expanding and fictualizing the story, I realized she might just be right.

I'd done a personal story about my family for a DC Comics anthology about cartoonists' experiences of 9/11 and made tracings from photographs for the backgrounds. So when it came time to do the illustrations for *Knuffle Bunny* I thought I would do the same. But the characters weren't popping and I couldn't get it to work. Then one of my drawings accidentally fell on top of one of the photographs on my light box, and I suddenly had the idea to combine the two.

This was a very exciting moment for me, because I knew I'd come up with something different. Plus, I thought I'd get out of the dull, laborious work of drawing backgrounds. Of course, I had to learn how to alter photographs digitally so they would look the way I wanted them to look and to convey the emotional truth I wanted, which took a good deal more time than just making some drawings.

Q: You set up a really interesting contrast between the realism of the photographs and the caricatures of the characters.

A: I think the cartoon characters in the Knuffle Bunny books are *more* real than the photographic backgrounds. They're purer than more realistic drawings of the characters would have been, because their design focuses on their emotional side. If the drawings had been more realistic, my audience would be asking narratively irrelevant questions like, "How did she get the pants on her head?"

Who cares? I want you to see my characters for who they actually are, to expose their core jealousy, anger, love, joy, and silliness. I want you to see yourself in them.

VERA B. WILLIAMS

Born 1927, Hollywood, California

Vera B. Williams recalls: "I was a child with a lot to say. When people grew tired of my talking, I drew pictures. But then I had to tell about the pictures. Even with acting and dancing, I couldn't get it all told."

Williams turned out to have a lot to say later in life, too. She has written poetry, worked as a printmaker and painter, designed magazine covers, been a teacher, and played an active role on behalf of political and social causes of concern to her. As an author and illustrator for children, she has created picture books (as well as poetry and the autobiographical novel *Scooter* [1993]) of rare emotional depth, crafting stories that, unlike most of those to be found in contemporary picture books, do not take the material well-being of their heroes for granted. Because Williams's recurring character,

273

young Rosa, and her family and friends cannot have everything they want, they must decide what matters most to them. As they make their choices, we come to know them all the better — and ourselves as well. At the same time, Williams's books never want for color and flashes of the street-smart, down-to-earth humor that also salts her conversation. Although at more than eighty years old she has long since put her roller skates on the shelf for good, Williams seems very close in spirit to the feisty ten-year-old who once went barreling helter-skelter down the Bronx, New York, streets of an eventful Depression-era childhood. A good twenty years after first meeting, we sat down to record this interview in her Greenwich Village apartment on November 9, 2009.

~~~~~~~~~~~~~~~~~~~~~~~~

LEONARD S. MARCUS: Tell me about the time you met Eleanor Roosevelt.

VERA B. WILLIAMS: I must have been eight, which was in 1935. I met her at an exhibition that was held at the old Museum of Modern Art, which was in a townhouse down the block from where it now is. The occasion was an exhibit of WPA art from classes for adults and for children. My sister had a sculpted horse that she had made at the Bronx House, which was a settlement house where we took art classes, and I had a painting that I had made there called *Yentas*. In my memory Mrs. Roosevelt was coming around the room looking at everything, followed by Movietone News. I was standing by my painting and she stopped to admire what I had done. I had a conversation with her, told her how to pronounce *yentas* [which means "gossipy women" in Yiddish], and what the yentas were saying. I think she called it "Yen-*TASS*" at first! Mrs. Roosevelt was a very big hero in our family. We loved her. She belonged to us. We were grateful for her work on behalf of the WPA, which had meant so much to us growing up poor in the Bronx.

Q: Tell me about your parents. Did they encourage your love of art?

A: My mother was very interested in having us paint and draw. She was interested in education. She had opened a little nursery school in our apartment. My father wasn't working, and so I thought it was because she needed to make some money that she started the school. But she was interested in progressive education.

Q: Did she have any training as a teacher?

A: No, she didn't. She had gone to work after eighth grade. But she educated herself by attending the free lectures at Cooper Union and was part of that group of radical immigrant women who had made it their business to learn. Both my parents tended toward an anarchist view of life and education and were very devoted to the idea of culture for poor people, to what came to be called "Bread and Roses."

Q: How did you happen to be born in Hollywood?

A: My parents were wanderers with poetic natures, and after World War I they set out on a cross-country trip in search of adventure. In the photographs they look like hippies, sitting in front of their tent in their big boots and headbands. Eventually they reached Los Angeles.

Q: What were you like as a child?

A: I was irrepressible, extremely talkative, and quite cute. I liked fun but I also had quite a developed sense of the tragic. I had some difficult things to put up with before I was even five. We moved a lot, and around the time I was four, my sister and I lived for about a year and a half in the Jewish Home for Children in San Francisco. My mother had a job at that time and my father was away, possibly in prison. I still don't know for sure. My sister and I heard conflicting stories, and we didn't have the sense to ask them directly.

Q: Were you enterprising like your character Rosa?

A: I took one of my first allowances, which must have been a nickel, and got on a bus whose route I had some vague idea about. This was after we had moved to the Bronx. I went by myself and stayed on for about as far as I thought I could walk back home from, as I didn't have the return fare.

As part of the Victory Garden program, I got myself a little plot of land in Crotona Park where I could grow vegetables. I had a proprietary attitude toward New York City and its parks and museums: I believed they belonged to me. I was very inspired by Ruth Sawyer's book *Roller Skates,* which I read over and over, and which I think is very much in the background of my book *Scooter.* I, too, roller-skated everywhere and appreciated the feeling of being free in New York.

Q: Did you know what you wanted to be when you grew up?

A: I wanted to be lots of things. I liked acting. I liked showing off. I first may have thought of becoming a painter after I became aware of Rosa Bonheur, who meant a great deal to me. My parents, who didn't have money for books, did buy us V. M. Hillyer's *A Child's History of Art.* I was very taken with it.

As a result of the WPA show where I met Eleanor Roosevelt, my sister was approached by an art educator named Florence Cane, who had an art school on the twenty-fourth floor of one of the buildings in Rockefeller Center. My sister began taking art classes there every Saturday when she was ten. I would come with my parents on the Third Avenue El to pick her up, and would just stand there and prattle. One day Mrs. Cane asked me if I would like to take classes, too. I said yes and continued to go there all the way through high school. We never had to pay anything.

We had wonderful art supplies, and I did my first oil painting there and also pastels and watercolors and prints. We would start each class with modern dance movements, just to loosen ourselves up. If the teachers thought we were getting timid or too tight or derivative in our drawing, they would encourage us to scribble. We didn't love Florence Cane, who was very formal and didn't have a way with little children. But we knew she was good for us.

As a teenager, I went to the High School of Music and Art in Manhattan. There I had a more traditional kind of training in drawing. As one of my projects, I made a children's book, which I bound myself. I can still see it! It was called *The Very Big Banana*.

Q: Did the public library play a part in your childhood?

A: Oh, yes. We went to the New York Public Library's Tremont Branch in the Bronx. That's where I signed up. They gave you a pen and you had to dip it in ink and show that you could write your name on the blue line in a big ledger. You also had to show you could read by reading out loud a statement saying you agreed to take good care of the books. It all felt very grand. I liked *The Poppyseed Cakes,* all the fairy-tale books, and *The Burgess Animal Book for Children* by Thornton Burgess, in which I would trace the pictures. I liked Maud and Miska Petersham's books — *The Story of Paper, The Story of Oil.* I enjoyed the combination of a story and something to do with how the world worked.

Q: Did you do well in school?

A: I did very well at anything I could do well without having to work at it too hard. I took remedial arithmetic, which I loved! They came and got you. They took you out of class and you went to this wonderful room and it was all very visual and full of colors. I did very well in remedial math. I loved everything that was imaginative and active. And I loved everything that had to do with words. From an early age I loved to write, and we wrote a composition every day at school.

Q: Looking back, what impact would you say the Depression had on your life?

A: I'm sure it had a lot to do with my father's trouble. He had always had a sketchy work history anyway. The Depression was responsible for a certain weight that settled on my mother, who was not a natural worrier or a gloomy person. Even so she managed to have quite a lot of spirit and be active in the neighborhood to try to make things a little better. But the fear of poverty had an enormous impact on everybody.

Despite my family's struggles, my parents were seriously involved in having a good life. My father sang very well. He liked to sing and dance. He liked to go for long walks. He swam. When we went walking with my father, we would walk across the Bronx, across the Harlem River to the George Washington Bridge, across the George Washington Bridge, and up the Palisades. Then we would take the Dyckman Street ferry and the trolley back to the Bronx. We went all over!

Q: Was it at the High School of Music and Art that you heard about Black Mountain College?

A: Probably. I went to Black Mountain, in Asheville, North Carolina, in the middle of World War II. We had only fifty-five students. Josef Albers headed the art department. Before the war, he had been assistant head of the Bauhaus in Germany. I studied drawing, painting, color, and design with Albers. It was a very good place for me. We learned to letter. We drew freehand Bodoni lettering, which we constructed by eye and drew by hand. This trained our eye and our measuring capacity. We made rectangles and drew 2's and 3's and 5's. I loved that. We covered every bit of paper with drawings and exercises, because you didn't just make a drawing and hang it on the wall. We were always experimenting, making more studies. We made newspapers in fake languages. We wrote backwards, did all sorts of graphic exercises as well as drawing from the model.

We had an old print shop with wooden type where I learned to set type. As one of my graduation projects, I designed and printed the posters, programs, and advertisements that were needed for the college. Inspired by the whiteness of the whale in *Moby-Dick,* I wrote an essay about the color black. It's funny because, except for *Scooter,* all my books are highly colored and all my paintings as a child were highly colored, but I was interested in black and white at the time. I also made a children's book called *The Man Who Lost His Birthday.*

At Black Mountain we had three areas of study: the arts, the liberal arts, and the daily arts. In the latter category, we repaired our own roads and ran our own farm. We grew corn, raised pigs, and milked the cows. I made butter and cheese and learned to work on a wood lathe. The students built the study building, which was a large contemporary structure. I installed the windows.

Q: Many years passed between the time you graduated from Black Mountain and the time you began making picture books. What were you doing during those years?

A: I had gotten married at Black Mountain. My husband was an architect and builder. I didn't have to make a living and I was interested in many, many things: gardening, cooking, learning about wild mushrooms and plants. I studied etching at the Boston Museum School. Then I took a print-making course at Pratt in New York. I did a lot of paintings and drawings and prints that were not for books.

After Black Mountain College a few of us started an intentional community of our own for people in the arts — the Gate Hill Co-op. I was twenty-three. If you lived in our community, you couldn't own your own house. We owned everything in common. Every Saturday we did repair work together on the property. I laid the stone floor in my building. I laid the cork tiles and painted the walls. The composer John Cage was our next-door neighbor, and together he and I built this quite odd stone wall between his house and ours. Neither of us had built a wall before, and when we got about three-quarters of the way up, John had to go on tour and I had to give birth to my baby. I started a day-care center for our community.

Later we started an elementary school, where I taught. It wasn't a utopia by any means, but we tried to support each other's art and it was a great place for little children.

I was very interested in politics, and for years I did the covers for *Liberation* magazine. I think I did some very innovative designs. Then I was divorced and moved to Ontario, Canada, where I became the cook for a group that was publishing an interesting magazine about elementary education. At that time I was also very interested in canoeing, and after a couple of years of that I took up with a man who was interested in canoeing, too. We decided to head West for a canoeing trip on the Little Nahanni River, which is in the Northwest Territories, in remote wilderness terrain that you have to fly into. The more I thought about it, the scareder and scareder I got. I'm adventurous, but I'm not a daredevil! Finally I had to admit that I was not up for the trip, and so we went down the Yukon River instead. Many of my experiences ended up in *Three Days on a River in a Red Canoe* (1981). That marriage ended, too, and after a while I found a houseboat in Vancouver to live in that happened to have a built-in drawing board, and I thought, *This is the life for me!*

Around that time I got in touch with Remy Charlip, who was an old friend from Black Mountain and by then a well-known picture-book artist. Remy showed me a picture-book manuscript he had co-written with Lilian Moore and didn't have time to illustrate. He asked if I would like to illustrate it. I said I yes, and the book that resulted is called *Hooray for Me!* (1975). Remy designed the book and I learned a lot from him. Then I illustrated a picture book by Barbara Brenner called *Ostrich Feathers* (1978) and then I did my own first book, *It's a Gingerbread House! Bake It! Build It! Eat It!* (1978).

Q: Why a book about gingerbread?

A: When I had the school at the Gate Hill Co-op we made fantastic gingerbread houses with the children. Then one year the American Craft Museum in New York was planning an international breads and cakes exhibition and invited us to make a piece for the show. The museum also needed a commemorative cookie for their black-tie fundraising affair, so I made it for them out of gingerbread. I was really into gingerbread! When it came Christmastime that year I wrote a nostalgic little story, never intending to publish it. But then an agent I had met offered to show my work to publishers.

Greenwillow Books looked at my story and said that if they could make a gingerbread house from my directions they would publish the book, and they did.

Q: Did you see making picture books as being connected, in a more general way, to the baking and building and canoeing and other activities you had been spending your time on up until then?

A: I've been very lucky in life in that I haven't experienced a great deal of separation between the things I do. I've been able to bake and cook and hike and have children and raise them and start schools and do politics and have love affairs and embroider and draw and paint and write poetry — and all of it seems connected to me. From early on, I was really devoted to the idea that it would be all connected. I think I'm like my parents in that regard. But I was also lucky because many people have that as an aim but can't do it because their economic situation is too difficult, or for some other reason.

Q: Did you look at other authors' picture books once you began writing and illustrating your own?

A: No, because I had taken such a long time to come around to it — I was forty-six and still living on my houseboat and writing lots of poetry at that time — that I felt I already knew how I wanted my books to look. Of course, I had to struggle to make them look that way. They didn't just come out.

Q: How would you describe what it was that you wanted?

A: There's a certain hands-on quality that I have wanted to preserve in my illustrations, but I would say there's quite a range to my work, depending on the graphic necessities of the story. *Three Days on a River in a Red Canoe,* and even more so *Stringbean's Trip to the Shining Sea* (1988), has a scrapbook quality that I wanted. The Chair books took a lot from my childhood paintings, except that they have a much more sophisticated sense of color. I've never been a real painter. Mine is a suit-the-need kind of graphic art in which I employ a lot of imagination, with built-in leaps from what you see to what you can then make out of it yourself. I don't draw from life and I don't draw from photographs. I just draw and draw and draw until it comes out the way I want. The thing I'm most interested in doing as an illustrator is to make emotion visible. Even with the details in the borders and with the furnishings in a scene, I have tried to render an environment that while not impoverished is also not well heeled, and in which affection and a sense of history are conveyed, without it being cute or cottage-y. The chair in the Chair books is a metaphorical chair. People ask me if I have a chair like that one. I don't and I wouldn't. My taste runs more toward Bauhaus furniture! What I have wanted in my illustrations is for the chair, the teapot, the shoes — everything — to *signify,* to convey a certain emotion and sense of reality.

Q: There's always an emotional intensity in the faces you draw — even in the faces of the little children in *"More, More, More," Said the Baby* (1990).

A: To illustrate that book, I drew a great deal, and ultimately I drew the final images on a high-quality red tracing paper. I then cut out the figures with manicuring scissors and glued them in place. I wanted the paint in that book to look like children's paint. When young children are painting they become mesmerized by the color. They're not really making a picture. They're playing with the color. I wanted to paint like that, too. I wanted a book that looked like it was painted. I'm very proud of it because I feel it wedded two different parts of my art experience. It owes a lot to my Albers training in that I played with color in the same way we did in our color studies at Black Mountain, putting together certain colors that are very close in light value in order to produce a certain effect. I also did the hand-lettering, which I had learned to do from Albers. At the same time, I used a very free method of painting and drawing. So it is both very well organized and quite spontaneous looking.

Of course I was also able to incorporate my ideas about how the world should be freely populated with people of different colors. I didn't design it that way initially. I was besotted with love for my first grandchild, who is Little Guy in the book, and it was all going to be about him. But as I continued to work, I realized that the book would be very limited if I made it all about a very blond little boy. So I redesigned it, giving the three parts of the story to three sets of characters. My "ideological" idea had the side benefit of giving the book a much wider graphic scope. At the last minute we added the subtitle *3 Love Stories*.

Q: Did you choose Rosa as the name for the girl in several of your books as a way of calling to mind the expression "Bread and Roses"?

A: I'm not sure why I chose that name. I myself was almost named Rosa, after Rosa Luxemburg, but my mother had objected, saying, "Let the child make her own name," so I became "Vera" instead. I love roses, and the rose, of course, is the flower of love. The "Bread and Roses" idea is very dear to me. But I can't really say why.

Q: Did you set out to do *A Chair for My Mother* (1982) and its sequels in part because you felt a need for picture books that were not about middle-class people living comfortable lives?

A: I did choose to do that, and I felt that it was an important choice. But *A Chair for My Mother* is also an expression of my life experience at the moment I was making it. I had finally come to a point in my life where I needed to make a living. *My* jar was empty! So the book is about Rosa's story and my story, too. I started those books during the peak years of the feminist movement, when there was increased awareness of the situation of single-parent families. But the emotional core of the book is simply love, and the chair and the jar are also about love.

Q: It's about values, too, isn't it — about making choices when you have to make choices?

A: I gave a talk at a private girls' school once, and one of the girls said of *Something Special for Me* (1983), "Why didn't they just buy *everything* they wanted?" A teacher said to me afterward, "*That* is one of the reasons we wanted you to come!"

Q: You mentioned the appeal of scrapbooks. Even *Amber Was Brave, Essie Was Smart* (2001) ends with a kind of family album of pictures.

A: In the case of that book, I hadn't wanted any illustrations at first. But the text was too short to be a book on its own, and that's how it evolved. *Stringbean* and the *Canoe* book are definitely scrapbooks.

Q: Isn't there an implied invitation to children to make scrapbooks of their experiences?

A: Yes. Many experiences besides my own travels lay behind the making of those books. When I was a child taking art classes at the Bronx House we made a post office one summer, with a wicket for buying and selling stamps. I carved the cancellation mark from linoleum, got a bad cut, and was rushed to Bronx Hospital! It was all very dramatic. We sent cards and letters throughout the building. I loved it. Years later Remy showed me a collection of sky postcards that he and another artist had made, and I spent time at the New York Public Library looking at old picture postcards in the library's picture collection. Also, I had a little tin box in which were saved all the postcards that I had sent to my mother during my trip to the Yukon. And finally, one of our family's prized possessions was an old photo album that was full of Kodak pictures of my parents' cross-country trip. I had always loved those photos, and so I wanted my travel books to look like albums, too.

Q: In *A Chair for Always* (2009), Rosa calls the chair a "lucky chair." The last words of *Stringbean's Trip* are "Good luck," and you've written a book called *Lucky Song*. *Luck* seems to be a very important word — and concept — for you.

A: Along with certain talents, the fairies, when they came when I was born, brought me luck. I feel that I have been a very lucky person. Is there a four-leaf clover in Stringbean's book?

Q: Yes, it's in the illustration on the back cover.

A: The girl in *Lucky Song* is a little Eve. I wanted her to stand for an Every Child who would get what she wanted in the sense that she would get what she needed. I feel very strongly that, if little children would be given what they really need in the way of love and adventures, then we would have a lot more happiness in the world. I wrote *Lucky Song* around the time that my grandson Hudson was born, and I thought of it as a kind of gift to toddlers. I've had children tell me, "Oh, she's so spoiled. She gets everything she wants." I think that's sad, because what *does* she want? She doesn't want anything extravagant. She wants to climb. She wants to fly a kite. She wants her mother to look. She wants to eat. She wants to sleep. She wants a song. It's nothing more than what everyone should have in life. The word *luck* had to be in the title because for many children, to get even half of those things is lucky. I was lucky. My children were lucky. So, I guess I would have to say I'm a fortunate soul, right?

LISBETH ZWERGER

Born 1954, Vienna, Austria

P ictures should be mysterious," Lisbeth Zwerger has said, "because it
makes you want to look at them again and again, to solve the riddle."
A largely self-taught artist, Zwerger was still in her twenties when
she gained worldwide renown for her haunting, fog-bound watercolor
illustrations for some of the most mysterious stories ever told: classic fairy
tales such as *Hansel and Gretel* (1979), *Little Red Cap* (1983), and *The Seven
Ravens* (1981). In these early books Zwerger reimagined as quirky, flesh-
and-blood individuals the characters — human, animal, and spirit alike —
who lurk or wander fatefully in the forest of the tales. At the same time
she left much to the reader's imagination. By indicating little about the

story's setting, Zwerger deliberately placed her apple-cheeked Hansel and Gretel, Thumbelina, and Swineherd in a world that might be anywhere or nowhere — or that just as likely might be a dream. Readers were captivated. Zwerger was only thirty-six when in 1990 she won children's literature's most coveted lifetime achievement award, the international Hans Christian Andersen Medal for illustration.

Since then, Zwerger has illustrated a variety of other classic texts, from *The Wizard of Oz* (1996) to the Bible, bringing ever more color and an increasingly adventurous sense of design to the page. She has done so even as her regular sightings of a young neighbor who appears to do nothing but play video games all day have prompted her to wonder about the future of the book. I first wrote about Zwerger's work in the *Washington Post* in the early 1990s, and met her when she came to New York for a tea party celebrating the American publication of *Alice in Wonderland* (1999). For this interview, Zwerger spoke by phone with me on November 6, 2009, from her apartment in Vienna.

LEONARD S. MARCUS: What were you like as a child?

LISBETH ZWERGER: A little bit lazy! That's basically what I was, and drawing and reading were my preferred pastimes.

Q: You didn't study hard in school?

A: That's right. One could say I was a real failure! I didn't want to work and I didn't imagine any future for myself. I didn't want to become anything. I was lucky that people, my parents in particular, helped me along and showed me a lot of understanding. It was they who thought I might want to study art and arranged for me to do so.

Q: Tell me about your experience at art school.

A: It was not very good. I had not yet decided, exactly, to become an illustrator, but I had begun to make pictures for fairy tales. Unfortunately, my teachers were not at all interested in illustration. I was not even seventeen then and I did not understand what they were after, but I think they hoped for modern art. We did have life-drawing classes, but the teachers were more after abstract things.

Q: Where did you learn to draw? Had you taught yourself by then?

A: In a way, yes, I had. I was drawing from the time I was very small, though I would not say I was a genius! I just grew up in the right surroundings. My father was a designer, and my mother was also very interested in drawing. My younger sister and I always drew a lot. My father had his studio two floors up from the flat where we lived, and we always used to go up there. It was full of paper and paint — just the right atmosphere.

Q: Sometimes the look and feel of art supplies, the smell of paint, can seem fascinating to a child.

A: Exactly! My father was an industrial designer. He designed cameras and projectors, all sorts of things. He also painted really nice paintings.

Q: Did you read the Grimm and Andersen fairy tales as a child?

A: Oh, yes. And my parents and grandparents read them to me, too.

Q: Did memories of World War II cast a shadow on your childhood in Vienna?

A: Vienna then, unlike now, was a very dreary city. Even in 1981, when I moved into the building where I still live, I could see across the street a building with shrapnel holes left over from World War II. But in the days when I was a school-aged child, the war wasn't spoken about much.

Maybe it was too soon. In Austria, that discussion didn't really open up properly until the 1980s.

Q: How did you find your style as an illustrator?

A: The first illustrator I admired was the Czech artist Jiří Trnka, who illustrated Andersen's fairy tales, among other things. Then I turned to the art of Arthur Rackham. I enjoyed his sense of line, his way of drawing animals, and the darkness in his paintings. Rackham's backgrounds are very busy, but I realized I didn't want that aspect of his style for my illustrations.

Q: In *The Seven Ravens* and other early books, the backgrounds are fog- or cloudlike — mysterious in a very evocative way.

A: I created them with liquid watercolor. It seemed like such a simple way to indicate landscape. I was very surprised that other illustrators had not thought to do the same before me. Critics would praise my illustrations, saying that I left so much to the viewer's imagination, and I wouldn't know what they meant. Now I do understand. If you just have a blur for the background — and of course you have to have an idea about how the blur should go — it does leave a lot to the imagination, and I do prefer that to Arthur Rackham's way of having so much detail, of even giving faces to the trees.

Q: Did you often find yourself redoing the blurs in order to get them exactly right?

A: I always had heart palpitations when I came to do that phase of an illustration. I would draw the figures first, and then it would be time to do the blur. You would hope and wish it would go well — and usually it did. That, of course, was exciting.

Q: Around the edges of some of your illustrations, the white of the page becomes mixed up with the image. It becomes unclear where the picture begins and ends.

A: I didn't plan that. I like having a white border around a picture.

Q: Do you do much research?

A: For *The Seven Ravens,* I had my brother-in-law take photographs of crows. My ravens are really crows! I didn't think it mattered so much. Since that time, I have clipped and collected a great many pictures from newspapers and magazines for use as reference. My picture files were very helpful, for example, when it came time to draw all the animals for *Noah's Ark* (1997).

Q: Your version of the witch's house in *Hansel and Gretel* is a lot plainer than what I think most children have come to expect. You have stayed close to the Grimms' original description of a simple house with a pancake roof.

A: Because the stories are so very well known, everyone already has a certain mental image of things like that. The image in America might even be different from what it is here.

I have always tried to avoid the clichés associated with fairy tales. I tend not to go for the first image that pops into the head but instead to follow the text.

Q: In some American versions, the witch's house is completely made of sweets — gingerbread men, candy canes, gumdrops, you name it. The house is sometimes the only detail of the story that children remember, with the result that they come away thinking of "Hansel and Gretel" as a happy story, and wishing they, too, could visit the house.

A: Yes, but that might be fatal!

Q: In your version you focus more on the witch herself, who looks a lot like someone's idea of a ghost.

A: I have given some workshops for young illustrators. One of the exercises was to do a picture of a princess or a witch or a giant. For the most part, people came up with such clichéd images. All the princesses had pinkish or pale blue dresses with puffed sleeves — and of course there are so many ways of picturing a character. I think it's a good exercise to become more aware of the clichés one carries around in one's head as a first step toward looking beyond them.

Q: Have you ever put yourself in an illustration? Are you perhaps your Thumbelina or Alice in Wonderland?

A: I suppose most illustrators end up, unknowingly, in their own picture books. I have put other people in my books but not myself, I don't think. My sister and her husband are in *A Christmas Carol* (1988). An old aunt of mine is the grandmother in *Little Red Cap*. My ex-husband, the illustrator John Rowe, is the dwarf in *The Seven Ravens*.

Q: Around the time that you began illustrating Grimms' fairy tales, a lot was being written about fairy tales. For instance, *The Uses of Enchantment,* by psychoanalyst Bruno Bettelheim, was widely discussed in America, and I think it had a big impact on American children's books for years to come. Were you aware of Bettelheim's book or others like it?

A: Yes, I read part of Bettelheim's book. In German it was called "Children Need Fairy Tales." It never one hundred percent convinced me. Traditional stories do seem to be a good thing. But it's hard to say whether children really *need* fairy tales. I didn't really have children in mind when I made my books, except insofar as I tried not to make really horrifying pictures that might frighten a child.

Q: Is seems that you have become increasingly interested in color.

A: I had a barrier to overcome that was left over from my bad art-school experience, and which had made me very timid. The teachers would criticize me for what I was doing, and by the end of my time there, I could hardly hold a pencil. Slowly my then-husband, John, helped me along with color. I started off dark, with just a tiny bit of color, and gradually added more and more. After my "gloomy" phase — the time of *Hansel and Gretel* and *Little Red Cap,* among others — I felt ready to try something new and a little bit more risky.

Q: In recent books like *Noah's Ark,* you seem also to have had fun with composition and proportion. Some details in the pictures are much too small, while others are much too big. Some images are placed off-center. You put umbrellas in the hands of biblical characters, which feels like a surreal touch.

A: Well, Magritte is one of my heroes, though there are so many heroes, Goya being the greatest of them all. But in the case of *Noah's Ark,* my interest went beyond surrealism. My big desire was to change Bible illustration for children. A number of years ago I published an illustrated Bible for children, but my edition did not find a big market. My publisher was worried about the project from the start. He said, "Nobody is interested in the Bible!" I find Bible stories very exciting, and it makes me so angry that the illustrated children's Bibles that I see in stores are so boring-looking.

Q: Does your family name, Zwerger, have a meaning in German?

A: Yes, *zwerg* means "dwarf." *Zwerg Nase* means "Dwarf Nose." Our family name is in fact a geographical reference. But for me growing up, it was not good to have a name like this. Children would tease me because of it, though not cruelly, I wouldn't say. They were just making an obvious joke. Even now sometimes it happens to me that I look at my name and think, *What a funny name.* I don't ever really forget what that part of my name means.

Q: Well, in a way it suits you, considering what you have done.

A: Yes, it's the perfect name for me!

BIBLIOGRAPHY

MITSUMASA ANNO

Anno's Alphabet: An Adventure in Imagination (New York: Crowell, 1975)

Anno's Britain (New York: Philomel, 1981)

Anno's Counting Book (New York: Crowell, 1975)

Anno's Faces (New York: Philomel, 1989)

Anno's Journey (New York: Philomel, 1978)

Anno's Math Games (New York: Philomel, 1987)

Anno's Medieval World (New York: Philomel, 1980)

Anno's Mysterious Multiplying Jar, written by Masaichiro Anno (New York: Philomel, 1983)

Anno's U.S.A. (New York: Philomel, 1983)

Topsy-Turvies: Pictures to Stretch the Imagination (New York: Weatherhill, 1970)

QUENTIN BLAKE

Charlie and the Chocolate Factory, written by Roald Dahl (New York: Knopf, 1964)

Clown (New York: Holt, 1996)

How Tom Beat Captain Najork and His Hired Sportsmen, written by Russell Hoban (New York: Atheneum, 1974)

Loveykins (Atlanta, GA: Peachtree, 2002)

The Marzipan Pig, written by Russell Hoban (New York: Farrar, Straus and Giroux, 1987)

Michael Rosen's Sad Book, written by Michael Rosen (Cambridge, MA: Candlewick, 2005)

Mrs. Armitage and the Big Wave (San Diego: Harcourt, Brace, 1998)

On Angel Wings, written by Michael Morpurgo (Cambridge, MA: Candlewick, 2007)

Patrick (New York: H. Z. Walck, 1969)

Quentin Blake's ABC (New York: Knopf, 1989)

Roald Dahl's Revolting Rhymes, written by Roald Dahl (New York: Knopf, 1982)

Wizzil, written by William Steig (New York: Farrar, Straus and Giroux, 2000)

Zagazoo (New York: Orchard, 1998)

ASHLEY BRYAN

Ashley Bryan: Words To My Life's Song (New York: Atheneum, 2009)

Ashley Bryan's African Tales, Uh-huh (New York: Atheneum, 1998)

Beautiful Blackbird (New York: Atheneum, 2003)

The Dancing Granny (New York: Atheneum, 1977)

I Greet the Dawn: Poems, written by Paul Laurence Dunbar (New York: Atheneum, 1978)

Let It Shine: Three Favorite Spirituals (New York: Atheneum, 2007)

Moon, For What Do You Wait? written by Rabindranath Tagore (New York: Atheneum, 1967)

The Night Has Ears: African Proverbs (New York: Atheneum, 1999)

The Ox of the Wonderful Horns and Other African Folktales, edited by Richard Lewis (New York: Atheneum, 1971)

The Sun Is So Quiet, written by Nikki Giovanni (New York: Henry Holt, 1996)

Turtle Knows Your Name (New York: Atheneum, 1989)

Walk Together Children: Black American Spirituals (New York: Atheneum, 1974)

JOHN BURNINGHAM

Borka: The Adventures of a Goose With No Feathers (New York: Random House, 1963)

Cloudland (New York: Crown, 1996)

Granpa (New York: Crown, 1984)

Hey! Get Off Our Train (New York: Crown, 1989)

Humbert, Mister Firkin & the Lord Mayor of London (Indianapolis: Bobbs-Merrill, 1965)

It's a Secret! (Somerville, MA: Candlewick, 2009)

John Patrick Norman McHennessy: The Boy Who Was Always Late (New York: Crown, 1987)

The Magic Bed (New York, Knopf, 2003)

Mr. Gumpy's Outing (New York: Holt, 1970)

There's Going to Be a Baby, illustrated by Helen Oxenbury (Somerville, MA: Candlewick, 2010)

Whaddayamean (New York: Crown, 1999)

ERIC CARLE

1, 2, 3 to the Zoo (Cleveland: World, 1968)

The Artist Who Painted a Blue Horse (New York: Philomel, 2011)

Brown Bear, Brown Bear, What Do You See? written by Bill Martin Jr. (New York: Holt, Rinehart & Winston, 1967)

Draw Me a Star (New York: Philomel, 1992)

Flora and Tiger: 19 Very Short Stories from My Life (New York: Philomel, 1997)

From Head to Toe (New York: HarperCollins, 1997)

A House for Hermit Crab (Saxonville, MA: Picture Book Studio, 1987)

The Mixed-Up Chameleon (New York: Crowell, 1975)

The Very Busy Spider (New York: Philomel, 1984)

The Very Hungry Caterpillar (New York: Collins World, 1969)

The Very Lonely Firefly (New York: Philomel, 1995)

The Very Quiet Cricket (New York: Philomel, 1990)

LOIS EHLERT

Color Zoo (New York: Lippincott, 1989)

Eating the Alphabet: Fruits and Vegetables from A to Z (San Diego: Harcourt Brace Jovanovich, 1989)

Fish Eyes: A Book You Can Count On (San Diego: Harcourt Brace Jovanovich, 1990)

Growing Vegetable Soup (San Diego: Harcourt, 1987)

Hands: Growing Up to Be an Artist (San Diego: Harcourt, Brace, 2004)

Leaf Man (Orlando: Harcourt, 2005)

Market Day: A Story Told with Folk Art (San Diego: Harcourt, Brace, 2000)

Nuts to You! (San Diego: Harcourt Brace Jovanovich, 1993)

Snowballs (San Diego: Harcourt, Brace, 1995)

Waiting for Wings (San Diego: Harcourt, 2001)

KEVIN HENKES

All Alone (New York: Greenwillow, 1981)

Crysanthemum (New York: Greenwillow, 1991)

A Good Day (New York: Greenwillow, 2007)

Julius, The Baby of the World (New York: Greenwillow, 1990)

Kitten's First Full Moon (New York: Greenwillow, 2004)

Lilly's Purple Plastic Purse (New York: Greenwillow, 1996)

Little White Rabbit (New York: Greenwillow, 2011)

Old Bear (New York: Greenwillow, 2008)

Owen (New York: Greenwillow, 1993)

A Weekend with Wendell (New York: Greenwillow, 1986)

YUMI HEO

A Is for Asia, written by Cynthia Chin-Lee (New York: Orchard, 1997)

Father's Rubber Shoes (New York: Orchard, 1995)

The Green Frogs: A Korean Folktale (Boston: Houghton Mifflin, 1996)

Henry's First-Moon Birthday, written by Lenore Look (New York: Atheneum, 2001)

Hey, Mr. Choo-choo, Where Are You Going? written by Susan Wickberg (New York: Putnam, 2008)

Moondog, written by Alice Hoffman and Wolfe Martin (New York: Scholastic, 2004)

One Sunday Morning (New York: Orchard, 1999)

The Rabbit's Judgment, written by Suzanne Crowder Han (New York: Holt, 1994)

So Say the Little Monkeys, written by Nancy Van Laan (New York: Atheneum, 1998)

Ten Days and Nine Nights: An Adoption Story (New York: Random House, 2009)

Uncle Peter's Amazing Chinese Wedding, written by Lenore Look (New York: Atheneum, 2006)

TANA HOBAN

26 Letters and 99 Cents (New York: Greenwillow, 1987)

Black on White (New York: Greenwillow, 1993)

Colors Everywhere (New York: Greenwillow, 1995)

I Read Signs (New York: Greenwillow, 1983)

Little Elephant, written by Miela Ford (New York: Greenwillow, 1994)

Look Again! (New York: Macmillan, 1971)

Look Book (New York: Greenwillow, 1997)

The Moon Was the Best, written by Charlotte Zolotow (New York: Greenwillow, 1993)

More, Fewer, Less (New York: Greenwillow, 1998)

Of Colors and Things (New York: Greenwillow, 1989)

One Little Kitten (New York: Greenwillow, 1979)

Shapes and Things (New York: Macmillan, 1970)

White on Black (New York: Greenwillow, 1993)

JAMES MARSHALL

Fox on the Job (New York: Dial, 1988)

George and Martha (Boston: Houghton Mifflin, 1972)

Goldilocks and the Three Bears (New York: Dial, 1988)

James Marshall's Cinderella, written by Barbara Karlin (Boston: Little, Brown, 1989)

James Marshall's Mother Goose (New York: Farrar, Straus and Giroux, 1979)

Miss Nelson Is Missing! written by Harry Allard (Boston: Houghton Mifflin, 1977)

Space Case, written by J. M. as Edward Marshall (New York: Dial, 1980)

The Stupids Step Out, written by Harry Allard (Boston: Houghton Mifflin, 1974)

Swine Lake, illustrated by Maurice Sendak (New York: HarperCollins, 1999)

Three by the Sea, written by J. M. as Edward Marshall (New York: Dial, 1981)

ROBERT McCLOSKEY

Blueberries for Sal (New York: Viking, 1948)

Centerburg Tales: More Adventures of Homer Price (New York: Viking, 1951)

Homer Price (New York: Viking, 1943)

Journey Cake, Ho! written by Ruth Sawyer (New York: Viking, 1953)

Lentil (New York: Viking, 1940)

Make Way for Ducklings (New York: Viking, 1941)

One Morning in Maine (New York: Viking, 1952)

Time of Wonder (New York: Viking, 1957)

HELEN OXENBURY

Alice's Adventures in Wonderland, written by Lewis Carroll (Cambridge, MA: Candlewick, 1999)

Big Mama Makes the World, written by Phyllis Root (Cambridge, MA: Candlewick, 2002)

The Birthday Party (New York: Dial, 1983)

The Car Trip (New York: Dial, 1983)

Clap Hands (New York: Simon and Schuster, 1987)

Dressing (New York: Wanderer Books/Simon and Schuster, 1981)

Eating Out (New York: Dial, 1983)

The Growing Story, written by Ruth Krauss (New York: HarperCollins, 2007)

Numbers of Things (New York: Franklin Watts, 1968)

So Much, written by Trish Cooke (Cambridge, MA: Candlewick, 1994)

Ten Little Fingers and Ten Little Toes, written by Mem Fox (New York: Harcourt, 2008)

There's Going to Be a Baby, written by John Burningham (Somerville, MA: Candlewick, 2010)

We're Going On a Bear Hunt, written by Michael Rosen (New York: Margaret K. McElderry/ Simon and Schuster, 1989)

Working (New York: Wanderer Books / Simon and Schuster, 1981)

JERRY PINKNEY

The Adventures of Spider: West African Folk Tales, written by Joyce Cooper Arkhurst (Boston: Little, Bown, 1964)

Aesop's Fables (New York: SeaStar, 2000)

Black Cowboy, Wild Horses: A True Story, written by Julius Lester (New York: Dial, 1998)

The Hired Hand: An African-American Folktale, written by Robert D. San Souci (New York: Dial, 1997)

John Henry, written by Julius Lester (New York: Dial, 1994)

Journeys with Elijah: Eight Tales of the Prophet, written by Barbara Diamond Goldin (San Diego: Harcourt, Brace, 1999)

The Lion & the Mouse (New York: Little, Brown, 2009)

The Little Match Girl (New York: Phyllis Fogelman, 1999)

Minty: A Story of Young Harriet Tubman, written by Alan Schroeder (New York: Dial, 1996)

Mirandy and Brother Wind, written by Patricia C. McKissack (New York: Knopf, 1988)

The Old African, written by Julius Lester (New York: Dial, 2005)

The Patchwork Quilt, written by Valerie Flournoy (New York: Dial, 1985)

Rabbit Makes a Monkey Out of Lion: A Swahili Tale, written by Verna Aardema (New York: Dial, 1989)

Sam and the Tigers: A New Telling of Little Black Sambo, written by Julius Lester (New York: Dial, 1996)

Sweethearts of Rhythm: The Story of the Greatest All-girl Swing Band in the World, written by Marilyn Nelson (New York: Dial, 2009)

The Talking Eggs: A Folktale From the American South, written by Robert D. San Souci (New York: Dial, 1989)

The Ugly Duckling, adapted from Hans Christian Andersen (New York: Morrow, 1999)

CHRIS RASCHKA

Charlie Parker Played Be Bop (New York: Orchard, 1992)

Five for a Little One (New York: Atheneum, 2006)

Grump Groan Growl, written by Bell Hooks (New York: Hyperion, 2008)

The Hello, Goodbye Window, written by Norton Juster (New York: Michael di Capua Books/ Hyperion, 2005)

Little Tree, written by E.E. Cummings (New York: Hyperion, 2001)

Moosey Moose (New York: Hyperion, 2000)

Mysterious Thelonious (New York: Orchard, 1997)

A Poke in the I: A Collection of Concrete Poems, selected by Paul B. Janeczko (Cambridge, MA: Candlewick, 2001)

A Primer About the Flag, written by Marvin Bell (Somerville, MA: Candlewick, 2011)

Yo! Yes? (New York: Orchard, 1993)

MAURICE SENDAK

Bumble-Ardy (New York: HarperCollins, 2011)

Dear Mili: An Old Tale, written by Wilhelm Grimm, translated by Ralph Mannheim (New York: Farrar, Straus and Giroux, 1988)

Hector Protector and *As I Went Over the Water* (New York: Harper and Row, 1965)

Higglety, Pigglety Pop! (New York: Harper and Row, 1967)

A Hole Is To Dig: A First Book of First Definitions, written by Ruth Krauss (New York: Harper, 1952)

I Saw Esau: The Schoolchild's Pocket Book, edited by Iona and Peter Opie (Cambridge, MA: Candlewick, 1992)

In the Night Kitchen (New York: Harper and Row, 1970)

The Juniper Tree and Other Tales From Grimm, translated by Lore Segal and Randall Jarrell (New York: Farrar, Straus and Giroux, 1973)

The Nutshell Library (New York: Harper and Row, 1962)

Outside Over There (New York: Harper and Row, 1981)

A Very Special House, written by Ruth Krauss (New York: Harper, 1953)

We Are All in the Dumps with Jack and Guy (New York: HarperCollins, 1993)

Where the Wild Things Are (New York: Harper and Row, 1963)

PETER SÍS

Beach Ball (New York: Greenwillow, 1990)

Fire Truck (New York: Greenwillow, 1998)

Follow the Dream: The Story of Christopher Columbus (New York: Farrar, Straus and Giroux, 2003)

Komodo! (New York: Greenwillow, 1993)

Madlenka (New York: Frances Foster / Farrar, Straus and Giroux, 2000)

Rainbow Rhino (New York: Knopf, 1987)

A Small Tall Tale from the Far Far North (New York: Knopf, 1993)

Starry Messenger: Galileo Galilei (New York: Farrar, Straus and Giroux, 1996)

Tibet Through the Red Box (New York: Farrar, Straus and Giroux, 1998)

The Tree of Life: Charles Darwin (New York: Farrar, Straus and Giroux, 2003)

The Wall: Growing Up Behind the Iron Curtain (New York: Farrar, Straus and Giroux, 2007)

Waving: A Counting Book (New York: Greenwillow, 1988)

WILLIAM STEIG

The Amazing Bone (New York: Farrar, Straus and Giroux, 1976)

Amos & Boris (New York: Farrar, Straus and Giroux, 1971)

Brave Irene (New York: Farrar, Straus and Giroux, 1986)

C D B! (New York: Windmill, 1968)

Consider the Lemming, written by Jeanne Steig (New York: Farrar, Straus and Giroux, 1988)

Doctor De Soto (New York: Farrar, Straus and Giroux, 1982)

Farmer Palmer's Wagon Ride (New York: Farrar, Straus and Giroux, 1974)

A Gift from Zeus: Sixteen Favorite Myths, written by Jeanne Steig (New York: Joanna Cotler/HarperCollins, 2001)

A Handful of Beans: Six Fairy Tales, written by Jeanne Steig (New York: HarperCollins, 1998)

The Lonely Ones (New York: Duell, Sloan and Pearce, 1942)

Pete's a Pizza (New York: HarperCollins, 1998)

The Real Thief (New York: Farrar, Straus and Giroux, 1973)

Roland, the Minstrel Pig (New York: Windmill, 1968)

Shrek! (New York: Farrar, Straus and Giroux, 1990)

Spinky Sulks (New York: Farrar, Straus and Giroux, 1988)

Sylvester and the Magic Pebble (New York: Windmill, 1969)

Tiffky Doofky (New York: Farrar, Straus and Giroux, 1978)

Zeke Pippin (New York: HarperCollins, 1994)

ROSEMARY WELLS

Benjamin & Tulip (New York: Dial, 1973)

Emily's First 100 Days of School (New York: Hyperion, 2000)

Lassie Come-Home, illustrated by Susan Jeffers (New York: Holt, 1995)

Love Waves (Somerville, MA: Candlewick, 2011)

Max's Birthday (New York: Dial, 1985)

Max's Dragon Shirt (New York: Dial, 1991)

Morris's Disappearing Bag (New York: Dial, 1975)

My Very First Mother Goose, edited by Iona Opie (Cambridge, MA: Candlewick, 1996)

Noisy Nora (New York: Dial, 1973)

Tell Me a Trudy, written by Lore Segal (New York: Farrar, Straus and Giroux, 1977)

Timothy Goes to School (New York: Dial, 1981)

Voyage of the Bunny Planet (New York: Viking, 1992)

Yoko (New York: Hyperion, 1998)

MO WILLEMS

Are You Ready to Play Outside? (New York: Hyperion, 2008)

City Dog, Country Frog, illustrated by Jon J Muth (New York: Hyperion, 2010)

Don't Let the Pigeon Drive the Bus! (New York: Hyperion, 2003)

Edwina, the Dinosaur Who Didn't Know She Was Extinct (New York: Hyperion, 2006)

Knuffle Bunny: A Cautionary Tale (New York: Hyperion, 2004)

Knuffle Bunny Free: An Unexpected Diversion (New York: Balzer and Bray/HarperCollins, 2010)

Knuffle Bunny Too: A Case of Mistaken Identity (New York: Hyperion, 2007)

Leonardo, the Terrible Monster (New York: Hyperion, 2005)

Naked Mole Rat Gets Dressed (New York: Hyperion, 2009)

There Is a Bird On Your Head! (New York: Hyperion, 2007)

VERA B. WILLIAMS

Amber Was Brave, Essie Was Smart: The Story of Amber and Essie Told Here in Poems and Pictures (New York: Greenwillow, 2001)

A Chair for Always (New York: Greenwillow, 2009)

A Chair for My Mother (New York: Greenwillow, 1982)

Cherries and Cherry Pits (New York: Greenwillow, 1986)

Hooray for Me! written by Remy Charlip and Lilian Moore (New York: Parents' Magazine Press, 1975)

It's a Gingerbread House: Bake It, Build It, Eat It! (New York: Greenwillow, 1978)

Lucky Song (New York: Greenwillow, 1997)

"More, More, More," Said the Baby: Three Love Stories (New York: Greenwillow, 1990)

Music, Music for Everyone (New York: Greenwillow, 1984)

Scooter (New York: Greenwillow, 1993)

Something Special For Me (New York: Greenwillow, 1983)

Stringbean's Trip to the Shining Sea, with Jennifer Williams (New York: Greenwillow, 1988)

Three Days on a River in a Red Canoe (New York: Greenwillow, 1981)

LISBETH ZWERGER

Alice in Wonderland, written by Lewis Carroll (New York: North-South, 1999)

A Christmas Carol, written by Charles Dickens (Saxonville, MA: Picture Book Studio, 1988)

Dwarf Nose, written by Wilhelm Hauff (New York: North-South, 1994)

The Gift of the Magi, written by O. Henry and Michael Neugebauer (Natick, MA: Picture Book Studio, 1982)

Hans Christian Andersen's Fairy Tales, text adapted from Hans Christian Andersen (New York: Simon and Schuster, 1991)

Hansel and Gretel, written by the Brothers Grimm, translated by Elizabeth D. Crawford (Natick, MA: Picture Book Studio, 1979)

The Little Mermaid, adapted from the text by Hans Christian Andersen (New York: Minedition/Penguin, 2005)

The Nightingale, adapted from the text by Hans Christian Andersen (Natick, MA: Picture Book Studio, 1984)

Noah's Ark, written by Heinz Janisch (New York: North-South, 1997)

The Seven Ravens, written by the Brothers Grimm, translated by Elizabeth D. Crawford (New York: Morrow, 1981)

ILLUSTRATION AND PHOTOGRAPHY CREDITS

ILLUSTRATIONS

Preliminary art for *Anno's Alphabet: An Adventure in Imagination* copyright © 1974 by Mitsumasa Anno, reproduced by permission of the Kerlan Collection, University of Minnesota Libraries, and by permission of the artist

Preliminary art for *Michael Rosen's Sad Book* copyright © 2005 by Quentin Blake, courtesy of Quentin Blake

Preliminary art for *Quentin Blake's ABC* copyright © 1989 by Quentin Blake, courtesy of Quentin Blake

Preliminary art for *The Night Has Ears: African Proverbs* copyright © 1999 by Ashley Bryan, courtesy of Ashley Bryan

Preliminary art for *Ashley Bryan's African Tales, Uh-huh* copyright © 1998 by Ashley Bryan, courtesy of Ashley Bryan

Preliminary art for *Turtle Knows Your Name* copyright © 1989 by Ashley Bryan, courtesy of Ashley Bryan

Preliminary art for *It's a Secret!* copyright © 2009 by John Burningham, courtesy of John Burningham

Preliminary and final cover art for *The Very Lonely Firefly* copyright © 1995 by Eric Carle, courtesy of The Eric Carle Museum of Picture Book Art

Preliminary art for *Waiting for Wings* copyright © 2001 by Lois Ehlert, courtesy of Lois Ehlert

Preliminary art for *Leaf Man* copyright © 2005 by Lois Ehlert, courtesy of Lois Ehlert

Preliminary art for *Old Bear* copyright © 2008 by Kevin Henkes, courtesy of Kevin Henkes

Preliminary art for *Henry's First-Moon Birthday* copyright ©2001 by Yumi Heo, courtesy of Yumi Heo

Preliminary art for *Colors Everywhere* copyright © 1995 by Tana Hoban, reproduced by permission of the Kerlan Collection, University of Minnesota Libraries, and by permission of the estate of Tana Hoban

Preliminary art for *One Little Kitten* copyright © 1979 by Tana Hoban, reproduced by permission of the de Grummond Collection, McCain Library, University of Southern Mississippi, and by permission of the estate of Tana Hoban

Preliminary art for *George and Martha Round and Round* copyright © 1988 by James Marshall, reproduced by permission of the Kerlan Collection, University of Minnesota Libraries, and by permission of the James Marshall Trust

Two unpublished notebooks of James Marshall, one undated and the other dated 1988, copyright © by James Marshall, reproduced by permission of the Kerlan Collection, University of Minnesota Libraries, and by permission of the James Marshall Trust

Dummy pages from an early draft of *Make Way for Ducklings*, by Robert McCloskey, reproduced by permission of the May Massee Collection, Emporia State University Archives, Emporia, Kansas, and by the estate of Robert McCloskey

Preliminary art for *We're Going on a Bear Hunt* copyright © 1989 by Helen Oxenbury, courtesy of Helen Oxenbury

Preliminary art for *John Henry* copyright © 1994 by Jerry Pinkney, courtesy of Jerry Pinkney

Preliminary art for *A Primer About the Flag* copyright © 2011 by Chris Raschka, courtesy of Chris Raschka

Preliminary art for *Five for a Little One* copyright © 2006 by Chris Raschka, courtesy of Chris Raschka

Final drawing for *I Saw Esau: The Schoolchild's Pocket Book*. Pencil, pen and ink, watercolor, copyright © 1992 by Maurice Sendak. Courtesy of Walker Books Ltd., London.

Preliminary drawing for *In the Night Kitchen*. Pencil on tracing paper, copyright © 1970 by Maurice Sendak. Courtesy of Maurice Sendak.

Study for "Hansel and Gretel," for *The Juniper Tree and Other Tales from Grimm*. Graphite pencil, copyright © 1972 by Maurice Sendak. Courtesy of Maurice Sendak.

Preliminary art for "Madlenka's Block," the prototype for *Madlenka*, copyright © 2000 by Peter Sís, courtesy of Peter Sís

Preliminary art for *Sylvester and the Magic Pebble* copyright © 1969 by William Steig. Collection of the Eric Carle Museum of Picture Book Art. Gift of Jeanne Steig.

Preliminary art for *Love Waves* copyright © 2011 by Rosemary Wells, courtesy of Rosemary Wells

Preliminary art for *Knuffle Bunny: A Cautionary Tale* copyright © 2004 by Mo Willems, by permission of Mo Willems and by permission of the Sheldon Fogelman Agency

Preliminary art for *"More, More, More," Said the Baby* copyright © 1990 by Vera B. Williams, courtesy of Vera B. Williams

Preliminary art for *Noah's Ark* copyright © 1997 by Lisbeth Zwerger, courtesy of Lisbeth Zwerger and Michael Neugebauer

PHOTOGRAPHS

Page 7: photograph courtesy of Mitsumasa Anno

Page 18: photograph courtesy of Quentin Blake

Page 28: photograph by Mathew Wysocki, courtesy of Simon and Schuster

Page 42: photograph courtesy of Candlewick Press

Page 52: photograph by Paul Shoul, courtesy of the Eric Carle Studio

Page 80: photograph by Lillian Schultz, courtesy of Lois Ehlert

Page 88: photograph courtesy of Kevin Henkes

Page 97: photograph by Steven Dana, courtesy of Yumi Heo

Page 105: photograph courtesy of Miela Ford

Page 116: photograph by William Gray, courtesy of William Gray

Page 141: photograph copyright © by Nancy Schön, courtesy of Nancy Schön

Page 153: photograph courtesy of Candlewick Press

Page 164: photograph copyright © by Myles C. Pinkney, courtesy of Little, Brown

Page 180: photograph courtesy of Candlewick Press

Page 191: photograph by Harrison Judd

Page 216: photograph courtesy of Peter Sís

Page 228: photograph courtesy of Maggie Steig

Page 246: photograph courtesy of Candlewick Press

Page 263: photograph courtesy of Hyperion Books

Page 273: photograph copyright © by Susan Kuklin, courtesy of HarperCollins

Page 286: photograph courtesy of Michael Neugebauer

SOURCE NOTES

MITSUMASA ANNO:
p. 7: "When I was a child . . . source of all my books": quoted in Doris de Montreville and Elizabeth D. Crawford, eds, *The Fourth Book of Junior Authors & Illustrators* (New York: H.W. Wilson, 1978), p. 11.

JOHN BURNINGHAM:
p. 42: "My true interest is in landscape and light": John Burningham, *John Burningham* (Somerville, MA: Candlewick Press, 2009), p. 104.

LOIS EHLERT:
p. 80: "Art supplies are really all around us": quoted in *Wondertime*, as cited in *Amie Hollman* (blog), January 23, 2009, http://amiehollmann.com/2009/01/23/lois-ehlert/.

KEVIN HENKES:
p. 88: "In the life . . . to eternity": Kevin Henkes, "Caldecott Medal Acceptance Speech," reprinted in *The Horn Book*, July/August 2005, p. 397.

JAMES MARSHALL:
p. 116: "A notorious perfectionist": Maurice Sendak, foreword to *George and Martha: The Complete Stories of Two Best Friends*, by James Marshall (Boston: Houghton Mifflin, 2008), p. 4.

p. 117: "Zany . . . I've ever done": quoted in "A Lost Art," Talk of the Town, *New Yorker*, November 2, 1992, p. 40.

CHRIS RASCHKA:
p. 180: "Usually a number . . . I want to get down": Chris Raschka biography, Scholastic website, http://www2.scholastic.com/browse/contributor.jsp?id=2847.

p. 181: "And for that . . . thankful": Chris Raschka, "Caldecott Medal Acceptance Speech," reprinted in *The Horn Book*, July/August 2006, p. 397.

PETER SÍS:
p. 216: "When I was a little boy . . . by its thick skin": Peter Sís, "Peter Sís," in *The Art of Reading: Forty Illustrators Celebrate RIF's 40th Anniversary*, by Reading Is Fundamental (New York: Dutton, 2005), p. 52.

VERA B. WILLIAMS:
p. 273: "I was a child . . . get it all told": Vera B. Williams, "Voices of the Creators" in *The Essential Guide to Children's Books and Their Creators*, ed. Anita Silvey (Boston: Houghton Mifflin, 2002), pp. 474–475.

LISBETH ZWERGER:
p. 286: "Pictures should be . . . the riddle": quoted in *Watercolor* magazine, fall 2005, as cited in *Eric Orchard* (blog), January 27, 2008, http://ericorchard.blogspot.com/2008_01_01_archive.html.

INDEX

Page citations in boldface indicate
subjects of interviews.

Daugherty, James, 141

d'Aulaire, Ingri and Edgar Parin, 141, 147

Daumier, Honoré, 23

Davis, Stuart, 236

Dewey, John, 115

Dial Press, 133, 174, 252, 255, 257, 258

Dickens, Charles, 117, 208

Diebenkorn, Richard, 79

Douglas, Helen Gahagan, 249

Drescher, Henrik, 100

du Bois, William Pène, 188–189

Dunbar, Paul Laurence, 39

Dürer, Albrecht, 216

Duvoisin, Roger, 188

Eco, Umberto, 100

Edwards, Amelia, 258

Ehlert, Lois, 5, **80–87**

Ehrlich, Amy, 258

Elijah (prophet), 178

Emerson, Ralph Waldo, 167–168

Eric Carle Museum of Picture Book Art, The, 53, 78–79

Escher, M. C., 10

Feiffer, Jules, 188

Field, Eugene, 31

Field, Rachel, 257, 258

Flack, Marjorie, 141

Fleischman, Sid, 223

Fleming, Ian, 46

Fogelman, Phyllis, 174, 252, 255, 257

Ford, Miela, 114

Forman, Milos, 220

Fortune (magazine), 68, 145

Foster, Frances, 223, 225

François, André, 20

Gág, Wanda, 1

Giovanni, Nikki, 39

Glaser, Milton, 170

Gnoli, Domenico, 118, 123

Goffstein, M. B., 95

Golden Books, 90, 91, 188

Gorey, Edward, 4, 123, 128

Grahame, Kenneth, 157, 163

Gramatky, Hardie, 141

Graphis (journal), 73, 222

Greenfield, Eloise, 165

Greenwillow Books, 106, 111, 113, 222–223, 281

Grimm, Wilhelm, 195

Grimm Brothers, 290, 291

Guston, Philip, 190

Hamilton, Virginia, 165

Hans Christian Andersen Medal, 8, 287

Harcourt (publisher), 86

Hardy, Oliver, 210, 211, 213

Harper (publisher), 86, 192, 215, 251, 252

Hayes, Regina, 256

Henkes, Kevin, 5, **88–96**

Henry Holt (publisher), 70–71

Heo, Yumi, 5, **97–104**

Hillyer, V. M., 276

Hirschman, Susan, 107, 111, 114, 222, 223–224, 251–252

Hoban, Russell, 106, 108–109, 110–111

Hoban, Tana, 4, **105–115**

Hokusai, Katsushika, 33

Homer, Winslow, 181

Houghton Mifflin (publisher), 123, 133

Hughes, Langston, 39

Ionesco, Eugene, 21

Irving, Washington, 31

Jackson, Richard, 181, 186

James, Henry, 198

Jeffers, Susan, 256–257

John Henry legend, 164, 174

Johnson, Crockett, 93, 239

ACKNOWLEDGMENTS

First, this note: the following interviews were first published in *Parenting* magazine: Mitsumasa Anno, Robert McCloskey, Helen Oxenbury (earlier portion only), and Maurice Sendak (parts one and two only). An abridged version of part three of my interview with Maurice Sendak appeared in *The Horn Book*.

I wish to thank each of the artists who agreed to be interviewed for this book. I am grateful for their interest, cooperation, and patience, without which these conversations could not have happened, and for all their help in making this the best possible book.

Thanks to all of the individuals and institutional staff members who were instrumental in making available the images reproduced here as illustrations: Lynn Caponera; the Eric Carle Museum of Picture Book Art (Kristin Angel and Nick Clark); Eric Carle Studio (Motoko Inoue); Steven Dana; the de Grummond Collection, University of Southern Mississippi (Ellen Ruffin); the Sheldon Fogelman Agency (Sheldon Fogelman, Sean McCarthy, and Marcia Warnick); Miela Ford; Fukuinkan Shoten (Rie Takagi); William Gray; HarperCollins (Stephanie Macy); Houghton Mifflin Harcourt (Karen Walsh); Hyperion (Dina Sherman); Harrison Judd; Motoo Ito; the Kerlan Collection, University of Minnesota Libraries (Meredith Gillies and Karen Nelson Hoyle); Nikki Mansergh; the May Massee Collection, Emporia State University (Heather Wade); Jane McCloskey; Sally McCloskey; Cecilia Milanesi; Minedition (Michael Neugebauer); the Northeast Children's Literature Collection, University of Connecticut (Terri Goldich); Myles C. Pinkney; Pippin Properties (Holly McGhee); Rosenbach Museum & Library (Patrick J. Rodgers and Karen Schoenewaldt); Nancy Schön; Simon and Schuster (Caityn Dlouhy); Jeanne Steig; Maggie Steig; Susan Valdina; and Walker Books (Louise Power).

I wish to express my deep gratitude to my editor at Candlewick Press, Deborah Wayshak, and to art director Sherry Fatla, for their tirelessness, patience, and professionalism at every stage of this immensely complex project, and to everyone at Candlewick — and Walker — who contributed to its completion.

As always, I wish to thank my agent, George M. Nicholson of Sterling Lord Literistic, for his friendship, guidance, and support. And a special thanks to my wife, Amy, and son, Jacob, for their love and friendship, and for many other things.

—L. S. M.